Shakespeare's Sonnets

or

How heavy do I journey on the way

Wes Jamroz

Troubadour Publications

Shakespeare's Sonnets

or

How heavy do I journey on the way

Editing:	*Dominique Hugon*
Cover design:	*Sandra Viscuso*
Illustrations:	*Jeff Burgess*

Copyright © 2014 by Troubadour Publications. All rights reserved.

No part of this work may be reproduced or transmitted in any form or by any means, electronic or mechanical, including photocopying and recording, or by any information storage or retrieval system without the prior written permission of Troubadour Publications.

Montreal, QC, Canada

TroubadourPubs@aol.com
http://www.troubadourpublications

ISBN: 978-0-9869673-9-9

Table of Contents

INTRODUCTION 5
    The Poet and his Guide 7
    Technical background 8
    Historical perspective 11
    Layout.. 12
    Punctuation, capitalization, italization 13
Prologue (the Dedication) 15
The Guide's first counsel (Sonnets 1 - 16) 19
Recognition (Sonnets 17 - 36) 55
The Guide's second counsel (Sonnet 37) 101
Initiation (Sonnets 38 - 47) 107
The Guide's third counsel (Sonnet 48) 137
Reformation (Sonnets 49 - 53) 141
The Guide's fourth counsel (Sonnets 54 - 55) 155
Separation (Sonnets 56 - 66) 161
The Guide's fifth counsel (Sonnets 67 - 70) 185
Detachment (Sonnets 71 - 72) 195
The Guide's sixth counsel (Sonnets 73 - 74) 201
Impermanency (Sonnets 75 - 76) 207
The Guide's seventh counsel (Sonnet 77) 213
Jealousy (Sonnets 78 - 81) 217
The Guide's eighth counsel (Sonnet 82) 229
Self-deception (Sonnets 83 - 93) 235
The Guide's ninth counsel (Sonnets 94 - 99) 259
Awakening (Sonnets 100 - 103) 275
The Guide's tenth counsel (Sonnet 104) 285
Wonderment (Sonnets 105 - 107) 289
The Guide's eleventh counsel (Sonnet 108) 299
Rebuke (Sonnets 109 - 125) 303
The Guide's twelfth counsel (Sonnet 126) 343
Unveiling (Sonnets 127 - 128) 349
The Guide's thirteenth counsel (Sonnet 129) 357
Purification (Sonnets 130 - 142) 361
The Guide's fourteenth counsel (Sonnet 143) 389
Dying (Sonnets 144 - 152) 393
Epilogue (Sonnets 153 - 154) 413
CONCLUSION 419
References 425

INTRODUCTION

The Poet and his Guide

The Sonnets contain a unique record of Shakespeare's experiences, which led him to become one of the world's greatest dramatist and poet. The interesting thing is that Shakespeare was taught why to write, how to write, when to write, and what to write about. According to the information provided in the Sonnets, at the beginning of his career, Shakespeare met his spiritual Guide.

The spiritual guide is a discernible feature of Shakespeare's plays. Let's make it clear though: Shakespeare's guide is not a guru, a preacher, or a facilitator of rituals. He is a living exemplar of human perfection. The Guide's function and his actions remain invisible to ordinary men. Depending on the environment in which he has to work, his appearance may vary. In Shakespeare plays, for example, he appears as a king, a queen, a husband, a wife, a rogue, a fool, a prince, a maiden, a nobleman, a bastard, a magician, a craftsman, a general, or a clown. In the Sonnets, the Guide appears as a young handsome man.

It was his Guide who pointed out to Shakespeare that he was wasting his time and talent on useless activities and meaningless writings. Then the Guide led Shakespeare through a sequence of experiences that allowed the poet to start to perceive the true value of his talent and the way in which his talent could be of use to a greater purpose.

The Sonnets are a record of the interactions between the poet and his Guide. In other words, there are two voices in the Sonnets. First we hear the Guide who appeals to the poet's conscience by pointing out how wasteful his life and his writing are. Then we hear the poet's reaction to the Guide's appeal. What follows are exchanges of arguments between the two men. Then we witness how the poet's intuition and his perception gradually develop and expand.

Although both the poet and his Guide are presented as young and handsome men, there is a distinct difference between them. The Guide speaks with authority and understanding; he is confident and his counsels follow a precise developmental methodology. The poet, on the other hand, is unsteady, immature, and moody; his reactions change quickly from highly enthusiastic to deeply depressed.

Shakespeare's Sonnets, like his plays, have an outward and an inner content. The outward content includes the full spectrum of emotional states such as loving, hatred, admiration, longing, jealousy, anger, rivalry, accusation, treachery, blame, forgiveness, etc. In ordinary life these various states appear randomly, chaotically, and with unpredictable outcome. The interpretations of the outward content based on "psychological realism" can be easily recognized because (i) they can be applied only to a few selected Sonnets and (ii) require exclusions of other Sonnets. This is why it is very difficult, or even impossible, to comprehend the Sonnets if their interpretation is limited to the outward content.

The inner content is based on a precise design. This design is governed by a set of rules that are not limited by intellectual or emotional barriers. At this level all Sonnets, like Shakespeare's plays, form a coherent narrative. The narrative describes the sequence of experiences that lead to a well-defined outcome: the development of higher states of mind.

Technical background

The Sonnets illustrate the process of the activation of higher states of mind and the formation of man's inner being. Allegorically, man's inner being may be referred to as the angelic soul.

Ordinary man's soul consists of manifest faculties, i.e., intellect, heart, and self. Understanding and knowledge, the capacity to perceive, to recollect the things of the past and plan for the things of the future - these are the qualities that are attributed to the intellect faculty. Entertaining feelings of love and hatred, showing bravery or cowardice, forming an intention and carrying out a particular action - these are the characteristics of the heart faculty. Survival, as well as the desire for and the pursuit of pleasure, ambitions, self-importance and greed - all these are the attributes of the self faculty.

The inner being is formed through the activation of latent layers of the intellect and the heart faculties. When activated, these inner layers form a new range of higher states of mind. The higher states, or subtle faculties, are latent in the ordinary mind. In the Sonnets the subtle faculties are referred to as roses of various colours.

The subtle faculties of the heart permit to recognize and experience love. But "love" here refers to objective love, and not its precognitive echo in emotional attachments and sensual attractions. In the Sonnets, the operation of these subtle faculties is indicated by an increased depth of intuitive feelings. The procedures leading to the activation of the subtle faculties of the heart are termed the Path of the Heart.

The correctly developed inner layers of the intellect faculty allow for a deeper understanding of man's origin and destiny. In the Sonnets, Shakespeare indicates the operation of the subtle aspects of the intellect as the means of perceiving the nature of time and death. The procedures leading to the activation of the subtle faculties of the intellect are called the Path of the Intellect.

The activation of the subtle faculties is possible when there is no interference from the self faculty, i.e., the centre which is responsible for all sorts of selfish and worldly attractions and desires. Spiritual reformation is a technical term describing this part of the process that aims at subduing the self faculty. The reformation is the first step towards the activation of the subtle faculties.

The actual activation of the subtle faculties is known as spiritual purification.

The process is completed when the subtle faculties are united. The unitive energy of love is needed for the unification of the subtle faculties. The unitive energy of love is the principle of all motion towards universal perfection and completion. When united, the subtle faculties are transmuted to form the angelic soul, i.e., a new inner being.

A particular subtle faculty may be activated by coming into contact with a specific element of evolutionary energy. By absorbing such energy, an inner layer becomes active. The entire process is directed by a guide. Therefore, the evolutionary process may be illustrated as the interaction between a guiding aspect, a latent or aspiring aspect, and an element of evolutionary energy. Shakespeare uses young women to represent various elements of evolutionary energy. In this symbolic representation a guide, an aspirant, and a young woman represent three parts of an evolutionary triad. The triad provides the needed arrangement within which an element of evolutionary energy may be effectively absorbed to activate a specific subtle faculty. Commitment to such an arrangement is called "marriage". Union of several marriages may lead to the formation of a new inner being. Allegorically, a new inner being is described as a child of such marriage(s).

There is a very precise methodology leading to the development of the inner being. The methodology is based on a specific sequence of reforming, purifying, and uniting experiences. Shakespeare's plays are a record of the implementation of such a methodology to the formation and the development of Western civilization. In the Sonnets, the same methodology is illustrated in the context of Shakespeare's personal journey. Therefore, the Sonnets and the plays are complementary. The Sonnets help to understand some episodes of the plays; the plays help to grasp the meaning of the Sonnets. This is why every Sonnet may be referenced to some episodes of the plays.

Historical perspective

Prior to the publications of Shakespeare's Sonnets, the operation of the evolutionary triad was illustrated in the Western literature by the various forms of "ménage à trois" of the Troubadours. Introduced in the 11th century, the triad of the Troubadours consisted of a king, a queen, and a young lover. The power figure of the king represented the guiding principle. The lover was an aspirant to higher knowledge. The evolutionary impulse to which the lover was drawn was represented by the queen. The queen was the lover's ideal mistress, whom he worshiped from afar, but who was essentially unattainable at that time. The lady was unattainable, for she was not a maid but a married woman. This particular triad represented a certain evolutionary potentiality, but it was a sterile triad. At that time the "lover", i.e., 11th century European man, was not ready yet for the actualization of this particular potentiality. Later on, the theme of the sterile triad was used by Petrarch and all sonneteers after him, who praised their unattainable mistresses.

Shakespeare's Sonnets were a form of announcement indicating that the evolutionary condition of European man changed around the 15th century. Namely, the Sonnets describe an active triad that includes the poet, the Guide, and a lady. The poet represents European man. The Guide, represented by the poet's friend, replaces the distant power figure of the king of the Troubadours. The unattainable queen is replaced by an attractive lady. The lady represents the currently available evolutionary impulse. Now, however, she is within the poet's reach.

Layout

The first 16 Sonnets are the Guide's appeal to the poet. They may be looked at as the introduction of the poet to the spiritual path. Although the Guide addresses the poet as his "dear love" and "my lovely boy", he describes him as selfish, egoistic, self-loving, niggardly, usurer, self-willed, insensitive, un-provident, etc. The Guide emphasizes the importance of entering onto the spiritual path. The poet may fulfil his destiny and achieve immortality by entering onto the path leading to the development of his inner being. The commitment to the spiritual path is referred to as "marriage". The outcome of the commitment is a "child", i.e., the birth of a new inner being. The Guide tells the poet that he has been granted a "bounteous gift", which not everybody is endowed with. It is the poet's responsibility to use the gift correctly. The Guide's appeal is a condensed projection of the developmental process. Through the remaining Sonnets, the poet will gradually experience all stages of the process that are encapsulated in the first 16 Sonnets.

Then is the time for the poet's answer. The poet's first reaction to the Guide's appeal is summarized in Sonnets 17 - 36. The poet's tone is very different from the Guide's appeal. The poet is respectful, admiring, and obedient. In the poet's words, the Guide is graceful, heavenly, eternal, gilding the object whereupon it gazeth, etc.

The following Sonnets illustrate the interactions between the Guide and the poet. Every time the poet makes a noticeable progress, or when he starts to deviate from the straight path, the Guide intercedes and delivers an approving or a rebuking counsel. The poet goes through two cycles of reformation and purification. Every cycle consists of seven stages. The stages are marked by the Guide's fourteen counsels.

Sonnet 127 marks the appearance of the Black Lady. The

appearance of the Black Lady symbolically represents experiences associated with the exposure to an evolutionary impulse, which may lead to the completion of the process. Such an experience is very challenging and confusing at first, because it leads to the realization of the limitation of ordinary knowledge and understanding. This is why such an experience is described as "tyrannous" and "cruel".

The challenges associated with the appearance of the Black Lady may be overcome through freeing oneself from sensual and emotional conditionings. In Shakespeare's presentation, Cupid is responsible for triggering such ordinary sensuality and emotions. Cupid's influence is greatly diminished at the moment when the poet is able to free himself from such worldly attractions and desires. It is only then that the poet may become immune to Cupid's interference and transmute his inner faculties into a new inner being. This stage of the process is indicated in the last two Sonnets.

Punctuation, capitalization, italization

The Sonnets are deliberately ambiguous. The purpose of this built-in ambiguity is to help the readers to identify their own intellectual and emotional conditionings that prevent them from recognizing the operation of more subtle states of mind. Shakespeare used punctuation, capitalization, and italization to help the readers to discern the Sonnets' inner content. Therefore, any changes to the punctuation corrupt the original form of the Sonnets and make it more difficult to grasp their inner meaning.

The punctuation, capitalization, and italization presented here have been reproduced in accordance with the original version of the Sonnets published in the 1609 Quarto.

Prologue (the Dedication)

THE DEDICATION

In accordance with the custom of the sonneteers, the first published edition of the Sonnets, i.e., the 1609 Quarto, was accompanied by a dedication:

> TO. THE. ONLY. BEGETTER. OF.
> THESE. ENSUING. SONNETS.
> Mr. W.H. ALL HAPPINESS.
> AND. THAT. ETERNITY.
> PROMISED.
> BY.
> OUR. EVER-LASTING. POET.
> WISHETH.
> THE. WELL-WISHING.
> ADVENTURER. IN.
> SETTING.
> FORTH.
>
> T.T.

This enigmatic dedication makes references to Mr. W.H., to our immortal poet, and to T.T., i.e., the author of the dedication. The dedication may be read as follows:

> "To the only Inspirer of the ensuing sonnets.
> I wish Mr. W.H. all the happiness and eternity
> promised by our immortal poet, the inspired
> adventurer who undertook the task of writing them,
>
> T.T."

The dedication serves as Prologue. It contains an outer and an inner meaning. Its inner meaning contains the outline of the process described in the Sonnets. The dedication is addressed to Master W.H. In its symbolic meaning, the letters W and H indicate the first and the final stages of a spiritual journey, i.e., from the initiation (W) to achieving an inner balance (H). This means that the dedication is addressed to any traveler, who enters onto the path. The symbolic meaning of the letter T is secret knowledge. It applies to the custodians of the secret knowledge. In other words, the dedication is signed by the Guide (see Sonnets 15 and 20). The Guide wishes the travellers all the happiness and eternity that have been promised by the author of the Sonnets.

The Guide's first counsel (Sonnets 1 - 16)

SONNET I

From fairest creatures we desire increase,
That thereby beauty's Rose might never die,
But as the riper should by time decease,
His tender heir might bear his memory:
But thou contracted to thine own bright eyes,
Feed'st thy light's flame with self substantial fuel,
Making a famine where abundance lies,
Thyself thy foe, to thy sweet self too cruel:
Thou that art now the world's fresh ornament,
And only herald to the gaudy spring,
Within thine own bud buriest thy content,
And, tender churl, mak'st waste in niggarding:
    Pity the world, or else this glutton be,
    To eat the world's due, by the grave and thee.

This is the Guide's first appeal to the poet. The Guide explains to the poet what his potential is and what his responsibilities are. In the Guide's vocabulary, "increase" refers to the development of the inner being. He compares the inner being to beauty's Rose.

The development of the inner being is the ultimate goal of human evolution. This is why the poet's primary responsibility is to fulfil his evolutionary potentiality ("from fairest creatures we desire increase, that thereby beauty's rose might never die"). The inner being allows to break through the limitations of time and space. The correctly developed inner being will supersede the poet's mortal body and will preserve his inner beauty ("but as the riper should by time decease, his tender heir might bear his memory"). But as long as the poet is preoccupied with his egotistic goals, he is just idly burning his life energy ("but thou contracted to thine own bright eyes, feed'st thy light's flame with self substantial fuel"). Right now, instead of actualizing his great potentiality, the poet is wasting his time ("making a famine where abundance lies"). In this way he is cruel to himself and his worst enemy ("thyself thy foe, to thy sweet self too cruel"). The Guide tells the poet that he is the world's newest jewel, but in his current state he is only an indication of such a potentiality ("thou that art now the world's fresh ornament, and only herald to the gaudy spring"). This potentiality is still buried within himself. But he is ruining all of that by his indolent behaviour ("within thine own bud buriest thy content, and, tender churl, mak'st waste in niggarding"). The Guide warns the poet that if he does not take pity on the world, he will finish like a miser who takes with him to his grave that which rightly belongs to the world ("pity the world, or else this glutton be, to eat the world's due, by the grave and thee").

Duke Senior in "As You Like It" describes the inner being as a precious jewel hidden in the head of an ugly and venomous toad[1]. In the following quote, ordinary man is compared to such an ugly toad:

> "Sweet are the uses of adversity,
> Which, like the toad, ugly and venomous,
> Wears yet a precious jewel in his head."

The "jewel" may be found through overcoming the challenges of the path ("Sweet are the uses of adversity").

---

[1] See "Technical background" (Shakespeare for the Seeker, Volume 2, Chapter 5.2).

SONNET II

When forty Winters shall besiege thy brow,
And dig deep trenches in thy beauty's field,
Thy youth's proud livery so gazed on now,
Will be a totter'd weed of small worth held:
Then being asked, where all thy beauty lies,
Where all the treasure of thy lusty days;
To say within thine own deep sunken eyes,
Were an all-eating shame, and thriftless praise.
How much more praise deserv'd thy beauty's use,
If thou couldst answer this fair child of mine
Shall sum my count, and make my old excuse
Proving his beauty by succession thine.
    This were to be new made when thou art old,
    And see thy blood warm when thou feel'st it cold.

Man has an incredible potentiality for evolutionary growth. However, there is a time limit within which such a progress may be realized. The Guide symbolically refers to this time limit as "forty winters". In this quote "winter" means a wasted window of opportunity. After living through forty idle seasons the poet will see wrinkles that will bruise his beautiful face, of which he is so proud now ("and dig deep trenches in thy beauty's field, thy youth's proud livery so gazed on now"). The poet's face, says the Guide, will become like a rotten weed, with no value at all ("will be a totter'd weed of small worth held"). Then, continues the Guide, the poet will be asked what happened to his beauty, and where are all those treasures of his youth ("then being asked, where all thy beauty lies, where all the treasure of thy lusty days"). And the poet will have to answer that he wasted all on shameful activities and worthless praises ("to say within thine own deep sunken eyes, were an all-eating shame, and thriftless praise"). In this context, beauty means the poet's inner being, which remains in its latent state. How much more valuable would be, argues the Guide, to answer that his efforts led to a lasting testimony of the poet's proper use of his inner potential ("how much more praise deserv'd thy beauty's use, if thou couldst answer this fair child of mine shall sum my count, and make my old excuse proving his beauty by succession thine"). The Guide concludes that it is this "child" that will survive him when the poet's body will be dead ("thy blood warm when thou feel'st it cold"). In other words, the "child" will make the poet a new man ("this were to be new made when thou art old").

A similar diagnosis about spiritual idleness was given by Perdita to King Polixenes in "The Winter's Tale". Polixenes was not able to live up to his potentiality. This is why, although it was spring in Bohemia, Perdita gave him "flowers of middle summer":

> "Here's flowers for you;
> Hot lavender, mints, savoury, marjoram;
> The marigold, that goes to bed wi' the sun
> And with him rises weeping: these are flowers
> Of middle summer, and I think they are given
> To men of middle age. You're very welcome."

In this way she indicated that Polixenes' potentiality had been exhausted. There was no possibility for his further development[2].

---

[2] See "Perdita" (Shakespeare for the Seeker, Volume 3, Chapter 6.1).

SONNET III

Look in thy glass and tell the face thou viewest,
Now is the time that face should form another,
Whose fresh repair if now thou not renewest,
Thou dost beguile the world, unbless some mother.
For where is she so fair whose uneared womb
Disdains the tillage of thy husbandry?
Or who is he so fond will be the tomb,
Of his self-love to stop posterity?
Thou art thy mother's glass and she in thee
Calls back the lovely April of her prime,
So thou through windows of thine age shalt see,
Despite of wrinkles, this thy golden time.
 But if thou live, remembered not to be,
 Die single and thine Image dies with thee.

The Guide tells the poet that it is the right time for him to make an effort towards his inner development. If he does not do it now, he will rob the world from its treasure ("now is the time that face should form another, whose fresh repair if now thou not renewest, thou dost beguile the world"). By being idle, the poet will prevent Nature from fulfilling her desire for growth ("for where is she so fair whose uneared womb disdains the tillage of thy husbandry"). So, who would be so stupid as to allow his own self-indulgence to cut him off from immortality ("who is he so fond will be the tomb, of his self-love to stop posterity"). The poet is Nature's greatest treasure, and it is his duty to preserve it and make good use of it ("thou art thy mother's glass and she in thee calls back the lovely April of her prime"). Within the poet's lifetime, and despite his aging, he is capable of fulfilling his evolutionary purpose ("so thou through windows of thine age shalt see, despite of wrinkles, this thy golden time"). But, warns the Guide, if the poet fails to arrive at the state of "to be", his potentiality will die with him ("but if thou live, remembered not to be, die single and thine Image dies with thee").

The state "not to be" mentioned in the concluding couplet is a reference to Hamlet's famous soliloquy "to be or not to be"[3]:

> "To be, or not to be: that is the question:
> Whether 'tis nobler in the mind to suffer
> The slings and arrows of outrageous fortune,
> Or to take arms against a sea of troubles
> And by opposing end them?

The soliloquy describes these two states of "to be" and "not to be" as "awakening" and "sleeping", respectively. The state "not to be" or "sleeping" is developmentally sterile. It corresponds to ordinary life driven by "self-love". On the other hand, the state "to be" corresponds to a spiritually awakened man, who is able to enjoy his "golden time".

---

[3] See "To be or not to be" (Shakespeare for the Seeker, Volume 4, Chapter 7.3).

SONNET IV

Unthrifty loveliness, why dost thou spend,
Upon thy self thy beauty's legacy?
Nature's bequest gives nothing, but doth lend,
And being frank she lends to those are free:
Then beauteous niggard why dost thou abuse,
The bounteous largess given thee to give?
Profitless usurer why dost thou use
So great a sum of sums yet canst not live?
For having traffic with thy self alone,
Thou of thy self thy sweet self dost deceive,
Then how when nature calls thee to be gone,
What acceptable *Audit* canst thou leave?
 Thy unused beauty must be tombed with thee,
 Which used lives th' executor to be.

The Guide asks the poet why he is such a wasteful person who spends all his inherited treasures on egoistic pursuits ("unthrifty loveliness, why dost thou spend, upon thy self thy beauty's legacy?") The poet has been given the potentiality to evolve. This potentiality is like Nature's loan that was freely given to him ("Nature's bequest gives nothing, but doth lend, and being frank she lends to those are free"). The Guide asks the poet why he misuses this gift that was given to him ("then beauteous niggard why dost thou abuse, the bounteous largess given thee to give"). And why the poet wastes this immense treasure in such a way that he is not even able to live from it ("profitless usurer why dost thou use so great a sum of sums yet canst not live?") By limiting the use of this bounty to himself only, the poet is cheating himself out of his most valuable treasure ("thou of thy self thy sweet self dost deceive"). So, when Nature will call up his time, he will not be able to show any gains on his account ("then how when nature calls thee to be gone, what acceptable audit canst thou leave?") In this way, continues the Guide, the poet's unused potentiality will be buried with his body, instead of being used to preserve the poet's life ("thy unused beauty must be tombed with thee, which used lives th' executor to be").

In accordance with Shakespeare's symbolic description, such a misuse of evolutionary responsibility corresponds to spiritual usury. This is why the Guide addresses the poet as "profitless usurer", who does not use correctly "so great a sum of sums". Shylock in "The Merchant of Venice" tried to substantiate his own selfish purpose by cleverly but incorrectly interpreting Laban's story[4]:

> "This was a way to thrive, and he was blest:
> And thrift is blessing, if men steal it not."

Shylock used a literary, i.e., artificial meaning of the story. In this context, Shylock committed a spiritual usury by corrupting the meaning of the story to his own personal benefit.

---

[4] See "Villains" (Shakespeare for the Seeker, Volume 3, Chapter 6.4).

SONNET V

Those hours, that with gentle work did frame,
The lovely gaze where every eye doth dwell
Will play the tyrants to the very same,
And that unfair which fairly doth excel:
For never resting time leads Summer on,
To hideous winter and confounds him there,
Sap checked with frost, and lusty leaves quite gone.
Beauty o'er-snowed and bareness every where,
Then were not summer's distillation left
A liquid prisoner pent in walls of glass,
Beauty's effect with beauty were bereft,
Nor it, nor no remembrance what it was.
    But flowers distilled, though they with winter meet,
    Leese but their show, their substance still lives sweet.

The Guide explains that the poet's life is like seasons. Summer follows spring; then summer is destroyed by tyrannical winter ("for never-resting time leads summer on to hideous winter"). Winter will freeze sap, remove leaves, cover everything with snow and make everything naked ("sap checked with frost, and lusty leaves quite gone, beauty o'er-snowed and bareness every where"). Similarly, the poet's beautiful face that is now admired by everybody, will turn into an ugly one ("the lovely gaze where every eye doth dwell will play the tyrants to the very same, and that unfair which fairly doth excel"). Only the distilled flowers of the summer will survive the frost and snow of the winter. Their beauty will be preserved through their perfume stored in glass vials ("then were not summer's distillation left a liquid prisoner pent in walls of glass"). The Guide explains that without perfume it would not be possible to preserve summer's beauty ("beauty's effect with beauty were bereft, nor it, nor no remembrance what it was"). But through distillation, it is possible to preserve its sweetness ("but flowers distilled, though they with winter meet, leese but their show, their substance still lives sweet").

A perfume of flowers is a poetical expression that is used to describe the transmutation of the subtle faculties into a new inner being. Like perfume, the inner being is immune to death. Viola, disguised as Cesario, alluded to such a transmutation in her conversation with Orsino ("Twelfth Night")[5]:

Orsino:

> "For women are as roses, whose fair flower
> Being once display'd, doth fall that very hour."

Cesario:

> "And so they are: alas, that they are so;
> To die, even when they to perfection grow!"

Viola pointed out that an experience known as "to die before dying" is part of the process leading to the distillation of roses, i.e., the transmutation of the subtle faculties into a new being.

---

[5] See "Cruel maid" (Shakespeare for the Seeker, Volume 4, Chapter 7.1).

SONNET VI

Then let not winter's ragged hand deface,
In thee thy summer, ere thou be distilled:
Make sweet some vial; treasure thou some place,
With beauty's treasure ere it be self-killed:
That use is not forbidden usury,
Which happies those that pay the willing loan;
That's for thy self to breed another thee,
Or ten times happier be it ten for one,
Ten times thy self were happier than thou art,
If ten of thine ten times refigured thee,
Then what could death do if thou shouldst depart,
Leaving thee living in posterity?
    Be not self-willed for thou art much too fair,
    To be death's conquest and make worms thine heir.

The Guide continues his appeal by saying that the poet should not let time destroy his potential before it is correctly fulfilled ("then let not winter's ragged hand deface, in thee thy summer, ere thou be distilled"). The Guide advises the poet to prepare a special place and a container in which he may store his inner beauty before it fades away ("make sweet some vial; treasure thou some place, with beauty's treasure ere it be self-killed"). Such a transaction is a noble activity that will make happy those who are willing to invest in it ("that use is not forbidden usury, which happies those that pay the willing loan"). It makes one truly happy to be transmuted into a new man ("that's for thy self to breed another thee, or ten times happier be it ten for one"). Because happiness expands in proportion to the degree of inner growth ("ten times thy self were happier than thou art, if ten of thine ten times refigured thee"). In this way, the poet will be able to escape from death ("then what could death do if thou shouldst depart, leaving thee living in posterity?") Therefore, the Guide concludes, the poet should not be driven by his self-love, because he has too much to lose by making himself just food for worms ("be not self-willed for thou art much too fair, to be death's conquest and make worms thine heir").

"To be distilled" refers to the technical term "to die before dying". Man should die to his worldly attachments before his physical death. In this way, he may pay back "the willing loan". Such a gain on the interest "is not forbidden usury". Quite contrary, this is the only way to gain true happiness by prolonging one's life into the eternity. It is in this context that Othello's remark may be understood[6]:

> "For, in my sense, 'tis happiness to die."

---

[6] See "Transition" (Shakespeare for the Seeker, Volume 3, Chapter 6.2).

SONNET VII

Lo in the Orient when the gracious light,
Lifts up his burning head, each under eye
Doth homage to his new-appearing sight,
Serving with looks his sacred majesty,
And having climbed the steep up heavenly hill,
Resembling strong youth in his middle age,
Yet mortal looks adore his beauty still,
Attending on his golden pilgrimage:
But when from high-most pitch with weary car,
Like feeble age he reeleth from the day,
The eyes ('fore duteous) now converted are
From his low tract and look another way:
    So thou, thyself out-going in thy noon:
    Unlooked on diest unless thou get a son.

The Guide compares the poet's life to the rising and setting down of the sun. The rising sun gradually increases his appearance and his impact ("in the Orient when the gracious light, lifts up his burning head"). It is then that each person on earth pays homage to his majestic appearance ("each under eye doth homage to his new-appearing sight, serving with looks his sacred majesty"). Upon reaching his zenith, the sun resembles a strong man in its prime time ("and having climbed the steep up heavenly hill, resembling strong youth in his middle age"). The people still keep admiring and following the sun's heavenly pilgrimage ("yet mortal looks adore his beauty still, attending on his golden pilgrimage"). But then, he starts to descend ("but when from high-most pitch with weary car, like feeble age he reeleth from the day"). And people who previously admired him, turn their eyes away and look somewhere else ("the eyes, before duteous, now converted are from his low tract and look another way"). The same will happen to the poet if he does not fulfil his evolutionary potentiality ("so thou, thyself out-going in thy noon: unlooked on diest unless thou get a son").

Henry VIII in the "History Plays" made a similar observation when he was told about the birth of his child[7]:

> "O lord archbishop,
> Thou hast made me now a man! never, before
> This happy child, did I get any thing."

The birth of the child turned Henry VIII into a new man.

---

[7] See "Activation of permanent consciousness" (Shakespeare for the Seeker, Volume 1, Chapter 1).

SONNET VIII

Music to hear, why hear'st thou music sadly,
Sweets with sweets war not, joy delights in joy:
Why lov'st thou that which thou receiv'st not gladly,
Or else receiv'st with pleasure thine annoy?
If the true concord of well-tuned sounds,
By unions married do offend thine ear,
They do but sweetly chide thee, who confounds
In singleness the parts that thou shouldst bear:
Mark how one string sweet husband to another,
Strikes each in each by mutual ordering;
Resembling sire, and child, and happy mother,
Who all in one, one pleasing note do sing:
    Whose speechless song being many, seeming one,
    Sings this to thee thou single wilt prove none.

The Guide points out that the poet's reaction to the Guide's music is an indication of his inner imbalance. In other words, the poet is missing something that would allow him to move forward. The Guide notices that the poet likes to listen to music, but music makes him sad ("music to hear, why hear'st thou music sadly"). This is strange, because balance attracts harmony, and joy delights in joyfulness ("sweets with sweets war not, joy delights in joy"). The Guide asks the poet why he likes things that make him unhappy and enjoys those things that annoy him ("why lov'st thou that which thou receiv'st not gladly, or else receiv'st with pleasure thine annoy?") Feeling sad is a sign of his inner disharmony ("they do but sweetly chide thee, who confounds in singleness the parts that thou shouldst bear"). The Guide draws a parallel between the harmony of strings and the inner balance of properly aligned manifest faculties, which symbolically may be represented by a father, a mother and a child ("mark how one string sweet husband to another, strikes each in each by mutual ordering; resembling sire, and child, and happy mother"). Then the Guide explores further this symbolism by making a reference to the unity of the trinity ("who all in one, one pleasing note do sing"). Such harmony of three, although seemingly one, is an indication that the poet himself counts as nobody ("whose speechless song being many, seeming one, sings this to thee thou single wilt prove none").

The fact that the poet cannot respond correctly to music points out that he is not yet correctly tuned to "the true concord of well-tuned sounds". Or, as pointed out by Lorenzo[8] in "The Merchant of Venice", the poet is still dominated by "this muddy vesture of decay":

> "Such harmony is in immortal souls;
> But whilst this muddy vesture of decay
> Doth grossly close it in, we cannot hear it."

The poet is still veiled by "this muddy vesture of decay", so he is not able to respond correctly to "such harmony".

---

[8] See "Awakening" (Shakespeare for the Seeker, Volume 3, Chapter 6.4).

SONNET IX

Is it for fear to wet a widow's eye,
That thou consum'st thy self in single life?
Ah; if thou issueless shalt hap to die,
The world will wail thee like a makeless wife,
The world will be thy widow and still weep,
That thou no form of thee hast left behind,
When every private widow well may keep,
By children's eyes, her husband's shape in mind:
Look what an unthrift in the world doth spend
Shifts but his place, for still the world enjoys it
But beauty's waste hath in the world an end,
And kept unused the user so destroys it:
    No love toward others in that bosom sits
    That on himself such murd'rous shame commits.

The Guide continues with his arguments against the poet's spiritual indolence. The Guide points out that the poet is too attached to his pleasures and this makes him unsuitable to the discipline of the path. The poet should differentiate between his attachments to worldly pleasures and his commitment to the path. The poet's attachments are driven by his fear of losing worldly pleasures ("is it for fear to wet a widow's eye, that thou consum'st thy self in single life"). These attachments are like a veil that does not allow the poet to see his evolutionary potentiality. This is why the poet does not realize that the entire world would be affected if he did not fulfill his potentiality ("if thou issueless shalt hap to die, the world will wail thee like a makeless wife"). Then the Guide points out the difference between ordinary marriage and spiritual marriage, i.e., the poet's commitment to the spiritual path. Namely, a widow may preserve an image of her husband through her children eyes ("when every private widow well may keep, by children's eyes, her husband's shape in mind"). But in the case of the poet, the entire world would be mourning the loss of universal beauty ("the world will be thy widow and still weep, that thou no form of thee hast left behind"). Reckless spending of material goods does not destroy them; they are just shifted from one hand to another ("look what an unthrift in the world doth spend shifts but his place, for still the world enjoys it"). But wasted inner beauty cannot be recovered. By not using it correctly, its owner destroys it ("but beauty's waste hath in the world an end, and kept unused the user so destroys it"). The Guide warns that by committing such a murderous act on himself, the poet demonstrates his lack of concern for others ("no love toward others in that bosom sits that on himself such murd'rous shame commits").

One required condition is to free oneself from worldly attachments. "To die before dying" refers to such a condition. In the same symbolic language, the term "marriage" describes an unconditional commitment to the spiritual path. The same theme is further explored in "Romeo and Juliet"[9]. Here is a quote from Friar Lawrence's comment:

> "She's not well married that lives married long;
> But she's best married that dies married young."

In this context, the Guide's message may be summarized as "a good marriage is completed with death".

---

[9] See "Trails and errors" (Shakespeare for the Seeker, Volume 3, Chapter 6.6).

SONNET X

For shame deny that thou bear'st love to any
Who for thy self art so unprovident
Grant if thou wilt, thou art beloved of many,
But that thou none lov'st is most evident:
For thou art so possessed with murderous hate,
That 'gainst thy self thou stick'st not to conspire,
Seeking that beauteous roof to ruinate
Which to repair should be thy chief desire:
O change thy thought, that I may change my mind,
Shall hate be fairer lodged than gentle love?
Be as thy presence is gracious and kind,
Or to thyself at least kind-hearted prove,
    Make thee another self for love of me,
    That beauty still may live in thine or thee.

The Guide gives the poet a set of instructions, which may allow him to start on his spiritual journey. He starts with an introduction to the Path of the Heart. Firstly, the poet has to realize that there is the difference between ordinary sensual love and the experience of the unitive energy of love. Right now the poet is capable only of ordinary love. This is why the Guide tells him that, if he has any sense of shame, he should admit that there is no love for anyone in his heart ("for shame deny that thou bear'st love to any"). This is so obvious because the poet is not even able to care correctly for himself ("who for thy self art so unprovident"). The Guide knows that the poet is loved by many, but the poet loves no one ("grant if thou wilt, thou art beloved of many, but that thou none lov'st is most evident"). The poet is so possessed with destruction that he even plots against himself. Instead of repairing his inner house he intends to destroy it ("for thou art so possessed with murderous hate, that 'gainst thy self thou stick'st not to conspire, seeking that beauteous roof to ruinate which to repair should be thy chief desire"). The Guide wishes to be able to change his opinion about the poet, but the poet will have to free himself from his conditioned thinking pattern first ("O change thy thought, that I may change my mind"). The Guide says that it does not make any sense that hate is located in a better place than true love ("shall hate be fairer lodged than gentle love?") The Guide insists that the poet should be as gracious as is his external appearance or at least he should be kind to himself ("be as thy presence is gracious and kind, or to thyself at least kind-hearted prove"). Only then the Guide, who is the carrier of the unitive energy of love, will be able to pass it to him ("make thee another self for love of me"). In this way, the poet may be able to develop and preserve his inner being and fulfill his ultimate evolutionary purpose ("that beauty still may live in thine or thee").

Helena in "All's Well That Ends Well" was also very selective while choosing a candidate to whom she would pass the unitive energy of love[10]:

"You are too young, too happy, and too good,
To make yourself a son out of my blood."

She knew that his particular young man was not ready for it.

---

[10] See "Modulation of beauty" (Shakespeare for the Seeker, Volume 2, Chapter 5.1).

SONNET XI

As fast as thou shalt wane so fast thou grow'st,
In one of thine, from that which thou departest,
And that fresh blood which youngly thou bestow'st,
Thou mayst call thine, when thou from youth convertest,
Herein lives wisdom, beauty, and increase,
Without this folly, age, and cold decay,
If all were minded so, the times should cease,
And threescore year would make the world away:
Let those whom nature hath not made for store,
Harsh, featureless, and rude, barrenly perish,
Look whom she best endowed, she gave the more;
Which bounteous gift thou shouldst in bounty cherish,
    She carved thee for her seal, and meant thereby,
    Thou shouldst print more, not let that copy die.

The Guide continues his explanation of the nature of evolutionary growth. He tells the poet that he may grow as fast as his body declines ("as fast as thou shalt wane so fast thou grow'st"). He specifies that the poet's growth refers to the development of his inner being, from which his physical body will be separated ("in one of thine, from that which thou departest"). The poet may think about his inner being as his new self, when he will be no longer young ("and that fresh blood which youngly thou bestow'st, thou mayst call thine, when thou from youth convertest"). This is why it is said that within man there is a seed of knowledge, beauty, and growth ("herein lives wisdom, beauty, and increase"). Without this seed, there would be only ignorance, destruction, and death ("without this folly, age, and cold decay"). If none would be taking care of the seed, then time would end and the entire world would collapse within life-time of a man ("if all were minded so, the times should cease, and threescore year would make the world away"). The Guide tells the poet that those, who do not make any effort to develop themselves, will perish ("let those whom nature hath not made for store, harsh, featureless, and rude, barrenly perish"). But those, whom Nature endowed with beauty, she also gave a valuable gift ("look whom she best endowed, she gave the more"). The poet is such a man. Therefore, the poet is obliged to use this gift correctly ("which bounteous gift thou shouldst in bounty cherish"). Nature made the poet as her stamp so he may preserve her ("she carved thee for her seal"). The Guide emphasizes that this stamp should be preserved and used; it should not be wasted ("and meant thereby, thou shouldst print more, not let that copy die"). This counsel also serves as an indication of why and what the poet should write about. By developing himself, the poet will be capable of recording his own experiences. In this way, he will be able to pass his experiences to the future generations.

Hamlet also recognized the existence of such a stamp of perfection within mankind[11]:

> "What a piece of work is a man! how noble in reason!
> how infinite in faculty! in form and moving how
> express and admirable! in action how like an angel!
> in apprehension how like a god! the beauty of the
> world! the paragon of animals!"

---

[11] See "To be or not to be" (Shakespeare for the Seeker, Volume 4, Chapter 7.3).

SONNET XII

When I do count the clock that tells the time,
And see the brave day sunk in hideous night,
When I behold the violet past prime,
And sable curls all silvered o'er with white:
When lofty trees I see barren of leaves,
Which erst from heat did canopy the herd
And Summer's green all girded up in sheaves
Borne on the bier with white and bristly beard:
Then of thy beauty do I question make
That thou among the wastes of time must go,
Since sweets and beauties do themselves forsake,
And die as fast as they see others grow,
    And nothing 'gainst Time's scythe can make defence
    Save breed to brave him, when he takes thee hence.

Now the Guide introduces the poet to the Path of the Intellect. The Path of the Intellect leads to a stage where one may free himself from the destructivity of time. He warns the poet that there is time limit within which he will have to complete his task. This time limit is compared to the changes of hours and seasons. The Guide tells the poet that he should pay attention to things around him and to observe how all are subject to change and decline. He should look at the clock and see how time is ticking away and how hideous night marks the end of bright day ("when I do count the clock that tells the time, and see the brave day sunk in hideous night"); or look at the violet and see when it turns white with age ("when I behold the violet past prime, and sable curls all silvered o'er with white"); or at tall trees when they lose their leafs, which once provided protection against heat ("when lofty trees I see barren of leaves, which erst from heat did canopy the herd"). The same happens to summer which is carried off to its grave when its crops are tied up and hauled to the barn ("and summer's green all girded up in sheaves borne on the bier with white and bristly beard"). The poet should question himself whether his potentiality will also follow such a time-controlled pattern ("then of thy beauty do I question make that thou among the wastes of time must go"). Because it is obvious that beautiful creatures don't last long, but die as fast as others are growing up ("since sweets and beauties do themselves forsake, and die as fast as they see others grow"). And nothing can stop the sweep of time's cutting blade ("and nothing 'gainst time's scythe can make defence"). Only by developing his inner being prior to his physical death, the poet may free himself from the passing of time ("save breed to brave him, when he takes thee hence").

In every Shakespeare's play such a time limit is precisely determined for a given stage of the process. For example, the process illustrated in "A Midsummer Night's Dream" has to be completed "by the next new moon"[12]:

> "Take time to pause; and, by the next new moon
> The sealing-day betwixt my love and me,
> For everlasting bond of fellowship
> Upon that day either prepare to die
> For disobedience to your father's will,
> Or else to wed Demetrius, as he would."

---

[12] See "Corrective action" (Shakespeare for the Seeker, Volume 4, Chapter 8.3).

SONNET XIII

O that you were your self, but love you are
No longer yours, than you your self here live,
Against this coming end you should prepare,
And your sweet semblance to some other give.
So should that beauty which you hold in lease
Find no determination, then you were
Your self again after your self's decease,
When your sweet issue your sweet form should bear.
Who lets so fair a house fall to decay,
Which husbandry in honour might uphold,
Against the stormy gusts of winter's day
And barren rage of death's eternal cold?
    O none but unthrifts, dear my love you know,
    You had a Father, let your Son say so.

The Guide emphasizes the main point of the process, i.e., the preservation of man's evolutionary growth. Although the poet is still alive, in reality he does not exist yet ("O that you were your self, but love you are no longer yours, than you your self here live"). There is a time limit within which the poet has to develop his inner being ("against this coming end you should prepare, and your sweet semblance to some other give"). Otherwise, the still latent potentiality that was given to him on loan will be lost ("so should that beauty which you hold in lease find no determination"). But if he manages to develop his inner being, then he will be able to prolong his life ("then you were your self again after your self's decease, when your sweet issue your sweet form should bear"). So, why such a beautiful house should be reduced to rubble, when prudent maintenance might make it outlast the furry of winter and the wrath of death's eternal cold? ("Who lets so fair a house fall to decay, which husbandry in honour might uphold, against the stormy gusts of winter's day and barren rage of death's eternal cold?"). Only the most reckless spender would do such a thing ("O none but unthrifts"). And the Guide concludes making a reference to the continuity of evolutionary growth. He reminds the poet that his inner growth was possible because he has been provided with guidance. In other words, he had a Father ("dear my love you know, you had a Father"). By the same token, he is obliged to pass the teaching onto the next generation ("let your Son say so").

The entire corpus of Shakespeare's plays is based on the concept of building, maintaining, and preserving the evolutionary process. The evolutionary transmission chain is described in various symbolic forms. For example, the seven kings of the "History Plays" represent the seven evolutionary stages within the English branch of the modern evolutionary cycle[13].

---

[13] See "Evolutionary cycle" (Shakespeare for the Seeker, Volume 1, Chapter 1).

SONNET XIV

Not from the stars do I my judgement pluck,
And yet methinks I have Astronomy,
But not to tell of good, or evil luck,
Of plagues, of dearths, or seasons' quality,
Nor can I fortune to brief minutes tell,
Pointing to each his thunder, rain and wind,
Or say with Princes if it shall go well
By oft predict that I in heaven find.
But from thine eyes my knowledge I derive,
And constant stars in them I read such art
As truth and beauty shall together thrive
If from thyself, to store thou wouldst convert:
    Or else of thee this I prognosticate,
    Thy end is Truth's and Beauty's doom and date.

The Guide makes a reference to an evolutionary triad. The triad consists of three parts that are symbolically referred to as kind, fair (beauty), and true. In this Sonnet, the Guide (kind) talks about the unity of truth and beauty. The poet himself represents "beauty".

The Guide does not base his judgement on the stars, yet he knows enough to foretell certain things ("not from the stars do I my judgement pluck, and yet methinks I have astronomy"). But his knowledge is not concerned with predicting good or bad events, plagues, famines, or what a season will be like ("but not to tell of good, or evil luck, of plagues, of dearths, or seasons' quality"). Nor can he predict down to the minutes each season's thunder, rain, or wind ("nor can I fortune to brief minutes tell, pointing to each his thunder, rain and wind"). Nor can he, by looking at the sky, tell the princes if their affairs will go well for them ("or say with princes if it shall go well by oft predict that I in heaven find"). But by looking in the poet's s eyes, which are like guiding stars, the Guide can tell what his evolutionary potentiality is ("but from thine eyes my knowledge I derive, and constant stars in them I read such art"). Namely, the poet is capable of forming an evolutionary triad that may preserve the evolutionary process. But he would have to dedicate himself entirely to the path ("if from thyself, to store thou wouldst convert"). The poet needs to unite his inner beauty with truth ("as truth and beauty shall together thrive"). Otherwise the evolutionary process would be interrupted ("or else of thee this I prognosticate, thy end is Truth's and Beauty's doom and date"). In the context of the triad, "truth" denotes an element of evolutionary energy; "beauty" corresponds to the poet's inner being. The Guide ("kind") represents the third part.

Hamlet, for example, sensed that he somehow misused his potentiality[14]. Because his developmental potential was not able to flourish, he was put on the rigid path of the inescapable fate of "readiness is all":

> "There's a special
> providence in the fall of a sparrow. If it be now,
> 'tis not to come; if it be not to come, it will be
> now; if it be not now, yet it will come: the
> readiness is all: since no man has aught of what he
> leaves, what is't to leave betimes?"

---

[14] See "The fencing match" (Shakespeare for the Seeker, Volume 4, Chapter 7.3).

SONNET XV

When I consider every thing that grows
Holds in perfection but a little moment.
That this huge stage presenteth nought but shows
Whereon the Stars in secret influence comment.
When I perceive that men as plants increase,
Cheered and checked even by the self-same sky:
Vaunt in their youthful sap, at height decrease,
And wear their brave state out of memory.
Then the conceit of this inconstant stay,
Sets you most rich in youth before my sight,
Where wasteful time debateth with decay
To change your day of youth to sullied night,
    And all in war with Time for love of you
    As he takes from you, I engraft you new.

The Guide continues his explanation of the evolutionary process. He compares human life to the one of other living organisms, which can manifest their perfection but only for a brief moment ("when I consider every thing that grows holds in perfection but a little moment"). The Guide says that the whole world is one big stage on which the stars secretly direct the show ("That this huge stage presenteth nought but shows whereon the stars in secret influence comment"). In a similar way the stars encourage and then thwart the lives of men ("when I perceive that men as plants increase, cheered and checked even by the self-same sky"). In their youth men cherish their vigour; but when they arrive at their height, they vanish leaving no memory of their previous glory ("vaunt in their youthful sap, at height decrease, and wear their brave state out of memory"). The Guide addresses the poet saying that when he looks at the whole world's inconstancy he thinks about him, whom Nature granted so rich a gift. And the Guide says that he can hear how time and death are debating with each other about how to corrupt the poet's potentiality and reduce it to nothing ("where wasteful time debateth with decay to change your day of youth to sullied night"). The Guide compares himself to a gardener who, by his skills of grafting, is able to grow new species in his garden. He is able to ennoble the poet by engrafting a sample of evolutionary matrix onto his inner being and in this way to protect him against the tyranny of time ("and all in war with time for love of you as he takes from you, I engraft you new"). The comment about defending oneself against the tyranny of time applies to the processes belonging to the Path of the Intellect.

Organic engrafting is a symbolic illustration of the initial stage of the evolutionary process, which often is referred to as "baptism" or "initiation". At this stage an aspirant receives an impression, just as wax receives the impression of the signet ring. This impression allows for holding and digesting the initial evolutionary impulse. Graphically this may be illustrated as a superimposition of two triangles. One triangle represents ordinary man with his manifest faculties of the self, the heart, and the intellect. When the aspirant is exposed to an impulse of evolutionary energy, then the second triangle is formed. Such an engrafted triangle consists of a guiding aspect, an aspiring aspect, and an element of evolutionary energy. The superposition of these two triangles takes the form of a six pointed star, or hexagon. In a system of equivalence of numbers and letters, such a figure corresponds to the letter "W". This is why the letter "W" or hexagon is used to indicate the stage of spiritual initiation.

In his Roman plays, Shakespeare used a three-person coalition known as the triumvirate to represent the ordinary triad of the manifest faculties. It included Caesar Octavius, Mark Antony, and Lepidus. The engrafted triad was formed when Mark Antony married Octavia, Octavius's sister. Here is Caesar Octavius' comment on that marriage:

> "There is my hand.
> A sister I bequeath you, whom no brother
> Did ever love so dearly: let her live
> To join our kingdoms and our hearts; and never
> Fly off our loves again!"

In this newly formed triad Caesar Octavius represented a guiding aspect, Mark Antony was an aspiring aspect, and Octavia represented an element of evolutionary energy[15].

---

[15] See "Meeting of triumvirs" (Shakespeare for the Seeker, Volume 1, Chapter 2.3).

"And you must live drawn by your own sweet skill" (Sonnet 16)

SONNET XVI

But wherefore do not you a mightier way
Make war upon this bloody tyrant time?
And fortify your self in your decay
With means more blessed than my barren rhyme?
Now stand you on the top of happy hours,
And many maiden gardens yet unset,
With virtuous wish would bear you living flowers,
Much liker than your painted counterfeit:
So should the lines of life that life repair
Which this (Time's pencil or my pupil pen)
Neither in inward worth nor outward fair
Can make you live your self in eyes of men,
    To give away yourself, keeps yourself still,
    And you must live drawn by your own sweet skill.

This is the last Sonnet of the Guide's initial appeal to the poet encouraging him to make war upon the tyranny of time ("but wherefore do not you a mightier way make war upon this bloody tyrant time?") The Guide indicates that his written counsels to the poet are not sufficient enough to prevent the poet from decay ("and fortify your self in your decay with means more blessed than my barren rhyme"). The poet may conquer time by developing his inner being. The inner being is formed as the result of the union of the subtle faculties. The subtle faculties are referred to as "living flowers". The subtle faculties are activated through the absorption of the corresponding impulses of evolutionary energy. "Many maiden gardens, yet unset, with virtuous wish would bear you living flowers" is a reference to the availability of such impulses. The flowers may be of specific colours, i.e., yellow, red, white, and black. Yellow and red "flowers" are associated with the inner layers of the heart; white and black "flowers" are designated for the inner layers of the intellect. Yellow and white corresponds to reformed aspects of the heart and the intellect; red and black are associated with purified aspects, respectively.

The Guide concludes saying that only by fully dedicating himself to the path the poet may fulfil his potential ("to give away yourself, keeps yourself still").

The last two lines express the previously referred formula to "die before dying" or "die to live" ("to give away yourself, keeps yourself still, and you must live"). This is an echo of Friar Francis' recipe[16] in "Much Ado About Nothing":

> "Come, lady, die to live."

The Guide emphasizes, however, that the poet will have to develop some new skills to be able to accomplish this task ("drawn by your own sweet skill").

---

[16] See "Invisible assistant" (Shakespeare for the Seeker, Volume 3, Chapter 6.3).

Recognition (Sonnets 17 - 36)

SONNET XVII

Who will believe my verse in time to come,
If it were filled with your most high deserts?
Though yet heaven knows it is but as a tomb
Which hides your life, and shows not half your parts:
If I could write the beauty of your eyes,
And in fresh numbers number all your graces,
The age to come would say this Poet lies,
Such heavenly touches ne'er touched earthly faces.
So should my papers (yellowed with their age)
Be scorned, like old men of less truth than tongue,
And your true rights be termed a Poet's rage,
And stretched metre of an Antique song.
> But were some child of yours alive that time,
> You should live twice in it, and in my rhyme.

The previous Sonnets were addressed by the Guide to the poet. The Guide outlined an entire program for the poet. First, the Guide insisted on "marriage" and on having a "child", i.e., the poet's need to enter onto the spiritual path and to develop his inner being. This is the only way that the poet may defeat the tyranny of time and fulfil his evolutionary function. Then the Guide informed the poet that he has been given an incredibly rich gift. But this gift is in the form of a loan. The poet has to return it. And there is a time limit for the repaying of the loan. The poet may achieve his goal through the experience called "to die before dying". Such "death" is like a distillation of life into another form of being. In order to "die" correctly he will have to form an evolutionary triad. Within the structure of the triad, the Guide will engraft onto the poet's inner being a sample of the evolutionary matrix and expose him to impulses of evolutionary energy. Through this experience, the poet may be able to activate the inner layers of his ordinary faculties of the heart and the intellect. These inner layers, or subtle faculties, will let him taste true love and break through the limitation of time and death. And, finally, the Guide told him that everything has already been prepared and arranged for him. Now the poet may enter onto his spiritual path.

In this Sonnet we hear the poet for the first time. The Guide has selected his disciple. But the important thing is that the poet has to recognize his Guide. Such recognition is a critical step in the process. Otherwise the Guide would not be able to guide him. Let's recall that Hamlet, for example, failed to recognize his guide and, because of that, he could not save Elsinore from its evolutionary fiasco[17].

Following the Guide's indication in Sonnet 11, the poet intends to record the Guide's teaching. He realizes, however, that if he describes the Guide and his wisdom, his future readers will not understand his verses ("who will believe my verse in time to come, if it were filled with your most high deserts?") He will not be able to describe convincingly enough the Guide, his function, and his ability ("though yet heaven knows it is but as a tomb which hides your life, and shows not half your parts"). If he attempts to describe the Guide's loving eyes and write verses listing the Guide's wonderful attributes, his future readers will accuse him of lying ("if I could write the beauty of your eyes, and in fresh numbers number all your graces, the age to come would say this poet lies"). They will say no such human ever existed ("such heavenly touches ne'er touched earthly faces"). The poet's verses will be scorned, like old men who talk too much without saying anything of substance ("so should my papers, yellowed with their age, be scorned, like old men of less truth than tongue"); the poet's description of the Guide's role and his function will be dismissed as madness ("and your true rights be termed a poet's rage"). So, the poet is afraid that his poems will be perceived as an exaggerated fantasy ("and stretched

---

[17] See "Encounter at the graveyard" (Shakespeare for the Seeker, Volume 4, Chapter 7.3).

metre of an antique song"). The poet hopes, however, that his poems will be understood by some readers in the future ("but was some child of yours alive that time"). In this way, the Guide's teaching will be preserved ("you should live twice in it, and in my rhyme"). It seems that Shakespeare knew from the very beginning that it was going to take some time before his Sonnets and his plays will be understood.

This Sonnet marks the poet's entry onto the spiritual path. The following Sonnets are a record of the poet's experiences while travelling along the path.

"Who will believe my verse in time to come" (Sonnet 17)

SONNET XVIII

Shall I compare thee to a Summer's day?
Thou art more lovely and more temperate:
Rough winds do shake the darling buds of May,
And Summer's lease hath all too short a date:
Sometime too hot the eye of heaven shines,
And often is his gold complexion dimm'd,
And every fair from fair some-time declines,
By chance, or nature's changing course untrimm'd:
But thy eternal Summer shall not fade,
Nor lose possession of that fair thou owest,
Nor shall death brag thou wander'st in his shade,
When in eternal lines to time thou growest,
    So long as men can breathe or eyes can see,
    So long lives this, and this gives life to thee.

Despite his worry about the adequacy of his description, the poet attempts to portray his Guide.

Shall he compare his Guide to a summer day? But the Guide is much lovelier and much more pleasant ("thou art more lovely and more temperate"). Rough winds are able to shake off the pretty buds of May, and summer doesn't last long enough ("rough winds do shake the darling buds of May, and summer's lease hath all too short a date"). Sometimes the sun is unpleasant because it is too hot, and often its golden face is covered by clouds ("sometime too hot the eye of heaven shines, and often is his gold complexion dimm'd"). And everything that is beautiful, at one point stops to be attractive, either by accident or as a result of seasonal changes ("and every fair from fair some-time declines, by chance, or nature's changing course untrimm'd"). But the Guide's presence is eternal and his beauty everlasting ("but thy eternal summer shall not fade, nor lose possession of that fair thou owest"). He is able to prolong lives, therefore death does not brag that is able to conquer him ("nor shall death brag thou wander'st in his shade, when in eternal lines to time thou growest"). The Guide is a link to the evolutionary transmission chain and in this way he preserves humanity. As long as the Guide is recognised by men, humanity will be provided with the means for evolutionary growth ("so long as men can breathe or eyes can see, so long lives this"). The Guide will be present as long as there are people who are able to recognize his functionality ("and this gives life to thee").

According to Shakespeare's presentation, a break of a link with the evolutionary transmission chain took place at the time of Julius Caesar. The break led to the fiasco of the Roman evolutionary cycle. Horatio in "Hamlet" described the symbolic signs of the break[18]:

> "In the most high and palmy state of Rome,
> A little ere the mightiest Julius fell,
> The graves stood tenantless and the sheeted dead
> Did squeak and gibber in the Roman streets:
> As stars with trains of fire and dews of blood,
> Disasters in the sun; and the moist star
> Upon whose influence Neptune's empire stands
> Was sick almost to doomsday with eclipse."

---

[18] See "Evolutionary impulse" (Shakespeare for the Seeker, Volume 4, Chapter 7.3).

SONNET XIX

Devouring time, blunt thou the Lion's paws,
And make the earth devour her own sweet brood,
Pluck the keen teeth from the fierce Tiger's jaws,
And burn the long-lived Phoenix in her blood,
Make glad and sorry seasons as thou fleet'st,
And do whate'er thou wilt swift-footed time
To the wide world and all her fading sweets:
But I forbid thee one most heinous crime,
O carve not with thy hours my love's fair brow,
Nor draw no lines there with thine antique pen,
Him in thy course untainted do allow,
For beauty's pattern to succeeding men.
    Yet do thy worst old Time despite thy wrong,
    My love shall in my verse ever live young.

The poet makes references to the various concepts which he has learnt from the Guide. In his initial appeal, the Guide told him about the inconstancy of ordinary things and the permanency of perfection, about the cruelty of time, about the poet's evolutionary potential and his responsibility. The following Sonnets contain the poet's initial response to these concepts. He is enthusiastic about these ideas. But his initial response is based only on what he has heard and not what he has experienced, on what he thinks and not what he knows.

Sonnet 19 is a meditation on the theme of the cruelty of time. We may notice that the poet's initial approach is rather childish and naive. Instead of making efforts towards improving himself, he tries to preach to time. So, he encourages the devouring time to go ahead with its destruction, i.e., blunt the lion's paws, make the earth swallow her own creatures, pluck out the sharp teeth out of the tiger's jaws, and burn the long-lived phoenix in its own blood. The poet says that time may do whatever it wants to the entire world and its attractions, whether it is to induce happy or sorry seasons ("make glad and sorry seasons as thou fleet'st, and do whate'er thou wilt swift-footed time to the wide world and all her fading sweets"). But the poet forbids time to commit one deed, i.e., to carve wrinkles into the Guide's lovely face ("but I forbid thee one most heinous crime, carve not with thy hours my love's fair brow"). Neither should time make the Guide grow old ("nor draw no lines there with thine antique pen"). The Guide should not be touched by time, because he is the quintessence of beauty for all future generations.

The poet realizes that he himself has been charged with the task of preserving the Guide's teaching. In this way the future generations of readers will be able to benefit from the Guide's wisdom ("do allow for beauty's pattern to succeeding men"). The poet announces, therefore, that he will dedicate his writing to the preservation of the Guide's teaching. In this way he will be able to outdo time's wrongdoings ("yet do thy worst old time despite thy wrong, my love shall in my verse ever live young").

Similarly, Peter Quince in "A Midsummer Night's Dream" was asked to preserve Nick Bottom's dream[19]:

> "I will get Peter Quince to write a ballad of this dream."

But the poet does not understand yet that in order to do this effectively, he will need to first develop his inner being.

---

[19] See "The guide" (Shakespeare for the Seeker, Volume 4, Chapter 8.3).

SONNET XX

A woman's face with nature's own hand painted,
Hast thou, the Master Mistress of my passion,
A woman's gentle heart but not acquainted
With shifting change as is false women's fashion,
An eye more bright than theirs, less false in rolling:
Gilding the object where-upon it gazeth,
A man in hue all *Hues* in his controlling,
Much steals men's eyes and women's souls amazeth,
And for a woman wert thou first created,
Till nature as she wrought thee fell a doting,
And by addition me of thee defeated,
By adding one thing to my purpose nothing.
    But since she prick'd thee out for women's pleasure,
    Mine be thy love and thy love's use their treasure.

As a result of the corruption of the evolutionary process that took place in antiquity, a separating veil was formed between the world of higher states and the world of ordinary man. Ordinary man was cut-off from access to evolutionary energy. To correct this situation, Nature provided mankind with a lineage of spiritual guides. The guides are exemplars of human perfection. They are like a perfected species among humans. They are not recognizable by ordinary men, because there is nothing special in their physical appearance. Yet, they are the custodians of the evolutionary process and the possessors of the currently projected cosmic matrix. They have been equipped with techniques, instruments, and methodologies allowing them to instruct men in how to fulfill their evolutionary potentiality by removing the separating veil and developing their inner being. At the same time, they are the carriers of all available elements of evolutionary energy.

Shakespeare uses young women to represent the various elements of evolutionary energy. In several plays a young woman represents both a guide and an element of evolutionary energy. Such a double role ("the Master Mistress of my passion") is symbolically indicated by a woman who is temporarily disguised as a man (e.g., Portia in "The Merchant of Venice", Rosalind in "As You Like It"). The poet refers frivolously to such a double role of the Guide in the following lines of the Sonnet:

> "And for a woman wert thou first created,
> Till nature as she wrought thee fell a doting,
> And by addition me of thee defeated,
> By adding one thing to my purpose nothing."

This is why the poet describes the Guide's face being as pretty as a woman's face; his heart is as gentle as a woman's heart, but it is constant; his eyes are brighter and truer than women's eyes, giving blessing to everything they look at.

The Sonnet contains a word play on two aspects of attraction, i.e., ordinary (sensual) and spiritual. Sensual attraction is described as false and inconstant ("with shifting change, as is false women's fashion"). On the other hand, spiritual attraction carries the developmental functionality that may be symbolically described as "gilding the object whereupon it gazeth". In this context, the "gilding" indicates the evolutionary process, whereby an ordinary metal (the manifest faculties) may be transmuted into gold (the subtle faculties). The poet distances himself from sensual attractions by concluding that his current interest is in spiritual matters ("mine be thy love and thy love's use their treasure").

Shakespeare uses a colour code to indicate the specific subtle faculties. As mentioned earlier, the four subtle faculties are indicated by the colours yellow, red, white, and black. In other words, the man who has fully developed his inner being may be described as a man who is in control of all colours. The Guide is such a man ("a man in hue all hues in his controlling"). Graphically, such a fully developed state which contains the four subtle faculties and the four corresponding elements of energy, is represented by the octagon. If this octagonal inner structure is correctly balanced and harmonized, then it is possible to transmute it into a new inner being. Such a transmutation is illustrated as the appearance of a ninth point within the octagon. In the system of equivalence of letters and numbers, the octagon is represented by the letter H and the enneagon by the letter T. In other words, the letter T may be used to indicate a fully developed man, i.e., the Guide.

The transmutation of the octagon into the enneagon is illustrated as a transition from the letter H into the letter T. In the episode with Scarus in "Antony and Cleopatra", Shakespeare made a reference to such a transition[20]:

> "I had a wound here that was like a T,
> But now 'tis made an H."

In the above quote, Scarus' wound indicated an inverse transition, i.e., from T to H. It was a message to Mark Antony that he was diverging from the straight path.

Shakespeare used the same system of equivalence of letters and numbers in the Dedication to the Sonnets.

---

[20] See "Rescue attempts" (Shakespeare for the Seeker, Volume 1, Chapter 2.3).

SONNET XXI

So is it not with me as with that Muse,
Stirred by a painted beauty to his verse,
Who heaven itself for ornament doth use,
And every fair with his fair doth rehearse,
Making a couplement of proud compare
With Sun and Moon, with earth and sea's rich gems:
With April's first born flowers and all things rare,
That heaven's air in this huge rondure hems,
O let me true in love but truly write,
And then believe me, my love is as fair,
As any mother's child, though not so bright
As those gold candles fixed in heaven's air:
    Let them say more that like of hearsay well:
    I will not praise that purpose not to sell.

The poet makes a clear and significant distinction between the object of his praise and those of the other poets ("so is it not with me as with that Muse"). The other poets worship worldly beauty and describe it by using divine attributes ("stirred by a painted beauty to his verse, who heaven itself for ornament doth use"). He declares that his poetry is not inspired by an ordinary beauty that is often compared to the sun, the moon, and gems ("making a couplement of proud compare with sun and moon, with earth and sea's rich gems"). He leaves this sort of overactive imagination, fantasies, and emotions to other poets ("let me true in love but truly write"). In accordance with the symbols introduced by the Guide, he refers to his objective as a child ("and then believe me, my love is as fair, as any mother's child"). But he would not compare his love to such heavenly objects like golden stars ("though not so bright as those gold candles fixed in heaven's air"). He does not intend to use those usual poetic clichés in his verses ("let them say more that like of hearsay well"). His purpose is neither to sell nor to praise ("I will not praise that purpose not to sell").

In this way the poet differentiates between two types of arts. One type is of an evolutionary nature, the other aims at different goals. The evolutionary or objective art is created by a fully developed man, who has overcome his own ego and acts in accordance with the evolutionary needs. Therefore, he is able to express the essence of true knowledge. The other forms of art can be as necessary as the objective art, but there is a functional difference between them. Duke Theseus in "A Midsummer Night's Dream" also made the same distinction[21]. He referred to ordinary art as driven by an exaggerated imagination disconnected from reality:

> "The poet's eye, in fine frenzy rolling,
> Doth glance from heaven to earth, from earth to heaven;
> And as imagination bodies forth
> The forms of things unknown, the poet's pen
> Turns them to shapes and gives to airy nothing
> A local habitation and a name."

---

[21] See "The lunatic, the lover, and the poet" (Shakespeare for the Seeker, Volume 4, Chapter 8.3).

SONNET XXII

My glass shall not persuade me I am old,
So long as youth and thou are of one date,
But when in thee time's furrows I behold,
Then look I death my days should expiate.
For all that beauty that doth cover thee,
Is but the seemly raiment of my heart,
Which in thy breast doth live, as thine in me,
How can I then be elder than thou art?
O therefore love be of thyself so wary,
As I not for myself, but for thee will,
Bearing thy heart which I will keep so chary
As tender nurse her babe from faring ill,
    Presume not on thy heart when mine is slain,
    Thou gav'st me thine not to give back again.

In his initial enthusiasm, the poet treats his relation with the Guide a bit naively and sentimentally. He says that he will not be persuaded by a mirror when it tells him that he is old ("my glass shall not persuade me I am old"). Because he knows that his new inner self was born when he met the Guide, therefore he is as young as his Guide is ("so long as youth and thou are of one date"). But when he will notice that the Guide's face is covered with wrinkles, for him it will be a sign of approaching death ("but when in thee time's furrows I behold, then look I death my days should expiate"). The poet realizes that his heart is partially within the Guide's heart ("beauty that doth cover thee is but the seemly raiment of my heart"). His heart is encompassed by the Guide's heart, and the Guide's heart is within his ("which in thy breast doth live, as thine in me"). Then how could the poet be elder than the Guide? ("How can I then be elder than thou art?") Therefore, the poet asks the Guide to take care of himself ("O therefore love be of thyself so wary"). At the same time, the poet will be looking after himself for the sake of the Guide's heart ("as I not for myself, but for thee will"). The poet promises to protect the Guide's heart as carefully as a nurse takes care of her baby ("bearing thy heart which I will keep so chary as tender nurse her babe from faring ill"). The poet finishes with the conclusion that when his heart is slain, the Guide's heart will also die ("presume not on thy heart when mine is slain"). After all, the Guide gave him his heart, so it cannot be given back to him ("thou gav'st me thine not to give back again").

The poet's conclusion indicates that he has not understood the process yet. The process may be completed when his heart will be completely submerged within the Guide's essence. Then, there will be no distinction between "thine" and "mine". This may happen only when the poet "dies to live", i.e., when his heart will be "slain".

Desdemona in "Othello" went through a similar experience of "dying before dying". At first she was fearful of the coming death, because she did not fully understand what was really happening to her[22]:

> "And yet I fear you; for you are fatal then
> When your eyes roll so: why I should fear I know not,
> Since guiltiness I know not; but yet I feel I fear."

---

[22] See "Transition" (Shakespeare for the Seeker, Volume 3, Chapter 6.2).

SONNET XXIII

As an unperfect actor on the stage,
Who with his fear is put beside his part,
Or some fierce thing replete with too much rage,
Whose strength's abundance weakens his own heart;
So I for fear of trust, forget to say,
The perfect ceremony of love's rite,
And in mine own love's strength seem to decay,
O'ercharged with burthen of mine own love's might:
O let my looks be then the eloquence,
And dumb presagers of my speaking breast,
Who plead for love, and look for recompense,
More than that tongue that more hath more express'd.
    O learn to read what silent love hath writ,
    To hear with eyes belongs to love's fine wit.

The poet admits that he, like an inexperienced actor on the stage, is becoming overwhelmed by the magnitude of his current task ("as an unperfect actor on the stage, who with his fear is put beside his part"). He compares himself to some brutal creature whose excessive fury weakens its courage ("or some fierce thing replete with too much rage, whose strength's abundance weakens his own heart"). So is the poet, who is frightened by the magnitude of his burden ("and in mine own love's strength seem to decay, o'ercharged with burthen of mine own love's might"). He hopes that his look may serve as his speech and his silence may be his voice in eloquent pleading for his love ("let my looks be then the eloquence, and dumb presagers of my speaking breast, who plead for love, and look for recompense, more than that tongue that more hath more express'd"). To do this, the poet would have to read in silence and to hear with eyes ("to read what silent love hath writ, to hear with eyes"). Symbolically, such a state would mark the appearance of a new inner being, i.e., experience which "belongs to love's fine wit".

The formation of a new inner being is realized through the development of subtle faculties. The subtle faculties transcend the ordinary physical senses. Allegorically, the operation of the subtle faculties may be described as an experience that is beyond the eye, beyond the ear, beyond touch, beyond taste, beyond smell. But the activation of the subtle faculties is only a stage of the process. The process is completed when the subtle faculties are united and they are fused together to form the new inner being. By using the same allegory, the operation of this new being may be described as "to read what silent love hath writ, to hear with eyes". Nick Bottom in "A Midsummer Night's Dream" described such an experience in the following way[23]:

> "But man is but a patched fool,
> if he will offer to say what methought I had.
> The eye of man hath not heard, the ear of man hath not
> seen, man's hand is not able to taste, his tongue
> to conceive, nor his heart to report, what my dream was."

---

[23] See "The guide" (Shakespeare for the Seeker, Volume 4, Chapter 8.3).

SONNET XXIV

Mine eye hath played the painter and hath steeled,
Thy beauty's form in table of my heart,
My body is the frame wherein 'tis held,
And perspective that is best Painter's art.
For through the Painter must you see his skill,
To find where your true Image pictured lies,
Which in my bosom's shop is hanging still,
That hath his windows glazed with thine eyes:
Now see what good-turns eyes for eyes have done,
Mine eyes have drawn thy shape, and thine for me
Are windows to my breast, where-through the Sun
Delights to peep, to gaze therein on thee
    Yet eyes this cunning want to grace their art
    They draw but what they see, know not the heart.

Previously, the Guide asked the poet to build a special container in a secret place where his treasure may be stored ("make sweet some vial; treasure thou some place, with beauty's treasure ere it be self-killed" - see Sonnet 6). Now we find out more about the container and the secret place where the treasure is to be stored.

The poet says that he was able to paint an image of true beauty. He has stored the painting in his inner heart ("mine eye hath played the painter and hath steeled, thy beauty's form in table of my heart"). His own body is just a frame that holds this painting and provides the means for looking at it ("my body is the frame wherein 'tis held, and perspective that is best painter's art"). Seeing where the painting is placed makes it possible to judge the spiritual state of its painter ("for through the Painter must you see his skill, to find where your true Image pictured lies"). Namely, such an experience is a mark of the operation of a reformed heart faculty, i.e., the subtle faculty indicated by the colour yellow. At this time, only the Guide may view it ("which in my bosom's shop is hanging still, that hath his windows glazed with thine eyes"). The poet implies that their eyes have done the favours to each other ("now see what good-turns eyes for eyes have done"). Namely, the poet's eyes have drawn the Guide's image and stored it in his inner heart, i.e., where the Guide's eyes may see it ("mine eyes have drawn thy shape, and thine for me are windows to my breast"). And now, through the Guide's eyes, Nature may look at it and be delighted by true beauty ("where-through the sun delights to peep, to gaze therein on thee"). But the poet also wants to see and admire his own art ("yet eyes this cunning want to grace their art"). But his eyes cannot see true beauty ("they draw but what they see, know not the heart"). The fact, that the poet is able to paint it and store it but is not able to see true beauty, indicates that his heart faculty has been reformed but the subtle faculties of his intellect are still non-operational.

Similarly, the actor playing Lucianus in "Hamlet" was able to paint the image of Claudius' heart[24]. In that case, however, the image was "black as death":

> "Thoughts black, hands apt, drugs fit, and time agreeing;
> Confederate season, else no creature seeing;
> Thou mixture rank, of midnight weeds collected,
> With Hecate's ban thrice blasted, thrice infected,
> Thy natural magic and dire property,
> On wholesome life usurp immediately."

As a result of the actor's projection, Claudius called exasperatedly for "some light" and rushed out of the room.

---

[24] See "The players' performance" (Shakespeare for the Seeker, Volume 4, Chapter 7.3).

SONNET XXV

Let those who are in favour with their stars,
Of public honour and proud titles boast,
Whilst I whom fortune of such triumph bars
Unlook'd for joy in that I honour most.
Great Princes' favourites their fair leaves spread,
But as the Marigold at the sun's eye,
And in them-selves their pride lies buried,
For at a frown they in their glory die.
The painful warrior famoused for fight,
After a thousand victories once foiled,
Is from the book of honour razed quite,
And all the rest forgot for which he toiled:
    Then happy I that love and am beloved
    Where I may not remove, nor be removed.

The poet starts to absorb gradually the teaching that was contained in the Guide's initial appeal. In this Sonnet, the poet meditates on the transience of worldly fortunes and honours.

The poet recognizes the folly of worldly pleasures, to which he includes holding high public positions and honorary titles ("let those who are in favour with their stars, of public honour and proud titles boast"). Such pleasures are at the mercy of other men, who are inconstant and incomplete. He considers himself to be lucky, because such worldly fortunes are beyond his reach ("whilst I whom fortune of such triumph bars"). Instead, he finds himself rewarded in rather unexpected joy, i.e., the constancy of the Guide's love. And that is what he honours most ("unlook'd for joy in that I honour most"). In comparison, courtiers who are basking in the favours of their princes are like marigolds, because marigolds bloom only as long as the sun shines on them ("great princes' favourites their fair leaves spread, but as the marigold at the sun's eye"). So it is with the courtiers' glory, which is killed by a single frown of their princes ("and in them-selves their pride lies buried, for at a frown they in their glory die"). Similarly, famous warriors who won their fame in a thousand battles, lose all their honours in a single defeat ("the painful warrior famoused for fight, after a thousand victories once foiled, is from the book of honour razed quite, and all the rest forgot for which he toiled"). But the poet's happiness derives from the constancy of the Guide's love, which is placed in the Guide's constant heart ("then happy I that love and am beloved where I may not remove, nor be removed").

Henry V arrived at a similar conclusion regarding worldly honours[25]. Here is his meditation on the value of honours, titles, and ceremony:

> " 'Tis not the balm, the sceptre and the ball,
> The sword, the mace, the crown imperial,
> The intertissued robe of gold and pearl,
> The farced title running 'fore the king,
> The throne he sits on, nor the tide of pomp
> That beats upon the high shore of this world,
> No, not all these, thrice-gorgeous ceremony,
> Not all these, laid in bed majestical,
> Can sleep so soundly as the wretched slave,
> Who with a body fill'd and vacant mind
> Gets him to rest, cramm'd with distressful bread."

---

[25] See "Dawn of perfection" (Shakespeare for the Seeker, Volume 1, Chapter 1).

SONNET XXVI

Lord of my love, to whom in vassalage
Thy merit hath my duty strongly knit;
To thee I send this written embassage,
To witness duty, not to show my wit.
Duty so great, which wit so poor as mine
May make seem bare, in wanting words to show it;
But that I hope some good conceit of thine
In thy soul's thought (all naked) will bestow it:
Till whatsoever star that guides my moving,
Points on me graciously with fair aspect,
And puts apparel on my tottered loving,
To show me worthy of thy sweet respect,
    Then may I dare to boast how I do love thee,
    Till then not show my head where thou mayst prove me.

The poet starts to realize what his true position versus his Guide is ("lord of my love, to whom in vassalage thy merit hath my duty strongly knit"). He is discovering that his responsibility towards the Guide takes the form of duty and not showing off his talent ("to thee I send this written embassage, to witness duty, not to show my wit"). The poet is finding out that his skills are not adequate enough to discharge his current duty ("duty so great, which wit so poor as mine may make seem bare, in wanting words to show it"). Therefore, the poet hopes that despite the inadequacy of his skills, the Guide will appreciate them ("but that I hope some good conceit of thine in thy soul's thought, all naked, will bestow it"). The poet promises that as soon as his guiding star bestows on him the needed inspiration, he will try again to earn the Guide's respect in a more effective manner ("till whatsoever star that guides my moving, points on me graciously with fair aspect and puts apparel on my tottered loving, to show me worthy of thy sweet respect"). Only then the poet will dare to boast about his love ("then may I dare to boast how I do love thee"). Until then he will keep quiet, afraid of being put to the test ("till then not show my head where thou mayst prove me").

Katharina in "The Taming of Shrew" also discovered the nature of duty to her guide[26]. She spelled it out in her famous speech, which she delivered at the end of the play:

> "Thy husband is thy lord, thy life, thy keeper,
> Thy head, thy sovereign; one that cares for thee,
> And for thy maintenance commits his body
> To painful labour both by sea and land,
> To watch the night in storms, the day in cold,
> Whilst thou liest warm at home, secure and safe;
> And craves no other tribute at thy hands
> But love, fair looks and true obedience."

---

[26] See "Taming school" (Shakespeare for the Seeker, Volume 3, Chapter 6.5).

SONNET XXVII

Weary with toil, I haste me to my bed,
The dear repose for limbs with travel tired,
But then begins a journey in my head
To work my mind, when body's work's expired.
For then my thoughts (from far where I abide)
Intend a zealous pilgrimage to thee,
And keep my drooping eye-lids open wide,
Looking on darkness which the blind do see.
Save that my soul's imaginary sight
Presents thy shadow to my sightless view,
Which like a jewel (hung in ghastly night)
Makes black night beauteous, and her old face new.
    Lo thus by day my limbs, by night my mind,
    For thee, and for myself, no quiet find.

Here the poet gives an insight into the many toils and perils that a traveler on the spiritual path is faced with ("weary with toil"). There are no breaks during this journey ("Lo thus by day my limbs, by night my mind, for thee, and for myself, no quiet find"). It involves physical exercises ("I haste me to my bed, the dear repose for limbs with travel tired") and meditations ("but then begins a journey in my head to work my mind, when body's work's expired"). It is seemingly a never ending pilgrimage ("for then my thoughts, from far where I abide, intend a zealous pilgrimage to thee"). It requires a continuous struggle and effort, with no visible end in sight ("and keep my drooping eye-lids open wide, looking on darkness which the blind do see"). The important thing is that the poet is under the tutelage of his Guide, who is like a guiding star that makes the black and old face of night look young and beautiful ("save that my soul's imaginary sight presents thy shadow to my sightless view, which like a jewel, hung in ghastly night, makes black night beauteous, and her old face new").

In his last words, Julius Caesar described himself as such a unique guiding star[27]:

> "But I am constant as the northern star,
> Of whose true-fix'd and resting quality
> There is no fellow in the firmament.
> The skies are painted with unnumber'd sparks,
> They are all fire and every one doth shine,
> But there's but one in all doth hold his place:
> So in the world; 'tis furnish'd well with men,
> And men are flesh and blood, and apprehensive;
> Yet in the number I do know but one
> That unassailable holds on his rank,
> Unshaked of motion: and that I am he,
> Let me a little show it, even in this."

---

[27] See "Spiritual king" (Shakespeare for the Seeker, Volume 1, Chapter 2.2).

SONNET XXVIII

How can I then return in happy plight
That am debarred the benefit of rest?
When day's oppression is not eas'd by night,
But day by night and night by day oppressed.
And each (though enemies to either's reign)
Do in consent shake hands to torture me,
The one by toil, the other to complain
How far I toil, still farther off from thee.
I tell the Day to please him thou art bright,
And dost him grace when clouds do blot the heaven:
So flatter I the swart-complexion'd night,
When sparkling stars twire not thou gild'st the even.
    But day doth daily draw my sorrows longer,
    And night doth nightly make grief's length seem stronger.

This Sonnet emphasizes one of the characteristic features of the spiritual process. At this stage of the journey the poet's experiences or the states described in the previous Sonnets are not permanent yet. This is why he is not able to reproduce them ("how can I then return in happy plight that am debarred the benefit of rest?") Neither his physical efforts nor meditations seem to bring back his previous experiences ("when day's oppression is not eas'd by night, but day by night and night by day oppressed"). The poet looks at day and night as mutual enemies, yet they both seem to work together to torture him by offering him more toils and more reasons to complain ("and each, though enemies to either's reign, do in consent shake hands to torture me, the one by toil, the other to complain"). The net result is that the poet is not able to bring in the presence of the Guide ("still farther off from thee"). So, the poet tries to bribe the day by telling that the Guide is bright and will light the day when the clouds darken the heaven ("I tell the Day to please him thou art bright, and dost him grace when clouds do blot the heaven"). And he flatters the night by promising it that the Guide will brighten the starless evenings ("so flatter I the swart complexion'd night, when sparkling stars twire not thou gild'st the even"). At the end, the poet admits that both day and night only prolong his sorrows and grief ("but day doth daily draw my sorrows longer, and night doth nightly make grief's length seem stronger"). This sort of fleetingness of states is a result of impatience. In other words, it is the poet's impatience that is the source of his current frustration and disappointment.

Similarly, Juliet's impatience and her insistence on a premature wedding with Romeo[28] was one of the causes of their tragic story:

> "If that thy bent of love be honourable,
> Thy purpose marriage, send me word to-morrow."

---

[28] See "Villain" (Shakespeare for the Seeker, Volume 3, Chapter 6.6).

SONNET XXIX

When in disgrace with Fortune and men's eyes,
I all alone beweep my out-cast state,
And trouble deaf heaven with my bootless cries,
And look upon myself and curse my fate.
Wishing me like to one more rich in hope,
Featured like him, like him with friends possessed,
Desiring this man's art, and that man's scope,
With what I most enjoy contented least,
Yet in these thoughts my self almost despising,
Haply I think on thee, and then my state,
(Like to the Lark at break of day arising)
From sullen earth, sings hymns at Heaven's gate,
    For thy sweet love remembered such wealth brings,
    That then I scorn to change my state with Kings.

The poet's description of perils and toils is the mark of another source of fleetingness of his inner states. Namely, the poet's difficulties described in the Sonnet are caused by the importance that he still gives to worldly pleasures. Previously he has paid lip service to the inadequacies of such attachments (see Sonnet 25). But now we are finding out that he is still driven by those worldly attractions. So, he sits alone and cries when he is out of luck or when disgraced by his friends ("when in disgrace with fortune and men's eyes, I all alone beweep my outcast state"). And he curses himself and bothers heaven with his useless complains ("and trouble deaf heaven with my bootless cries, and look upon myself and curse my fate"). Then he lists a number of worldly pleasures that are still important to him, i.e., promising hopes, good look, having more friends, having certain skills and new opportunities ("wishing me like to one more rich in hope, featured like him, like him with friends possessed, desiring this man's art, and that man's scope"). Yet, he admits, he is least content with things he enjoys most ("with what I most enjoy contented least"). The poet discovers that he may distance himself from these destructive attachments by focussing his attention on the Guide. During such moments his inner state changes, like a lark at daybreak that starts to sing hymns to heaven ("in these thoughts my self almost despising, haply I think on thee, and then my state, like to the lark at break of day arising from sullen earth, sings hymns at heaven's gate"). At such moments the poet is able to experience a different kind of riches, which he would not exchange for anything else ("for thy sweet love remembered such wealth brings, that then I scorn to change my state with kings").

Ferdinand in "The Tempest" went through a similar experience. He was able to overcome his sorrows by focussing his attention on Ariel's music[29]:

> "Weeping again the king my father's wreck,
> This music crept by me upon the waters,
> Allaying both their fury and my passion
> With its sweet air: thence I have follow'd it,
> Or it hath drawn me rather."

Guided by Ariel's music, Ferdinand met Miranda.

---

[29] See "Process" (Shakespeare for the Seeker, Volume 4, Chapter 8.1).

SONNET XXX

When to the Sessions of sweet silent thought,
I summon up remembrance of things past,
I sigh the lack of many a thing I sought,
And with old woes new wail my dear time's waste:
Then can I drown an eye (unused to flow)
For precious friends hid in death's dateless night,
And weep afresh love's long since cancelled woe,
And moan the expense of many a vanished sight.
Then can I grieve at grievances foregone,
And heavily from woe to woe tell o'er
The sad account of fore-bemoaned moan,
Which I new pay as if not paid before.
    But if the while I think on thee (dear friend)
    All losses are restor'd, and sorrows end.

The poet indicates that he is learning about the nature of constructive meditation. He refers to his meditations as "sessions" ("when to the Sessions of sweet silent thought"). If during his meditations the poet allows his thoughts to wonder freely, they go back into the past and bring memories of all kind of unfulfilled desires ("I summon up remembrance of things past, I sigh the lack of many a thing I sought"). This makes him depressed and tearful ("and with old woes new wail my dear time's waste: then can I drown an eye, unused to flow"). He laments about old grievances and sadly recounts each woe of the past ("for precious friends hid in death's dateless night, and weep afresh love's long since cancelled woe, and moan the expense of many a vanished sight"). He realizes, that this is like paying again for something that he has already paid ("the sad account of fore-bemoaned moan, which I new pay as if not paid before"). Then he discovers that the only way to free himself from such idle commemorations is to focus his attention on his Guide. In this way the poet's meditation can lead to a constructive outcome ("but if the while I think on thee, dear friend, all losses are restor'd, and sorrows end").

Such an approach could also help Antonio[30] in "The Merchant of Venice" to deal with his sadness:

> "In sooth, I know not why I am so sad:
> It wearies me; you say it wearies you;
> But how I caught it, found it, or came by it,
> What stuff 'tis made of, whereof it is born,
> I am to learn;
> And such a want-wit sadness makes of me,
> That I have much ado to know myself."

Antonio, however, was not able to recognize the Guide. His attention was focussed on a shadow of the primary cause. Therefore, his inner state could not be changed.

---

[30] See "Villains" (Shakespeare for the Seeker, Volume 3, Chapter 6.4).

SONNET XXXI

Thy bosom is endeared with all hearts,
Which I by lacking have supposed dead,
And there reigns Love and all Love's loving parts,
And all those friends which I thought buried.
How many a holy and obsequious tear
Hath dear religious love stol'n from mine eye,
As interest of the dead, which now appear,
But things removed that hidden in thee lie.
Thou art the grave where buried love doth live,
Hung with the trophies of my lovers gone,
Who all their parts of me to thee did give,
That due of many, now is thine alone.
    Their images I loved, I view in thee,
    And thou (all they) hast all the all of me.

The poet makes a reference to the unbroken line of the transmission, mentioned by the Guide in Sonnet 13. The Guides are the carriers and the transmitters of the entire spectrum of evolutionary energy. The poet has just realized that his Guide represents all spiritual guides of the past ("thy bosom is endeared with all hearts"). Therefore, all modes of evolutionary energy are encompassed within the Guide's essence ("and there reigns love and all love's loving parts"). Because of his spiritual ignorance, the poet was assuming that the guides of the past were gone ("which I by lacking have supposed dead"). It seems that the poet used to follow a doctrine that was focused on an outdated teaching from previous times ("how many a holy and obsequious tear hath dear religious love stol'n from mine eye, as interest of the dead"). And only now he has realized that all what he needs he may find in his Guide ("which now appear, but things removed that hidden in thee lie"). The poet refers to the previous guides as lovers, whose essence has been preserved within his Guide's heart ("thou art the grave where buried love doth live, hung with the trophies of my lovers gone"). All love that the poet offered them previously, was inherited by his Guide ("who all their parts of me to thee did give, that due of many, now is thine alone"). The poet has recognized that all what he was looking for previously is contained within the heart of the presently living Guide ("their images I loved, I view in thee, and thou, all they, hast all the all of me").

Prince Morocco in "The Merchant of Venice" made a similar remark about Portia[31], i.e., the living saint of Belmont:

> "Why, that's the lady; all the world desires her;
> From the four corners of the earth they come,
> To kiss this shrine, this mortal-breathing saint."

---

[31] See "Pilgrimage" (Shakespeare for the Seeker, Volume 3, Chapter 6.4).

SONNET XXXII

If thou survive my well contented day,
When that churl death my bones with dust shall cover
And shalt by fortune once more re-survey:
These poor rude lines of thy deceased Lover:
Compare them with the bett'ring of the time,
And though they be out-stripped by every pen,
Reserve them for my love, not for their rhyme,
Exceeded by the height of happier men.
Oh then vouchsafe me but this loving thought,
Had my friend's Muse grown with this growing age,
A dearer birth than this his love had brought:
To march in ranks of better equipage:
    But since he died and Poets better prove,
    Theirs for their style I'll read, his for his love.

The poet starts to perceive the difference between container and content. A container may have many forms. In the case of poetry, it is its outward form, i.e., style, rhyme, composition, elegance, etc. The content, on the other hand, is the essence of truth, which may be stored or transmitted through poetry. The poet hopes that his poems' content will be remembered. So he asks the Guide that he should judge the poems for their content, and should not pay attention to their outward form ("reserve them for my love, not for their rhyme"). He says that there are many more talented poets than he is himself ("and though they be out-stripped by every pen"). He asks the Guide to excuse him for not being able to write better poetry. Had the poet's Muse grown together with him, his love would inspire him to write much better verses ("had my friend's Muse grown with this growing age, a dearer birth than this his love had brought"). The poet hopes that the Guide will judge his poems not by their style, but by the degree of the poet's love ("but since he died and Poets better prove, theirs for their style I'll read, his for his love").

Petruchio in "The Taming of the Shrew" also alluded to the subjective value of external appearances[32]:

> "What is the jay more precious than the lark,
> Because his fathers are more beautiful?
> Or is the adder better than the eel,
> Because his painted skin contents the eye?
> O, no, good Kate; neither art thou the worse
> For this poor furniture and mean array."

---

[32] See "Taming school" (Shakespeare for the Seeker, Volume 3, Chapter 6.5).

SONNET XXXIII

Full many a glorious morning have I seen,
Flatter the mountain tops with sovereign eye,
Kissing with golden face the meadows green;
Gilding pale streams with heavenly alchemy:
Anon permit the basest clouds to ride,
With ugly rack on his celestial face,
And from the forlorn world his visage hide
Stealing unseen to west with this disgrace:
Even so my Sun one early morn did shine,
With all triumphant splendour on my brow,
But out alack, he was but one hour mine,
The region cloud hath mask'd him from me now.
    Yet him for this, my love no whit disdaineth,
    Suns of the world may stain, when heaven's sun staineth.

This Sonnet emphasizes the impermanency of the poet's current experiences. The poet has encountered such fleeting states previously (see Sonnet 28). He compares these fleeting states to the inconstancy of the sun, whose radiant presence benefits the entire world ("flatter the mountain tops with sovereign eye, kissing with golden face the meadows green, gilding pale streams with heavenly alchemy"). The poet's inconstancy is the reason that he is not able to hold onto the presence of the Guide's radiance ("anon permit the basest clouds to ride, with ugly rack on his celestial face"). At this stage, therefore, the interaction between the Guide and the poet may be compared to the sun occasionally veiled by clouds ("but out alack, he was but one hour mine, the region cloud hath mask'd him from me now"). Yet, the poet says that these occasional separations from the Guide do not affect his love ("yet him for this, my love no whit disdaineth"). And he demonstrates his ignorance by implying that the Guide's disappearances are like great men's mistakes, which are induced by heavenly influences ("suns of the world may stain, when heaven's sun staineth"). The poet has not understood yet that his inconstancy is the cause of the Guide's disappearances.

Pericles in "Pericles, Prince of Tyre", for example, was able to be constant in his approach despite a seemingly unfavourable treatment by heaven[33]:

> "Yet cease your ire, you angry stars of heaven!
> Wind, rain, and thunder, remember, earthly man
> Is but a substance that must yield to you;
> And I, as fits my nature, do obey you."

---

[33] See "Inspirational vision" (Shakespeare for the Seeker, Volume 2, Chapter 4.1).

SONNET XXXIV

Why didst thou promise such a beauteous day,
And make me travel forth without my cloak,
To let base clouds o'ertake me in my way,
Hiding thy bravery in their rotten smoke.
'Tis not enough that through the cloud thou break,
To dry the rain on my storm-beaten face,
For no man well of such a salve can speak,
That heals the wound, and cures not the disgrace:
Nor can thy shame give physic to my grief,
Though thou repent, yet I have still the loss,
The offender's sorrow lends but weak relief
To him that bears the strong offence's cross.
    Ah but those tears are pearl which thy love sheds,
    And they are rich, and ransom all ill deeds.

To help the disciple discover his shortcomings, the Guide leads him though a series of very difficult and sometimes painful experiences. The challenge for the disciple is to realize that he should observe his own reaction to such deliberately arranged situations. This time the Guide points out that the poet's disappointments and suffering are a result of his false expectations. The Sonnet indicates that instead of focusing his attention on his own reactions, the poet preoccupies himself with accusations of the Guide.

As in the previous Sonnet, the poet compares the Guide to the sun. The poet was expecting to meet with him ("why didst thou promise such a beauteous day, and make me travel forth without my cloak"). Because his approach was not correct, the meeting did not take place ("to let base clouds o'ertake me in my way, hiding thy bravery in their rotten smoke"). Instead of reflecting on the event, the poet starts to complain and blame the Guide ("'tis not enough that through the cloud thou break, to dry the rain on my storm-beaten face"). The poet feels that he has been wounded and disgraced ("for no man well of such a salve can speak, that heals the wound, and cures not the disgrace"). He says that neither the Guide's embarrassment nor repentance are enough to heal the poet's grief and repair his loss ("nor can thy shame and give physic to my grief, though thou repent, yet I have still the loss"). If something is lost, being sorry does not help much ("the offender's sorrow lends but weak relief to him that bears the strong offence's cross"). And again, the poet arrives at a completely wrong conclusion. Namely, he says that the Guide's tears are signs of the Guide's repentance, and they make up for all his offences ("but those tears are pearl which thy love sheds, and they are rich, and ransom all ill deeds"). The poet misinterprets the Guide's embarrassment and his sorrow. The Guide is crying because the poet has not understood the lesson.

Pericles in "Pericles, Prince of Tyre" also misunderstood what was happening to him[34]: Here is his reaction to the death of Thaisa, his wife:

> "O you gods!
> Why do you make us love your goodly gifts,
> And snatch them straight away? We here below
> Recall not what we give, and therein may
> Use honour with you."

Only at the end of the play does he understand the reason of Thaisa's "death".

---

[34] See "Advanced techniques" (Shakespeare for the Seeker, Volume 2, Chapter 4.1).

SONNET XXXV

No more be grieved at that which thou hast done,
Roses have thorns, and silver fountains mud,
Clouds and eclipses stain both Moon and Sun,
And loathsome canker lives in sweetest bud.
All men make faults, and even I in this,
Authorizing thy trespass with compare,
Myself corrupting salving thy amiss,
Excusing their sins more than their sins are:
For to thy sensual fault I bring in sense,
Thy adverse party is thy Advocate,
And 'gainst myself a lawful plea commence,
Such civil war is in my love and hate,
    That I an accessary needs must be,
    To that sweet thief which sourly robs from me.

The poet is still preoccupied with a supposed offence committed by the Guide ("no more be grieved at that which thou hast done"). He does not realize that his false expectations are the cause of his current disappointment and unhappiness. So, it is interesting to see how such ignorance leads to further complications. The poet attempts to recover from his disappointment by trying to excuse the Guide for his apparent faults. He quotes the usual cliché about roses with thorns, fountains with mud, the sun and the moon obstructed by clouds, and a despicable worm living in a beautiful blossom ("roses have thorns, and silver fountains mud, clouds and eclipses stain both moon and sun, and loathsome canker lives in sweetest bud"). Then, the poet goes even deeper into his self-deception. He claims that nobody is perfect, and he blames himself for trying to excuse the Guide's wrongdoing ("all men make faults, and even I in this, authorizing thy trespass with compare"). He argues that he has corrupted himself by applying such grandeur measures to wipe out his friend's minor offence ("myself corrupting salving thy amiss, excusing their sins more than their sins are"). The poet realizes that by following his reason he turned himself into the Guide's defender ("for to thy sensual fault I bring in sense, thy adverse party is thy advocate"). Therefore, the poet ended up pleading the case against himself ("and 'gainst myself a lawful plea commence"). In this way, the poet has become a helper of the thief who robbed him from his love ("that I an accessary needs must be, to that sweet thief which sourly robs from me").

The poet's conclusion is an illustration of his multi-layered deception. A struggle between love and hate is a sign of his unbalanced emotional state ("such civil war is in my love and hate"). It is obvious that, at this time, the poet is incapable of recognizing the source of his troubles.

The city of Verona at the time of "Romeo and Juliet" was also caught up in such an unbalanced state. Here is Romeo's comment about it [35]:

> "Here's much to do with hate, but more with love.
> Why, then, O brawling love! O loving hate!"

---

[35] See "Villain" (Shakespeare for the Seeker, Volume 3, Chapter 6.6).

SONNET XXXVI

Let me confess that we two must be twain,
Although our undivided loves are one:
So shall those blots that do with me remain,
Without thy help, by me be borne alone.
In our two loves there is but one respect,
Though in our lives a separable spite,
Which though it alter not love's sole effect,
Yet doth it steal sweet hours from love's delight,
I may not ever-more acknowledge thee,
Lest my bewailed guilt should do thee shame,
Nor thou with public kindness honour me,
Unless thou take that honour from thy name:
 But do not so, I love thee in such sort,
 As thou being mine, mine is thy good report.

After satisfying himself with his own explanation of the situation in which he has found himself, the poet decides to take action. The poet decides to distance himself from his Guide ("let me confess that we two must be twain"). In the name of his love for the Guide, he will deal by himself alone with those stains that they both have incurred ("so shall those blots that do with me remain, without thy help, by me be borne alone"). Although their love bears mutual respect, there is some issue that forces them to separate their lives ("in our two loves there is but one respect, though in our lives a separable spite"). The poet says that his action does not alter his love, yet it robs him from the pleasure of enjoying the Guide's company ("which though it alter not love's sole effect, yet doth it steal sweet hours from love's delight"). The poet announces that he will never approach the Guide openly, because such a lamenting gesture would bring shame upon the Guide ("I may not ever-more acknowledge thee, lest my bewailed guilt should do thee shame"). Nor the Guide should say anything good about the poet, because that might also disgrace him ("nor thou with public kindness honour me, unless thou take that honour from thy name"). The poet claims that his love is of such nature, that he considers the Guide and himself as one ("I love thee in such sort, as thou being mine"). The Guide's honour is also his, therefore it should not be questioned ("mine is thy good report").

Although seemingly altruistic, the last verse is another illustration of the poet's ignorance. Despite being buried within his multi-layered deception, the poet's egoistic-self comes to the surface quite obviously. After all it is his own honour that he cares about. Now, therefore, it is time for the Guide to intervene in the process to prevent the poet from going further astray from the straight path.

Mark Antony in "Antony and Cleopatra" went through a similar deception as the result of his misunderstanding of Octavius' role[36]. Here is Octavius' comment about their strained relationship:

> "We could not stall together
> In the whole world: but yet let me lament,
> With tears as sovereign as the blood of hearts,
> That thou, my brother, my competitor
> In top of all design, my mate in empire,
> Friend and companion in the front of war,
> The arm of mine own body, and the heart
> Where mine his thoughts did kindle, -that our stars,
> Unreconciliable, should divide
> Our equalness to this."

---

[36] See "Octavius' transformation" (Shakespeare for the Seeker, Volume 1, Chapter 2.3).

The Guide's second counsel (Sonnet 37)

SONNET XXXVII

As a decrepit father takes delight,
To see his active child do deeds of youth,
So I, made lame by Fortune's dearest spite
Take all my comfort of thy worth and truth.
For whether beauty, birth, or wealth, or wit,
Or any of these all, or all, or more
Entitled in thy parts, do crowned sit,
I make my love ingrafted to this store:
So then I am not lame, poor, nor despised,
Whilst that this shadow doth such substance give,
That I in thy abundance am sufficed,
And by a part of all thy glory live:
    Look what is best, that best I wish in thee,
    This wish I have, then ten times happy me.

In this Sonnet we hear again the Guide. The Guide speaks with confidence and authority. His words are in stark contrast to the unsure, distraught, and wavering lamentations of the poet. The Guide acts like Chorus in the plays. He comments on the overall process, explains the achieved progress and, if required, advises the poet.

The Guide explains that his role is to pass his knowledge onto the poet. It is only in this way that the evolutionary process may be sustained and continued. The Guide himself cannot maintain the process. This is why he compares himself to a feeble father who is delighted by watching his teenage child exploring life ("as a decrepit father takes delight, to see his active child do deeds of youth"). At this stage of the process, the poet still behaves like a spoiled teenager, who does many foolish things. Yet, it is the poet's potentiality that is of interest to the Guide ("so I, made lame by fortune's dearest spite take all my comfort of thy worth and truth"). The Guide takes his comfort from the fact that the poet has been granted "beauty, birth, or wealth, or wit". These four aspects constitute the poet's evolutionary potentiality. These four aspects are a symbolic representation of the latent subtle faculties, which are symbolically associated with the four colours, i.e., yellow, red, white, and black (see Sonnet 16). The activation of any of these subtle faculties, or four of them, or more of them - will fulfil the poet's potentiality ("or any of these all, or all, or more entitled in thy parts, do crowned sit").

It may help to understand the Guide's comment to recall the following conversation between Don Adriano and his page Moth[37] in "Love's Labour's Lost":

Don Adriano:

"Who was Samson's love, my dear Moth?"

Moth:

"A woman, master."

Don Adriano:

"Of what complexion?"

Moth:

"Of all the four, or the three, or the two, or one of the four."

Shakespeare uses young women to represent various elements of evolutionary energy. In the above quote, Moth refers to these various elements as women of various complexions or colours. As a result of the assimilation of evolutionary energy, "of all the four, or the three, or the two, or one of the four" subtle faculties may be activated. The Guide refers to these still latent states as "beauty, birth, or wealth, or wit". Through the process of evolutionary

---

[37] See "Technical background" (Shakespeare for the Seeker, Volume 2, Chapter 5.3).

engrafting, the Guide may activate them ("I make my love ingrafted to this store"). As pointed out in Sonnet 20, the Guide is a carrier of all colours or shadows of the spectrum. By exposing the poet to his shadow, the Guide will provide him with a new substance, which is like a source of spiritual abundance ("whilst that this shadow doth such substance give, that I in thy abundance am sufficed"). In other words, the poet may gain his inner perfection through exposure to a part of the evolutionary spectrum ("and by a part of all thy glory live"). In this way the evolutionary process will be preserved ("so then I am not lame, poor, nor despised").

The Guide appeals to the poet to do his best to fulfil his potentiality ("look what is best, that best I wish in thee"). If the poet does so, then the Guide will be fully satisfied ("this wish I have, then ten times happy me"). The most important thing to notice is the fact that the poet's previous teenager-like experiences were needed to prepare him for more challenging stages of the process. Now the Guide will initiate the poet into the path, i.e., he will expose him to a sequence of evolutionary energy. The Guide will administer such an exposure in accordance with the poet's initial state and the current projection of the cosmic matrix.

Initiation (Sonnets 38 - 47)

SONNET XXXVIII

How can my Muse want subject to invent
While thou dost breathe, that pour'st into my verse
Thine own sweet argument, too excellent,
For every vulgar paper to rehearse:
Oh give thy self the thanks if aught in me,
Worthy perusal stand against thy sight,
For who's so dumb that cannot write to thee,
When thou thy self dost give invention light?
Be thou the tenth Muse, ten times more in worth
Than those old nine which rhymers invocate,
And he that calls on thee, let him bring forth
Eternal numbers to out-live long date.
    If my slight Muse do please these curious days,
    The pain be mine, but thine shall be the praise.

The poet's statement "thine own sweet argument, too excellent" summarizes the effect of the Guide's last counsel. Once again, the poet appears to be an enthusiastic and unwavering follower of the Guide's teaching. We may notice that the depth of his reflection and understanding has greatly improved. But there is still a long way in front of him.

The poet goes back to the theme of inspiration, which he has explored previously. Namely, in Sonnet 21 he was criticizing other poets for focussing their attention on secondary causes. He had made a clear distinction between the object of his praise and those of the other poets. Now the poet makes a subtle but a significant shift. Namely, instead of focussing his attention on others, he takes a critical look at his own writing.

The poet declares that as long as he is in the presence of the Guide, he does not need other sources of inspiration ("how can my Muse want subject to invent while thou dost breathe"). The Guide's arguments are too subtle to be grasped by ordinary readers ("thine own sweet argument, too excellent, for every vulgar paper to rehearse"). Therefore, the Guide should take credit if he notices anything of value in the poet's verses ("give thy self the thanks if aught in me, worthy perusal stand against thy sight"). For who would be so insensitive not to be inspired by the Guide's presence ("for who's so dumb that cannot write to thee, when thou thy self dost give invention light?") He promotes the Guide to the status of the tenth Muse, i.e., much more worthy than the classic Nine Greek Muses ("be thou the tenth Muse, ten times more in worth than those old nine which rhymers invocate"). And whoever writes about the Guide, let him compose verses that will last forever ("and he that calls on thee, let him bring forth eternal numbers to out-live long date"). The poet states that he would be ashamed if his verse pleased ordinary readers ("if my slight Muse do please these curious days"). But such pain would contribute to the Guide's further praise ("the pain be mine, but thine shall be the praise").

In his plays and Sonnets, Shakespeare consistently indicates the limited value of ancient myths and traditions. Ancient myths and traditions belong to other times and other places. Previous projections of spiritual teaching become sterile as the cosmic matrix changes. Therefore, certain developmental approaches from previous times and places may only be of use to historical and literary investigations. An updated approach and methodology is needed if the evolutionary process is to be successfully implemented[38].

Such an updated approach is presented in the following Sonnets. Similarly to the process illustrated in Shakespeare's plays, the implemented methodology includes banishment, modulation of beauty, and rebuke.

---

[38] See "Introduction" (Shakespeare for the Seeker, Volume 4, Chapter 8.1).

SONNET XXXIX

O how thy worth with manners may I sing,
When thou art all the better part of me?
What can mine own praise to mine own self bring;
And what is't but mine own when I praise thee,
Even for this, let us divided live,
And our dear love lose name of single one,
That by this separation I may give:
That due to thee which thou deserv'st alone:
Oh absence what a torment wouldst thou prove,
Were it not thy sour leisure gave sweet leave,
To entertain the time with thoughts of love,
Which time and thoughts so sweetly doth deceive.
    And that thou teachest how to make one twain,
    By praising him here who doth hence remain.

The poet has been separated from his Guide ("O absence"). Although physically separated from the Guide, the poet knows that they are two parts of the same being ("thou art all the better part of me"). This is why he complains that he cannot glorify the Guide in his poems, because this would be seen as self-indulgence ("what can mine own praise to mine own self bring, and what is't but mine own when I praise thee"). He uses this concept to explain and justify to himself the separation. The poet pursues the following line of thoughts: it is better to be separated, because then he has time to write praising verses about his friend ("that by this separation I may give that due to thee which thou deserv'st alone"). Therefore, the separation is not be so painful, because it gives the poet a chance to spend more time to think about his love ("Oh absence what a torment wouldst thou prove, were it not thy sour leisure gave sweet leave, to entertain the time with thoughts of love"). The poet concludes that the Guide teaches him how to divide himself into two parts, so he may praise him. By praising him he makes him stay ("and that thou teachest how to make one twain, by praising him here who doth hence remain").

The poet's conclusion indicates that he has not understood the purpose of separation. The purpose of separation is to learn how to overcome the divide between himself and the Guide, i.e., how to become truly united with the Guide. The poet is still thinking in the terms of two physical parts, while the Guide teaches him about unity of essence.

In the plays a separation of a disciple from his guide is referred to as banishment. During banishment it may be possible for the disciple to deepen his understanding of the path. This is why Princess in "Love's Labour's Lost" sent Ferdinand to "some naked hermitage"[39]:

> "Your oath I will not trust; but go with speed
> To some forlorn and naked hermitage,
> Remote from all the pleasures of the world;
> There stay until the twelve celestial signs
> Have brought about the annual reckoning.
> If this austere insociable life
> Change not your offer made in heat of blood;
> If frosts and fasts, hard lodging and thin weeds
> Nip not the gaudy blossoms of your love,
> But that it bear this trial and last love;
> Then, at the expiration of the year,
> Come challenge me, challenge me by these deserts,
> And, by this virgin palm now kissing thine
> I will be thine."

---

[39] See "Recipe" (Shakespeare for the Seeker, Volume 2, Chapter 5.3).

SONNET XL

Take all my loves, my love, yea take them all,
What hast thou then more than thou hadst before?
No love, my love, that thou mayst true love call,
All mine was thine, before thou hadst this more:
Then if for my love, thou my love receivest,
I cannot blame thee, for my love thou usest,
But yet be blam'd, if thou thy self deceivest
By wilful taste of what thyself refusest.
I do forgive thy robbery, gentle thief
Although thou steal thee all my poverty:
And yet love knows it is a greater grief
To bear love's wrong, than hate's known injury
    Lascivious grace, in whom all ill well shows,
    Kill me with spites yet we must not be foes.

The Guide is a carrier of the entire spectrum of evolutionary energy. Therefore, he is able to control and administer the poet's exposure to such energy. In the Guide's previous counsel, Shakespeare indicated that the elements of the impulse may be presented symbolically as women of various colours. Therefore, depending on the specific inner state of his disciple, the Guide will modulate accordingly the exposure to evolutionary energy. In this Sonnet, the poet describes his first experience with such a modulated exposure. An initial exposure to the impulse is symbolically illustrated as the poet's encounter with an attractive woman. But then the Guide takes her away from him. The poet perceives this particular experience as the Guide stealing his love ("take all my loves, my love, yea take them all"). In his ignorance, the poet calls the Guide's action a sort of robbery ("I do forgive thy robbery"), thievery ("gentle thief") and stealing ("thou steal thee all my poverty").

As pointed out in the Introduction, the overall design of the

Sonnets is based on the updated triad of the Troubadours. The triad was updated to reflect the changes within the currently projected cosmic matrix. Namely, the evolutionary potentiality of ordinary man has been greatly advanced. Now the lady of the triad is available. But the poet is not ready yet to correctly assimilate the impulse. This is why the Guide has to modulate accordingly the poet's exposure to such an impact. The Guide does it by allowing the poet to have a taste of it, but then he removes it. This is why the poet accuses the Guide of stealing his love. The poet bitterly questions his friend why he did it and what he gained from it ("what hast thou then more than thou hadst before?") Then he claims that the Guide did not gain anything, because the poet has already given him everything he had ("no love, my love, that thou mayst true love call, all mine was thine, before thou hadst this more"). The poet does not blame his friend for taking away his love ("then if for my love, thou my love receivest, I cannot blame thee, for my love thou usest"). But he blames the Guide for deceiving himself, because the Guide has allowed himself to be driven by sensuality ("but yet be blam'd, if thou thy self deceives by wilful taste of what thyself refusest").

Let's remember that the Guide acts as a mirror for the poet's actions. Therefore, the poet's accusations are a precise description of his own doing. The poet's reactions are still of an emotional and sentimental nature. He is driven by his emotions in the same manner as an ordinary lover would react to the loss of his or her beloved. He claims that it hurts more to be injured by a lover than by an enemy ("and yet love knows it is a greater grief to bear love's wrong, than hate's known injury"). And he accuses the Guide of hypocrisy for succumbing to lust with such grace that it makes him look good, even though he is hurting the poet's feeling ("lascivious grace, in whom all ill well shows, kill me with spites"). Yet, and this is very important, the poet is able to overcome the Guide's apparent treachery ("yet we must not be foes"). But the poet is still unaware that the Guide's purpose is to help him to identify and get rid of his emotional attachments.

Don Pedro in "Much Ado About Nothing" administered a similar recipe to cure Claudio's inner state. Don Pedro seemingly stole Hero from Claudio. Afterwards he explained that the purpose of such a "robbery" was to teach true love[40]:

> "I will but teach them to sing, and restore them to the owner."

---

[40] See "The guide" (Shakespeare for the Seeker, Volume 3, Chapter 6.3).

"Hers by thy beauty tempting her to thee,
Thine by thy beauty being false to me" (Sonnet 41)

SONNET XLI

Those pretty wrongs that liberty commits,
When I am some-time absent from thy heart,
Thy beauty, and thy years full well befits,
For still temptation follows where thou art.
Gentle thou art, and therefore to be won,
Beauteous thou art, therefore to be assailed.
And when a woman woos, what woman's son,
Will sourly leave her till he have prevailed.
Ay me, but yet thou mightst my seat forbear,
And chide thy beauty and thy straying youth,
Who lead thee in their riot even there
Where thou art forced to break a two-fold truth:
    Hers by thy beauty tempting her to thee,
    Thine by thy beauty being false to me.

Exposure to an element of evolutionary impulse has to be gradual. "Modulation of beauty" is a technical term to describe such a gradual exposure. This is why, after an initial encounter, the impulse has to be withdrawn. In the Sonnet, this is described as the disappearance of the Guide with the woman, who represents such an impulse. Such disappearances are part of the process. They allow the Guide to observe how the poet has been affected by his initial exposure to the modulated impact.

The poet tries to come to terms with his current situation. He accuses the Guide of forgetting about him and committing some infidelities ("those pretty wrongs that liberty commits, when I am some-time absent from thy heart"). He tries to justify the Guide's "betrayal" by the Guide's good look and his young age ("thy beauty, and thy years full well befits, for still temptation follows where thou art"). The Guide is noble, so women look at him as an attractive catch ("Gentle thou art, and therefore to be won"). He is handsome; therefore it is natural that he is pursued by women ("beauteous thou art, therefore to be assailed"). And when a woman is the pursuer, what man will refuse to triumph over her? ("And when a woman woos, what woman's son, will sourly leave her till he have prevailed"). But, demands the poet, his friend should stay away from his mistress and keep his youthful urges under control ("but yet thou mightst my seat forbear, and chide thy beauty and thy straying youth"). Because they're leading him into wantonness, which breaks two bonds ("who lead thee in their riot even there where thou art forced to break a two-fold truth"). The poet accuses the Guide of breaking the poet's bond with his mistress by tempting her, and of breaking his bond with the poet by being false to him ("hers by thy beauty tempting her to thee, thine by thy beauty being false to me").

Claudio in "Much Ado About Nothing" laid a similar accusation against Don Pedro[41]:

> "Friendship is constant in all other things
> Save in the office and affairs of love:
> Therefore, all hearts in love use their own tongues;
> Let every eye negotiate for itself
> And trust no agent; for beauty is a witch
> Against whose charms faith melteth into blood."

---

[41] See "Villain" (Shakespeare for the Seeker, Volume 3, Chapter 6.3).

SONNET XLII

That thou hast her it is not all my grief,
And yet it may be said I loved her dearly,
That she hath thee is of my wailing chief,
A loss in love that touches me more nearly.
Loving offenders thus I will excuse ye,
Thou dost love her, because thou know'st I love her,
And for my sake even so doth she abuse me,
Suffering my friend for my sake to approve her,
If I lose thee, my loss is my love's gain,
And losing her, my friend hath found that loss,
Both find each other, and I lose both twain,
And both for my sake lay on me this cross,
    But here's the joy, my friend and I are one,
    Sweet flattery, then she loves but me alone.

The poet is trying to come to terms with his situation within this ménage a trois. He is not able to perceive that the Guide, the lady, and himself are one. The three of them constitute an evolutionary triad. They all have to be transmuted into one being. Therefore, as long as the poet treats the Guide and the lady as separate entities, he will have to suffer. This is why the poet complains that he has been hurt by the Guide, who apparently run away with the poet's mistress ("that thou hast her it is not all my grief, and yet it may be said I loved her dearly"). But the fact that the lady took away his friend is even more painful ("That she hath thee is of my wailing chief, loss in love that touches me more nearly"). The poet cannot accept such a double loss. Therefore, he comes up with an explanation that satisfies his hurt ego. He presumes that the Guide took the lady because he knew that the poet loves her ("loving offenders thus I will excuse ye, thou dost love her, because thou know'st I love her"). And the lady loves the Guide for the same reason, i.e., because she knows that the Guide is the poet's dearest friend ("and for my sake even so doth she abuse me, suffering my friend for my sake to approve her"). If the poet loses his friend, it's a win for his mistress ("If I lose thee, my loss is my love's gain"). And by losing the lady, his friend will get what the poet has lost ("and losing her, my friend hath found that loss"). Both of them, therefore, have found each other. But the poet lost both, and both losses cause him pain ("both find each other, and I lose both twain, and both for my sake lay on me this cross"). The poet tries to use a rational approach to explain the situation. He applies the concept of I and my friend are one, but the lady is still outside of his equation ("but here's the joy, my friend and I are one"). By using such a convoluted justification, the poet arrives at a self-flattering conclusion: the lady loves only him ("sweet flattery, then she loves but me alone").

The poet would have to bring himself onto a higher state to perceive the true nature of his experience. Claudio in "Much Ado About Nothing" went through a similar process. It was only after a similar painful experience that Claudio was able to realize that Don Pedro was helping him win Hero[42]:

> "Here, Claudio, I have wooed in thy name, and
> fair Hero is won."

---

[42] See "Villain" (Shakespeare for the Seeker, Volume 3, Chapter 6.3).

SONNET XLIII

When most I wink then do mine eyes best see,
For all the day they view things unrespected,
But when I sleep, in dreams they look on thee,
And darkly bright, are bright in dark directed.
Then thou whose shadow shadows doth make bright,
How would thy shadow's form, form happy show,
To the clear day with thy much clearer light,
When to unseeing eyes thy shade shines so?
How would (I say) mine eyes be blessed made,
By looking on thee in the living day?
When in dead night thy fair imperfect shade,
Through heavy sleep on sightless eyes doth stay?
    All days are nights to see till I see thee,
    And nights bright days when dreams do show thee me.

After a brief exposure to an element of evolutionary energy, the poet experiences the first sign of a partially operational subtle faculty of the intellect. This particular experience is described as deepened inspiration. Such experience points out that the poet was exposed to a reforming impulse. Such an impulse is indicated by the colour white. Therefore, the lady of Sonnets 40 - 42 may be referred to as the White Lady.

This particular inspirational experience is described as dreaming. When the poet is in his ordinary state, he does not experience anything of importance ("for all the day they view things unrespected"). When he manages to enter into the inspirational state, he finds himself in the presence of the Guide ("but when I sleep, in dreams they look on thee"). This is why he says that his eyes work best when he is dreaming ("when most I wink then do mine eyes best see"). Let's recall that previously the poet did not think that he could compare the Guide to golden stars (see Sonnet 21). Now, however, the Guide's image shines brightly in the dark.

The image of the Guide further brightens the darkness of dead night ("and darkly bright, are bright in dark directed; then thou whose shadow shadows doth make bright"). Then, he wonders, what happiness would he experience if the Guide's radiance would illuminate the bright day? ("How would thy shadow's form, form happy show, to the clear day with thy much clearer light, when to unseeing eyes thy shade shines so?")

Prior to his encounter with the White Lady, the poet could paint and store the Guide's image in his inner heart. But he was not able to look at it (Sonnet 24). In other words, he had no means of communication with his inner heart. Now, however, he can see a blurred image of the Guide ("in dead night thy fair imperfect shade, through heavy sleep on sightless eyes doth stay"). This means that his intuitive feeling can be translated into thoughts and then communicated to the newly activated subtle faculty of his intellect ("to unseeing eyes"). This experience marks the activation of a reformed aspect of the intellect. It establishes a link between the poet's inner heart and his inner intellect.

The poet wonders how blessed his eyes would be if he could look at the Guide in the daytime ("how would, I say. mine eyes be blessed made, by looking on thee in the living day?") The poet concludes with the observation that he experiences reality when he is in an inspirational state; his ordinary life, i.e., the waking state, is only an illusion ("all days are nights to see till I see thee, and nights bright days when dreams do show thee me").

When Prospero in "The Tempest" perfected his inner state, he was able to control the goddesses. He explained his vision in the following way[43]:

---

[43] See "Prospero's challenges" (Shakespeare for the Seeker, Volume 4, Chapter 8.1).

> "We are such stuff
> As dreams are made on, and our little life
> Is rounded with a sleep."

Prospero's explanation also applies to the poet's dreams. The ordinary world is perceived through physical senses. The physical senses belong to the ordinary or mortal state. In accordance with Prospero's vocabulary, the ordinary state corresponds to "sleeping" or "dreaming", i.e., a form of illusion. In other words, any sensation provided by the ordinary senses is a product of the underdeveloped mind. This is why it may be said that men "are such stuff as dreams are made on". On the other hand, the invisible world is accessible through the subtle faculties. With the development of the subtle faculties man may make a breakthrough through the limitations of time and space and in this way enter into the invisible world, because "our little life is rounded with a sleep". By waking up from his "sleep", man may experience true life.

SONNET XLIV

If the dull substance of my flesh were thought,
Injurious distance should not stop my way,
For then despite of space I would be brought,
From limits far remote, where thou dost stay,
No matter then although my foot did stand
Upon the farthest earth removed from thee,
For nimble thought can jump both sea and land,
As soon as think the place where he would be.
But ah, thought kills me that I am not thought
To leap large lengths of miles when thou art gone,
But that so much of earth and water wrought,
I must attend, time's leisure with my moan.
    Receiving naughts by elements so slow,
    But heavy tears, badges of either's woe.

The poet realizes that he is still attached to worldly pleasures, which prevent him from making progress. He calls these attachments "the dull substance of my flesh". It is this dull substance that acts as "this muddy vesture of decay", which according to the Guide, does not allow him to hear "the true concord of well-tuned sounds" (see Sonnet 8). The poet describes this blocking barrier as "injurious distance" ("if the dull substance of my flesh were thought, injurious distance should not stop my way"). In this Sonnet the poet uses the term *thought* to indicate (i) inner "thought", referred to in Sonnet 43; and (ii) ordinary thought.

If he could be as light as "thought", then he would be able to bring himself in the presence of the Guide ("for then despite of space I would be brought, from limits far remote, where thou dost stay"). It wouldn't matter how far away he was from the Guide ("no matter then although my foot did stand upon the farthest earth removed from thee"). Because such "thought" is quick enough to jump over both sea and land as fast as one may think about the place where he or she wants to be ("for nimble thought can jump both sea and land, as soon as think the place where he would be"). But this very thought makes the poet to be even more distraught, because he realizes that he is not made of "thought" and he cannot leap over the distance separating him from the Guide ("thought kills me that I am not thought to leap large lengths of miles when thou art gone"). So, as long as the poet is made only from earth and water he has to wait patiently, filling time with his laments ("but that so much of earth and water wrought, I must attend, time's leisure with my moan").

Earth, water, air, and fire symbolically indicate the stages of the development of higher states of mind. These terms are chosen partly because they consecutively represent items in increasing degree of refinement or decreasing density. They correspond to the exposure to the specific elements of the spectrum of evolutionary energy. The higher the stage, the more refined is the energy to which a disciple is exposed to. An ordinary man remains at the stage of "earth". "Earth" is static; at this stage there is no internal movement. Man gains the first degree of spiritual "mobility" through initiation. After the initiation, sometimes referred to as "baptism", man enters the stage of "water". Man goes then through the process of spiritual reformation. In this way he reaches the stage of "air". The process of spiritual purification brings him to the stage of "fire". When his subtle faculties are purified and united by the unitive energy of love, they may form a new inner being. In this symbolic representation "earth" and "water" denote lower stages. As long as the poet is driven by earthly and watery attachments, he will remain at the lower stages. These attachments act as a veil separating him from enhanced perception and deeper intuition. The stage of "water" may be overcome through the reformation of his inner self. Till such a time, the poet may only convert water into heavy tears ("receiving naughts by elements so slow, but heavy tears, badges of either's woe").

In her comment to Olivia in "Twelfth Night", Cesario also alluded to a transition from one stage onto another[44]:

> "And make the babbling gossip of the air
> Cry out 'Olivia! O, You should not rest
> Between the elements of air and earth."

Cesario tells Olivia that she needs to be placed within a specific ambience that could be provided by "the babbling gossip of the air". (In Old English the word "gossip" means a godparent, i.e., a reference to baptism or initiation.) Then, "the babbling gossip of the air" would carry a "cry" that would free Olivia from the bounds of water, i.e., she would not remain any longer "between the elements of air and earth".

---

[44] See "Evolutionary impulse" (Shakespeare for the Seeker, Volume 4, Chapter 7.1).

SONNET XLV

The other two, slight air, and purging fire,
Are both with thee, wherever I abide,
The first my thought, the other my desire,
These present absent with swift motion slide.
For when these quicker Elements are gone
In tender Embassy of love to thee,
My life being made of four, with two alone,
Sinks down to death, oppress'd with melancholy.
Until life's composition be recured,
By those swift messengers return'd from thee,
Who even but now come back again, assured,
Of thy fair health, recounting it to me.
    This told, I joy, but then no longer glad,
    I send them back again and straight grow sad.

The poet uses the symbols of earth, water, air, and fire to describe his present state of separation. He says that the reforming air and purifying fire are always with the Guide, regardless of wherever the poet may be ("the other two, slight air, and purging fire, are both with thee, wherever I abide"). At the stage of "air" the poet would be free from the limitations of ordinary intellect; at the stage of "fire" he would be able to break away from his emotional desires ("the first my thought, the other my desire"). Because of the poet's worldly attachments, he is not able to preserve the permanency of his higher states; he slides back and forth between his ordinary and higher states ("these present absent with swift motion slide"). The required condition for inner balance is the harmonious presence of the four subtle faculties ("my life being made of four"). As pointed in the discussion of Sonnet 20, such "life made of four" is symbolically indicated by the octagon, i.e., when four elements of evolutionary energy are effectively absorbed by the four subtle faculties.

When the lighter elements of air and fire are gone ("for when these quicker elements are gone"), the poet falls back into his ordinary state ("my life ... sinks down to death, oppress'd with melancholy"). His inner balance is restored as soon as these two elements are back ("until air and fire return to restore the proper balance within me"). The poet is able to recognize his inner state, because at such moments he is able to perceive messages from the Guide ("who even but now come back again, assured, of thy fair health, recounting it to me"). Such an inspirational state, or awakening state, is also referred to as the state "to be".

The last two lines of the Sonnet explain why the poet is not able to sustain the state "to be" and almost immediately falls back to the state "not to be". At such moments of idolatrous joy, the poet's sentimental attraction diverts his attention towards the earthly form of the Guide. This results in the immediate withdrawal of the two lighter elements. Afterwards, the poet grows gloomy again ("this told, I joy, but then no longer glad, I send them back again and straight grow sad"). At the moments of idolatrous joy he realizes that he is still separated from the Guide, therefore he is "no longer glad". "These present absent" states of going and returning mark the poet's spiritual inconstancy. These two states of "present absent" correspond to Hamlet's "to be" and "not to be", respectively (see Sonnet 3). It was also such inconstancy that was holding Proteus back from recognizing the inner beauty of Julia in "Two Gentlemen of Verona"[45]:

> "Were man
> But constant, he were perfect. That one error
> Fills him with faults; makes him run through all the sins."

---

[45] See "Implementation" (Shakespeare for the Seeker, Volume 3, Chapter 6.7).

SONNET XLVI

Mine eye and heart are at a mortal war,
How to divide the conquest of thy sight,
Mine eye, my heart their picture's sight would bar,
My heart, mine eye the freedom of that right,
My heart doth plead that thou in him dost lie,
(A closet never pierced with crystal eyes)
But the defendant doth that plea deny,
And says in him thy fair appearance lies.
To side this title is impannelled
A quest of thoughts, all tenants to the heart,
And by their verdict is determined
The clear eye's moiety, and the dear heart's part.
    As thus, mine eye's due is thine outward part,
    And my heart's right, thine inward love of heart.

In Sonnets 40 – 43 the poet described the first signs of the operation of a reformed aspect of the intellect faculty. Now the poet describes in greater details the operation of the subtle aspects of the heart. This means that the Guide leads the poet through the experiences that belong to both, the Path of the Intellect and the Path of the Heart. As illustrated by Shakespeare in his plays, such methodology was implemented in the development of modern Western European society.

The first sign of the operation of a subtle aspect of the heart faculty is recorded in Sonnet 24. At that time the poet was able to store the image of true beauty, but was not able to look at it. Such experience belongs to a reformed aspect of the heart. This subtle faculty is symbolically indicated by the colour yellow. After his exposure to the White Lady, the poet was able to translate feelings coming from his inner heart into "thoughts" and then deliver them to his inner intellect. At that time, he was able to perceive only a blurred ("imperfect") image of the Guide (see Sonnet 43).

In this Sonnet the poet is able to admire a clear sight of the Guide. The blurring effect has been removed from the poet's inner heart. This is a sign of the operation of a purified aspect of the heart. This particular subtle faculty is indicated by the colour red. This means that, at the present time, the poet experiences the operation of three subtle faculties, which are symbolically indicated by the colours yellow, white, and red.

The poet describes the operation of his inner heat and his inner intellect. He refers to the subtle faculty of the intellect as "crystal eyes". The subtle faculty of the heart is described as "the dear heart". The poet compares his states to a war between these two subtle faculties, which fight between themselves for the sight of the Guide ("mine eye and heart are at a mortal war, how to divide the conquest of thy sight"). He says that his eye does not allow his inner heart to keep the Guide's image ("mine eye, my heart their picture's sight would bar"). The poet's inner heart, on the other hand, disputes whether the eye has the rights to the Guide's image ("my heart, mine eye the freedom of that right"). The inner heart pleads that the image is stored in him, i.e., a place beyond the eye's reach ("my heart doth plead that thou in him dost lie, a closet never pierced with crystal eyes"). But the defending eye denies that claim, and argues that the image is stored in him ("but the defendant doth that plea deny, and says in him thy fair appearance lies"). To decide whose claim is right, the poet has set-up a panel of jurors consisting of envoys ("thoughts"). As in Sonnet 43, "thoughts" serve as the means of communication of the subtle aspect of the heart. This is why the poet refers to "thoughts" as "all tenants to the heart" ("to side this title is impannelled a quest of thoughts, all tenants to the heart").

The jurors have delivered a verdict according to which part of the image belongs to the eye and which portion to the inner heart ("and by their verdict is determined the clear eye's moiety, and the dear heart's part"). The jurors have declared that the poet's eye has the right to admire the Guide's beautiful form, while the inner heart has the duty to immerse in the Guide's essence ("as thus, mine eye's due is thine outward part, and my heart's right, thine inward love of heart").

Olivia in "Twelfth Night" delivered a similar verdict. She recognized the perfection of Orsino's outward form. Here is her description of Orsino[46]:

> "Yet I suppose him virtuous, know him noble,
> Of great estate, of fresh and stainless youth;
> In voices well divulged, free, learn'd and valiant;
> And in dimension and the shape of nature
> A gracious person: but yet I cannot love him."

At the same time she intuitively felt Cesario's inner perfection.

---

[46] See "Cruel maid" (Shakespeare for the Seeker, Volume 4, Chapter 7.1).

SONNET XLVII

Betwixt mine eye and heart a league is took,
And each doth good turns now unto the other,
When that mine eye is famish'd for a look,
Or heart in love with sighs himself doth smother;
With my love's picture then my eye doth feast,
And to the painted banquet bids my heart:
Another time mine eye is my heart's guest,
And in his thoughts of love doth share a part.
So either by thy picture or my love,
Thy self away, art present still with me,
For thou not farther than my thoughts canst move,
And I am still with them, and they with thee.
    Or if they sleep, thy picture in my sight
    Awakes my heart, to heart's and eyes' delight.

The poet seems to be self-satisfied with his solution of bringing into peace his two previously competing experiences. He claims that his eye and his inner heart have reached an agreement ("betwixt mine eye and heart a league is took, and each doth good turns now unto the other"). When his eye desires to look at the Guide's image or his inner heart is overwhelmed with loving sighs, then the image admiring eye invites the heart to join the feast ("when that mine eye is famish'd for a look, or heart in love with sighs himself doth smother; with my love's picture then my eye doth feast, and to the painted banquet bids my heart"). At other times, the eye is the heart's invited guest with whom it shares its feeling of love ("another time mine eye is my heart's guest, and in his thoughts of love doth share a part"). So, the Guide is always present with the poet, either as his image or in the poet's loving thoughts ("so either by thy picture or my love, thy self away, art present still with me"). The poet claims that the Guide cannot escape from his thoughts. Because the poet is always with his thoughts, and his thoughts are with his Guide ("for thou not farther than my thoughts canst move, and I am still with them, and they with thee"). By the same token, when his thoughts are asleep, the poet's eyes may awaken his heart by bringing in the Guide's image ("or if they sleep, thy picture in my sight awakes my heart, to heart's and eyes' delight"). The poet happily concludes that it does not matter any longer that the Guide is away. The poet boasts that now he may be in the Guide's presence at his own pleasure, "either by thy picture or my love". In other words, "my friend and I are one" (Sonnet 42) and they are locked-up within the Guide's chest. Such an understanding is driven by the egotistic-self. There is a substantial difference between having access to the Guide's image and being annihilated within the Guide's essence. Although seemingly self-satisfying, the poet's conclusion is another illustration of his spiritual immaturity. Similarly to the concluding lines in Sonnet 36, the poet's boasting is an indication of the interference of his egoistic-self. Previously the poet was trying to protect his own honour. Now he thinks that he can control the Guide's presence.

Orlando in "As You Like It" realized that such a form of self-satisfaction was far away from the fulfilment of his inner need:

"I can live no longer by thinking."

It was at this point that Rosalind was able to initiate the next stage of the process[47]. This is why the Guide has to intervene with a corrective counsel (see the next Sonnet).

---

[47] See "The process" (Shakespeare for the Seeker, Volume 2, Chapter 5.2).

The Guide's third counsel (Sonnet 48)

SONNET XLVIII

How careful was I when I took my way,
Each trifle under truest bars to thrust,
That to my use it might unused stay
From hands of falsehood, in sure wards of trust?
But thou, to whom my jewels trifles are,
Most worthy comfort, now my greatest grief,
Thou best of dearest, and mine only care,
Art left the prey of every vulgar thief.
Thee have I not locked up in any chest,
Save where thou art not, though I feel thou art,
Within the gentle closure of my breast,
From whence at pleasure thou mayst come and part,
    And even thence thou wilt be stol'n I fear,
    For truth proves thievish for a prize so dear.

The Guide scorns the poet for straying off from the straight path. The Guide says that he prepared very carefully the poet's journey, taking into account every detail ("how careful was I when I took my way, each trifle under truest bars to thrust"). So there would be no interference with the poet's journey ("that to my use it might unused stay from hands of falsehood, in sure wards of trust"). But the poet, who is the Guide's most valuable treasure and his most worthy comfort, has become the source of the Guide's sadness and worry because he allows himself to be influenced by his vulgar and egotistic-self ("but thou, to whom my jewels trifles are, most worthy comfort, now my greatest grief, thou best of dearest, and mine only care, art left the prey of every vulgar thief"). The Guide clearly indicates that the poet has not been locked up in any chest ("thee have I not locked up in any chest"). He has kept a place for him in his breast, but the poet is not there yet ("save where thou art not, though I feel thou art, within the gentle closure of my breast"). Although sometimes the Guide feels that the poet is coming in and going out, as he is allowed to do at his own will ("from whence at pleasure thou mayst come and part"). The Guide fears, however, that the poet will go astray ("and even thence thou wilt be stol'n I fear"). Because experience shows that the poet's egotistic self is too greedy to let him go anywhere ("for truth proves thievish for a prize so dear").

In a similar manner Rosalind in "As You Like It" scorned Orlando, her disciple[48]:

> "your hose should be ungartered, your
> bonnet unbanded, your sleeve unbuttoned, your shoe
> untied and every thing about you demonstrating a
> careless desolation; but you are no such man; you
> are rather point-device in your accoutrements as
> loving yourself than seeming the lover of any other."

---

[48] See "The process" (Shakespeare for the Seeker, Volume 2, Chapter 5.2).

Reformation (Sonnets 49 - 53)

SONNET XLIX

Against that time (if ever that time come)
When I shall see thee frown on my defects,
When as thy love hath cast his utmost sum,
Called to that audit by advis'd respects,
Against that time when thou shalt strangely pass,
And scarcely greet me with that sun, thine eye,
When love converted from the thing it was
Shall reasons find of settled gravity.
Against that time do I ensconce me here
Within the knowledge of mine own desert,
And this my hand, against my self uprear,
To guard the lawful reasons on thy part,
    To leave poor me, thou hast the strength of laws,
    Since why to love, I can allege no cause.

The Guide's criticism has visibly sobered up the poet from his previous self-satisfying boasting. The poet realizes that he has misunderstood his situation and made errors ("against that time, if ever that time come, when I shall see thee frown on my defects"). Now he starts to worry that the Guide may start to ignore him, passing by him like a stranger and not looking at him ("when as thy love hath cast his utmost sum, called to that audit by advis'd respects, against that time when thou shalt strangely pass, and scarcely greet me with that sun, thine eye"). The poet anticipates that the Guide will exclude him from his heart ("when love converted from the thing it was shall reasons find of settled gravity"). In his anticipation of such a situation, the poet testifies against himself ("against that time do I ensconce me here within the knowledge of mine own desert"). So the Guide will be in a position to judge him correctly ("and this my hand, against my self uprear, to guard the lawful reasons on thy part"). The poet concludes that the Guide has every right to leave him, since he cannot keep up with the discipline of the path ("to leave poor me, thou hast the strength of laws, since why to love, I can allege no cause").

Desdemona experienced a similar despair when faced with an enforced separation from Othello's physical presence[49]. Here is an exchange between Othello and Desdemona:

Othello:

"Think on thy sins."

Desdemona:

"They are loves I bear to you."

Othello:

"Ay, and for that thou diest."

Like the poet of the Sonnet, Desdemona mistook her emotional attachments for true love.

---

[49] See "Advanced methodology" (Shakespeare for the Seeker, Volume 3, Chapter 6.2).

SONNET L

How heavy do I journey on the way,
When what I seek (my weary travel's end)
Doth teach that ease and that repose to say
Thus far the miles are measured from thy friend.
The beast that bears me, tired with my woe,
Plods dully on, to bear that weight in me,
As if by some instinct the wretch did know
His rider lov'd not speed being made from thee:
The bloody spur cannot provoke him on,
That some-times anger thrusts into his hide,
Which heavily he answers with a groan,
More sharp to me than spurring to his side,
    For that same groan doth put this in my mind,
    My grief lies onward and my joy behind.

"How heavy do I journey on the way" is an accurate description of the poet's experiences. His current stage corresponds to spiritual reformation. This is described symbolically as a journey driven by a beast. The reformation aims at subduing this beast.

The poet contemplates the difficulties of his current stage of journey. He has used the symbols of earth and water to describe the ordinary state; air and fire to indicate the higher states (see Sonnets 44 and 45). The higher states are his destination, i.e., his "weary travel's end". Now the poet describes his situation while travelling from the ordinary state to the higher state. Previously he was not able to overcome the "injurious distance" separating these two states. The ordinary state is where the Guide's outward form is. The Guide's inner heart is the higher state, i.e., the poet's ultimate destination. The poet is still attached to the physical presence of his Guide. This is why his journey is slowed down as the poet is hesitant to leave the Guide behind. The poet's attachment is driven by his egotistic-self. In the Sonnet, the egotistic-self is compared to a beast, which carries him ("the beast that bears me"). It is this beast that prevents the poet from reaching his destination.

The poet complains that the travel makes him distraught as he experiences how difficult it is to separate himself from the Guide's company ("how heavy do I journey on the way, when what I seek ... doth teach that ease and that repose to say thus far the miles are measured from thy friend"). The beast that carries him moves very slowly. The beast's behaviour is a reflection of the poet's hesitance. The poet implies that the poor beast somehow knows that he does not want to move quickly away from his worldly pleasures ("plods dully on, to bear that weight in me, as if by some instinct the wretch did know his rider lov'd not speed being made from thee"). Even with angry blows, the poet is not able to force his beast to move faster ("the bloody spur cannot provoke him on, that sometimes anger thrusts into his hide"). The beast answers with a groan, which hurts the poet even more, because it reminds him that his challenges and difficulties are ahead of him, and all his worldly pleasures are left behind ("for that same groan doth put this in my mind, my grief lies onward and my joy behind"). As long as the poet is driven by his dull beast, he will not be able to reach his destination.

It may help to grasp the meaning of the Sonnet to recall Falstaff's quote from "The Merry Wives of Windsor":

> "O powerful love! that, in some respects,
> makes a beast a man, in some other, a man a beast."

In this quote the term "beast" refers to an undeveloped man that is entirely driven by his base needs and desires[50]. The other part of the quote "O powerful love! that, in some respects, makes a beast a man" applies to the unitive energy of love that can transmute an ordinary man ("beast") into a fully developed man.

---

[50] See "Impurities" (Shakespeare for the Seeker, Volume 4, Chapter 8.2).

SONNET LI

Thus can my love excuse the slow offence,
Of my dull bearer, when from thee I speed,
From where thou art, why should I haste me thence,
Till I return of posting is no need.
O what excuse will my poor beast then find,
When swift extremity can seem but slow,
Then should I spur though mounted on the wind,
In winged speed no motion shall I know,
Then can no horse with my desire keep pace,
Therefore desire (of perfect'st love being made)
Shall neigh no dull flesh in his fiery race,
But love, for love, thus shall excuse my jade,
    Since from thee going, he went wilful-slow,
    Towards thee I'll run, and give him leave to go.

The poet continues his meditation on his current stage of his journey. He tries to excuse the slow progress of his tedious egoistic-self, to which he refers as his slow-moving bearer ("thus can my love excuse the slow offence, of my dull bearer"). Why should he, asks the poet, be in hurry while leaving the place where the Guide is? ("When from thee I speed, from where thou art, why should I haste me thence"). The poet predicts that when he returns, there will be no need for post horses ("till I return of posting is no need"). At the time of his return his stage will correspond to "air" and "fire". The poet wonders what excuse his dull bearer will be able to come up with, when even extreme swiftness will seem to be slow in comparison to travelling through air and fire ("what excuse will my poor beast then find, when swift extremity can seem but slow"). At that future time, the poet will be riding with such speed that even Pegasus' flight would look like standing still ("then should I spur though mounted on the wind, in winged speed no motion shall I know"). In other words, no mortal beast will be able to keep up pace with the poet's speed ("then can no horse with my desire keep pace"). Therefore, no neigh of mortal flesh but the poet's "perfected love" will be racing fierily towards the Guide's heart ("therefore desire, of perfect'st love being made, shall neigh no dull flesh in his fiery race, but love, for love"). The poet says that he will excuse his egotistic-self from deliberately slowing his departure from the ordinary state ("thus shall excuse my jade, since from thee going, he went wilful-slow"). Because the poet has realized that to arrive at the higher state, he will have to leave behind his dull bearer ("towards thee I'll run, and give him leave to go").

At such a time, the poet will have to distance himself from his egotistic-self. Only then, like in Feste's song in "Twelfth Night", the journey will end in lowers meeting[51]:

> "Journeys end in lovers meeting,
> Every wise man's son doth know."

The leaving of the "dull bearer" behind is a symbolic description of spiritual reformation. Its aim is to subdue the influence of the self faculty.

Initially humanity was in such a condition that the self faculty was totally engrossed in preserving the body. At that time, therefore, the developmental methodology was limited to spiritual reformation. It was for this reason that the ancient mystics used to place emphasis on the reforming of the self and regarded the purification of the faculties merely as the end-product and eventual consummation of such training. Such an approach required a very long time for its completion. A man's lifetime or a culture time-span was often not long enough to complete the process. This is why, after some time had passed, there appeared certain people who immersed themselves in an indiscriminate application of

---

[51] See "Feste" (Shakespeare for the Seeker, Volume 4, Chapter 7.1).

procedures that aimed at subduing the "dull bearer". These people started to show signs of extreme rigidity in their meticulous obedience to customs and rituals. Thus, without taking into account the question of proportion, and without making a proper diagnosis, they proposed one single medicine for every ailment. They maintained that man's only obstacle was his own self, his habits and behaviour. It was this methodology that was recorded in ancient mystical texts.

Shakespeare indicates that the overall evolutionary situation of man has been changed. Now man may benefit from the previously achieved evolutionary gains. The gains are reflected in the currently implemented developmental methodology. This advanced methodology allows for a simultaneous implementation of the reforming and the purifying processes. In this approach, purification may be used to accelerate reformation. Such an advanced approach is symbolically presented in the Sonnets 50 and 51. The "dull bearer" or an unreformed self is used to deliver the poet to his "weary travel's end". The "weary travel's end" is a higher state, which has been partially activated through the poet's previous exposure to a purifying impact (Sonnet 46). This partially activated state was needed to serve as a pointer for the current stage of the journey. Now, therefore, even the poet's unwilling "beast" may deliver him over there. Afterwards, his "beast" will not be needed anymore, because the poet will continue his journey "mounted on the wind".

"The beast that bears me, tired with my woe,
Plods dully on, to bear that weight in me" (Sonnet 50)

SONNET LII

So am I as the rich whose blessed key,
Can bring him to his sweet up-locked treasure,
The which he will not every hour survey,
For blunting the fine point of seldom pleasure.
Therefore are feasts so solemn and so rare,
Since seldom coming in the long year set,
Like stones of worth they thinly placed are,
Or captain Jewels in the carconet.
So is the time that keeps you as my chest,
Or as the ward-robe which the robe doth hide,
To make some special instant special blest,
By new unfolding his imprisoned pride.
 Blessed are you whose worthiness gives scope,
 Being had to triumph, being lacked, to hope.

Previously the poet was only able to talk about the possibility of entering into a space within the Guide's inner heart. As the result of his exposure to a purifying impact (Sonnet 46), he may now occasionally enter it. He compares himself to a rich man, who has got the key to a treasure chest ("so am I as the rich whose blessed key, can bring him to his sweet up-locked treasure"). However, because of his still imperfect inner state, he can access this treasure only on certain occasions. This is why he thinks about himself as a miser, i.e., a comparison which was indicated to him by the Guide in the first counsel (Sonnet 1). A miser will seldom look at his treasure from fear that it may lose its attraction if viewed too often ("the which he will not every hour survey, for blunting the fine point of seldom pleasure"). Such happy occasions occur very seldom; they are just like the seasonal festivals that only take place annually ("therefore are feasts so solemn and so rare, since seldom coming in the long year set"). Or as rare as the prime jewel among other stones in a necklace ("like stones of worth they thinly placed are, or captain Jewels in the carconet"). Or like a ceremonial robe that is hidden in a closet and taken out only on special occasions. So, in the same manner, time controls the poet's viewing of his treasure chest ("so is the time that keeps you as my chest"). The poet compares such viewing occasions to victories. And when they are gone, one hopes for their reappearance ("blessed are you whose worthiness gives scope, being had to triumph, being lacked, to hope").

An episode with three chests in "The Merchant of Venice" may help to understand the overall context of the Sonnet. Portia was also symbolically locked-up in one of the chests[52]. Only her true lover was able to find in which one:

> "I am lock'd in one of them:
> If you do love me, you will find me out."

Any pretending or false lovers were sent away.

---

[52] See "Trial" (Shakespeare for the Seeker, Volume 3, Chapter 6.4).

SONNET LIII

What is your substance, whereof are you made,
That millions of strange shadows on you tend?
Since every one, hath every one, one shade,
And you but one, can every shadow lend:
Describe *Adonis* and the counterfeit,
Is poorly imitated after you,
On *Helen's* cheek all art of beauty set,
And you in *Grecian* tires are painted new:
Speak of the spring, and foison of the year,
The one doth shadow of your beauty show,
The other as your bounty doth appear,
And you in every blessed shape we know.
  In all external grace you have some part,
  But you like none, none you, for constant heart.

After being allowed to experience the Guide's inner heart, the poet is able to give a more precise description of the Guide's functionality. Previously, the poet described the Guide as "the Master Mistress of my passion" (see Sonnet 20). Now, however, the poet is able to discern the whole spectrum of "Mistresses" in his Master. The Mistresses, or the young ladies, are a symbolic representation of the various elements of the spectrum of evolutionary energy. As indicated in the analysis of Sonnet 37, the Guide is a carrier of the full spectrum of evolutionary energy. In other words, he is made of a substance containing multiple combinations of colours ("what is your substance, whereof are you made, that millions of strange shadows on you tend"). Ordinary man, on the other hand, carries within himself a potentiality, which corresponds to his dominating combination of colours ("since every one hath, every one, one shade"). This is why it may be said that the Guide is the reality that sustains humanity ("and you but one, can every shadow lend").

In this context, there is no comparison between the Guide and the famous ancient beauties such as Adonis or Helen of Troy ("describe Adonis and the counterfeit, is poorly imitated after you; on Helen's cheek all art of beauty set, and you in Grecian tires are painted new"). The Guide's beauty is functional and his actions are bountiful, like the spring that leads to abundance at the time of harvest ("speak of the spring, and foison of the year, the one doth shadow of your beauty show, the other as your bounty doth appear"). The Guide's features are manifested in all known holy attributes and in all graceful forms ("and you in every blessed shape we know, in all external grace you have some part"). The Guide's unique feature, however, is the constancy of his aim and effort ("but you like none, none you, for constant heart").

The evolutionary dysfunctionality of the mythological and ancient heroes and heroines is consistently emphasized by Shakespeare in his plays. For example, here is Mercutio's summary in "Romeo and Juliet" of the famous ancient heroines[53]:

> "Dido a dowdy; Cleopatra a gipsy;
> Helen and Hero hildings and harlots; Thisbe a grey eye or so, but not to the purpose."

---

[53] See "Dido" (Shakespeare for the Seeker, Volume 4, Chapter 8.1).

The Guide's fourth counsel (Sonnets 54 - 55)

SONNET LIV

Oh how much more doth beauty beauteous seem,
By that sweet ornament which truth doth give,
The Rose looks fair, but fairer we it deem
For that sweet odour, which doth in it live:
The Canker blooms have full as deep a dye,
As the perfumed tincture of the Roses,
Hang on such thorns, and play as wantonly,
When summer's breath their masked buds discloses:
But for their virtue only is their show,
They live unwoo'd, and unrespected fade,
Die to themselves. Sweet Roses do not so,
Of their sweet deaths, are sweetest odours made:
    And so of you, beauteous and lovely youth,
    When that shall vade, by verse distills your truth.

The previous two Sonnets have shown signs of the poet's spiritual sobriety. So, we could expect that he would earn some commendation from the Guide. Indeed, this and the following Sonnet describe the Guide's praises of the poet's progress ("how much more doth beauty beauteous seem, by that sweet ornament which truth doth give"). In the Guide's praises we may discern the themes that were contained in his initial appeal to the poet, i.e., the beauty's Rose (Sonnet 1) and its preservation through the process of distillation ("the rose looks fair, but fairer we it deem for that sweet odour, which doth in it live" - Sonnets 5 and 6). The Guide emphasizes the poet's potentiality by comparing the ordinary and the subtle faculties to the wildflowers and the rose ("the canker blooms have full as deep a dye, as the perfumed tincture of the roses"). The wildflowers' only virtue is their outward look. They do not have such a sweet fragrance as the rose; only their external appearance is similar ("hang on such thorns, and play as wantonly, when summer's breath their masked buds discloses"). The wildflowers are sterile; they grow idly and fade away unnoticed ("but for their virtue only is their show, they live unwoo'd, and unrespected fade"). Left to themselves, they die alone leaving no traces ("die to themselves"). But when the rose dies, its essence is transmuted into the sweetest fragrance ("sweet roses do not so, of their sweet deaths, are sweetest odours made"). The same applies to the poet's mortal form and his inner essence. The Guide encourages the poet by telling him that his essence will be distilled and preserved in his verses ("and so of you, beauteous and lovely youth, when that shall vade, by verse distills your truth").

Olivia in "Twelfth Night" was also able to discern such an inner perfection in Cesario[54]:

> "Methinks I feel this youth's perfections
> With an invisible and subtle stealth
> To creep in at mine eyes."

---

[54] See "The Being of Illyria" (Shakespeare for the Seeker, Volume 4, Chapter 7.1).

SONNET LV

Not marble, nor the gilded monuments,
Of Princes shall outlive this powerful rhyme,
But you shall shine more bright in these contents
Than unswept stone, besmear'd with sluttish time.
When wasteful war shall *Statues* over-turn,
And broils root out the work of masonry,
Nor *Mars* his sword, nor war's quick fire shall burn:
The living record of your memory.
'Gainst death, and all oblivious enmity
Shall you pace forth, your praise shall still find room,
Even in the eyes of all posterity
That wear this world out to the ending doom.
    So till the judgment that yourself arise,
    You live in this, and dwell in lovers' eyes.

The Guide continues with his praise of the poet's progress. He indicates that the poet, in a constructive way, has absorbed the initial impact delivered by the Guide in his first 16 Sonnets. Specifically, the Guide refers to the poet's winning the war over time (Sonnets 15 and 16). The poet's progress and the essence of his inner beauty will be preserved in his verses. This is why he has to write his poetry. Because neither marble nor gold plated monuments of various human heroes will outlive his poetry ("not marble, nor the gilded monuments, of princes shall outlive this powerful rhyme"). The poet's inner beauty will shine more brightly than those dusty monuments blackened by time ("but you shall shine more bright in these contents than unswept stone, besmear'd with sluttish time"). While devastating wars will overturn those monuments and battles will damage the work of masons, neither swords nor fires shall destroy the essence living in the poet's verses ("when wasteful war shall statues over-turn, and broils root out the work of masonry, nor Mars his sword, nor war's quick fire shall burn the living record of your memory"). Despite death and hostilities, the poet will be living surrounded by glory ("against death and all oblivious enmity shall you pace forth, your praise shall still find room"). He will be praised by the future generations, all the way to the very end ("even in the eyes of all posterity that wear this world out to the ending doom"). Until the Last Judgment, when the poet will be raised up, he will live in these verses and in the eyes of true lovers ("so till the judgment that yourself arise, you live in this, and dwell in lovers' eyes").

The Guide indicates that the poet will preserve his teaching, i.e., the poet's intention expressed in Sonnet 17. Also, the Sonnet is the confirmation of the poet's hope, expressed in Sonnets 32 and 38, that his poetry would earn the Guide's appreciation.

The episode of bringing to life Hermione's statue in "The Winter's Tale" is another example of the functionality of objective art[55]:

> "A piece many
> years in doing and now newly performed by that rare
> Italian master, Julio Romano, who, had he himself
> eternity and could put breath into his work, would
> beguile Nature of her custom, so perfectly he is her ape."

---

[55] See "Final steps" (Shakespeare for the Seeker, Volume 3, Chapter 6.1).

Separation (Sonnets 56 - 66)

SONNET LVI

Sweet love renew thy force, be it not said
Thy edge should blunter be than appetite,
Which but today by feeding is allay'd,
Tomorrow sharpen'd in his former might.
So love be thou, although today thou fill
Thy hungry eyes, even till they wink with fullness,
Tomorrow see again, and do not kill
The spirit of Love, with a perpetual dullness:
Let this sad *Interim* like the Ocean be
Which parts the shore, where two contracted new,
Come daily to the banks, that, when they see:
Return of love, more blest may be the view.
  As call it Winter, which being full of care,
  Makes Summer's welcome, thrice more wish'd, more rare.

It is part of the developmental methodology that after acknowledging the poet's progress, the Guide would withdraw. Previously, the Guide would disappear occasionally. Now, however, the Guide disappears for a much longer period. This forces the poet to exercise his newly activated subtle faculties. In this way he may learn how to establish an invisible but more permanent link with his Guide. In the Sonnet, the period of the Guide's withdrawal is referred to as Interim.

The poet appeals to his love to be as strong as it used to be ("sweet love renew thy force"). So it be not said that true love is easier quenched than ordinary appetite ("be it not said thy edge should blunter be than appetite"). Appetite may be easily satiated, but on the next day it returns even hungrier than before ("which but today by feeding is allayed, tomorrow sharpened in his former might"). The poet wishes that his feeling of love, although now fully satisfied with the image of the beloved, should not be weakened tomorrow because of his Guide's absence ("although today thou fill thy hungry eyes, even till they wink with fullness, tomorrow see again, and do not kill the spirit of love, with a perpetual dullness"). The poet compares this sad period of absence to two lovers separated by an ocean ("let this sad interim like the ocean be which parts the shore, where two contracted new, come daily to the banks"). They both stand on the opposite shores hoping that their reunion will bring them even more happiness ("when they see return of love, more blest may be the view"). The poet refers to the absence as the gloom of winter, which makes him even more desirous of summer ("as call it winter, which being full of care, makes summer's welcome, thrice more wish'd, more rare").

Shakespeare used the same symbolic meaning of "winter" in the title "The Winter's Tale", i.e., the play illustrating how a period of absence was induced and how it was possible to overcome it. In that case the "winter" lasted sixteen years. Here is Autolycus' song in which he says good bye to "the winter's pale" and welcomes the arrival of a spiritual spring[56]:

> "When daffodils begin to peer,
> With heigh! the doxy over the dale,
> Why, then comes in the sweet o' the year;
> For the red blood reigns in the winter's pale."

---

[56] See "Bohemian forest" (Shakespeare for the Seeker, Volume 3, Chapter 6.1).

SONNET LVII

Being your slave what should I do but tend,
Upon the hours, and times of your desire?
I have no precious time at all to spend
Nor services to do, till you require.
Nor dare I chide the world without end hour,
Whilst I (my sovereign) watch the clock for you,
Nor think the bitterness of absence sour,
When you have bid your servant once adieu.
Nor dare I question with my jealous thought,
Where you may be, or your affairs suppose,
But like a sad slave stay and think of nought
Save, where you are, how happy you make those.
    So true a fool is love, that in your Will,
    (Though you do any thing) he thinks no ill.

The poet continues to describe his inner struggle caused by the absence of his Guide. His troubles are the result of misunderstanding of the nature of servanthood. He should have understood that his function is to be a servant of the process. However, he wrongly assumes that is he is a servant of the Guide ("being your slave what should I do but tend, upon the hours, and times of your desire"). Even if the Guide is not present, the poet has a job to do. Instead, the poet complains that he does not have anything to do ("I have no precious time at all to spend nor services to do, till you require"). He wastes his valuable time watching how much time has passed since the Guide's departure ("whilst I, my sovereign, watch the clock for you, nor think the bitterness of absence sour, when you have bid your servant once adieu"). And he speculates where the Guide may be or what he may be doing ("I question with my jealous thought, where you may be, or your affairs suppose"). The poet thinks about himself as a sad slave, who thinks about nothing else, except how happy are those who are now in the presence of their Master ("but like a sad slave stay and think of nought save, where you are, how happy you make those"). The poet's conclusion is a correct evaluation of his current state: he is a fool. He is a fool because he thinks that by doing nothing he does not do any harm ("so true a fool is love, that in your will, though you do any thing, he thinks no ill").

Grumio's comment about Gremio in "The Taming of the Shrew" may very well apply to the poet's current state[57]:

"O this woodcock, what an ass it is!"

---

[57] See "State of Padua" (Shakespeare for the Seeker, Volume 3, Chapter 6.5).

SONNET LVIII

That God forbid, that made me first your slave,
I should in thought control your times of pleasure,
Or at your hand the account of hours to crave,
Being your vassal, bound to stay your leisure.
Oh let me suffer (being at your beck)
The imprison'd absence of your liberty,
And patience tame, to sufferance bide each check,
Without accusing you of injury.
Be where you list, your charter is so strong,
That you yourself may privilege your time
To what you will, to you it doth belong,
Yourself to pardon of self-doing crime.
    I am to wait, though waiting so be hell,
    Not blame your pleasure be it ill or well.

The poet continues to agonize because of the Guide's absence. Although he is able to come up with satisfying rationale of his situation, his emotions do not allow him to perform any constructive action. In other words, he is still wasting his time.

The poet claims that he is not going to control or judge the Guide's actions ("that God forbid, that made me first your slave, I should in thought control your times of pleasure"). As a servant, he will wait until he is called for ("or at your hand the account of hours to crave, being your vassal, bound to stay your leisure"). The poet decides to wait patiently within the prison imposed upon him by the Guide's absence ("let me suffer, being at your beck, the imprison'd absence of your liberty"). And his efforts will be directed towards keeping in control his impatience and suffering, without blaming the Guide for anything ("and patience tame, to sufferance bide each check, without accusing you of injury"). The poet arrogantly gives the Guide freedom to go where he wants and do whatever he wishes ("be where you list, your charter is so strong, that you yourself may privilege your time to what you will, to you it doth belong"). After all, according to the poet, the Guide is privileged to pardon himself for any supposed wrongdoing ("yourself to pardon of self-doing crime"). The poet bitterly concludes that he has to wait, even if such waiting feels like hell ("I am to wait, though waiting so be hell"). But he will not accuse the Guide, regardless of his doing being right or wrong ("not blame your pleasure be it ill or well").

The poet would be better off if he could learn from Katharina in "The Taming of the Shrew"[58]. Here is Katharina's answer to Petruchio, which demonstrated her unconditional obedience to her guide:

> "Then, God be bless'd, it is the blessed sun:
> But sun it is not, when you say it is not;
> And the moon changes even as your mind.
> What you will have it named, even that it is;
> And so it shall be so for Katharina."

---

[58] See "Taming school" (Shakespeare for the Seeker, Volume 3, Chapter 6.5).

SONNET LIX

If there be nothing new, but that which is,
Hath been before, how are our brains beguil'd,
Which labouring for invention bear amiss
The second burthen of a former child?
Oh that record could with a back-ward look,
Even of five hundred courses of the Sun,
Show me your image in some antique book,
Since mind at first in character was done.
That I might see what the old world could say,
To this composed wonder of your frame,
Whether we are mended, or where better they,
Or whether revolution be the same.
    Oh sure I am the wits of former days,
    To subjects worse have given admiring praise.

After the initial period of anguish, the poet focuses his attention on a more constructive subject. Namely, he starts to look at the Guide from a much deeper perspective.

The Sonnet makes a reference to an evolutionary millennium that symbolically is described as "five hundred courses of the Sun". Each new millennium marks certain evolutionary gains. Therefore, these are not some repetitious sequences of events. This is underlined in the first two lines: "if there be nothing new, but that which is, hath been before, how are our brains beguil'd". The poet says that such understanding of the millennia does not make sense, because it would be like experiencing the same thing again and again ("which labouring for invention bear amiss the second burthen of a former child"). The initiation of each cycle is marked by the appearance of a new Guide. The Guide introduces new techniques and adjusts the developmental methodology. In this way it is possible to optimize the outcome of each evolutionary cycle. The poet says that any progress would be reflected in the image of the Guide. Therefore, he asks the Guide to show him images from his previous appearances ("show me your image in some antique book, since mind at first in character was done"). By looking at such an image it would be possible to tell whether mankind made any progress, or whether men are caught up in a vicious circle ("that I might see what the old world could say, to this composed wonder of your frame, whether we are mended, or where better they, or whether revolution be the same"). The poet is sure that the witty writers of the past did devote their admiration to much more inferior subjects than his Guide ("sure I am, the wits of former days to subjects worse have given admiring praise").

Katharine in "Love's Labour's Lost" alluded to such an evolutionary cycle when she sent Dumain away for "a twelvemonth and a day", i.e., till the time when the next evolutionary opportunity would occur[59]:

> "A twelvemonth and a day
> I'll mark no words that smooth-faced wooers say:
> Come when the king doth to my lady come;
> Then, if I have much love, I'll give you some."

---

[59] See "Recipe" (Shakespeare for the Seeker, Volume 2, Chapter 5.3).

SONNET LX

Like as the waves make towards the pebbled shore,
So do our minutes hasten to their end,
Each changing place with that which goes before,
In sequent toil all forwards do contend.
Nativity once in the main of light,
Crawls to maturity, wherewith being crown'd,
Crooked eclipses 'gainst his glory fight,
And time that gave, doth now his gift confound.
Time doth transfix the flourish set on youth,
And delves the parallels in beauty's brow,
Feeds on the rarities of nature's truth,
And nothing stands but for his scythe to mow.
    And yet to times in hope, my verse shall stand
    Praising thy worth, despite his cruel hand.

After recognizing the Guide's evolutionary function, the poet continues his meditation on the possibility of avoiding the cruelty of time. This theme was introduced to him by the Guide in Sonnet 12. At the beginning of his spiritual journey, the poet's approach was naïve and childish: instead of making efforts towards improving himself, he was trying to preach to time (Sonnet 19).

The poet compares the passing of time to sea waves breaking off on the rocky shore ("like as the waves make towards the pebbled shore, so do our minutes hasten to their end"). Similarly, each minute disappears as soon as the next one arrives, moving forward with unwavering efforts ("each changing place with that which goes before, in sequent toil all forwards do contend"). Then the poet repeats the allegory of ordinary life that was presented to him by the Guide in Sonnet 7. Namely, a new born appears, like a new wave, and then gradually crawls to maturity ("nativity once in the main of light, crawls to maturity, wherewith being crown'd"). After reaching his apogee, its glory becomes overshadowed by age ("crooked eclipses 'gainst his glory fight"). In this way, time gives its gift of life and then takes it away ("and time that gave, doth now his gift confound"). Time transfixes the growth of youth by digging wrinkles in his forehead ("time doth transfix the flourish set on youth, and delves the parallels in beauty's brow"). It devours the choicest specimens of nature; and nothing may be saved from its scythe ("feeds on the rarities of nature's truth, and nothing stands but for his scythe to mow"). The poet concludes by repeating the Guide's counsel about the immortality of his verses. The poet hopes that his verses will be able to overcome the cruelty of time ("and yet to times in hope, my verse shall stand praising thy worth, despite his cruel hand").

Orlando in "As You Like It" expressed a similar hope by carving his verses on trees in the Forest of Arden[60]:

> "Hang there, my verse, in witness of my love:
> And thou, thrice-crowned queen of night, survey
> With thy chaste eye, from thy pale sphere above,
> Thy huntress' name that my full life doth sway.
> O Rosalind! these trees shall be my books
> And in their barks my thoughts I'll character;
> That every eye which in this forest looks
> Shall see thy virtue witness'd every where."

---

[60] See "The process" (Shakespeare for the Seeker, Volume 2, Chapter 5.2).

SONNET LXI

Is it thy will, thy Image should keep open
My heavy eyelids to the weary night?
Dost thou desire my slumbers should be broken,
While shadows like to thee do mock my sight?
Is it thy spirit that thou send'st from thee
So far from home into my deeds to pry,
To find out shames and idle hours in me,
The scope and tenure of thy Jealousy?
O no, thy love though much, is not so great,
It is my love that keeps mine eye awake,
Mine own true love that doth my rest defeat,
To play the watch-man ever for thy sake.
> For thee watch I, whilst thou dost wake elsewhere,
> From me far off, with others all too near.

Once again, the poet misinterprets his experience. He complains about an exercise that he has been asked to perform. Namely, he has been asked that when meditating he should focus his attention on the Guide's image ("is it thy will, thy image should keep open my heavy eyelids to the weary night?") In this way the poet may strengthen up the newly activated subtle faculties of his heart. The poet, however, complains that he is required to keep awake at night to face the Guide's phantom ("dost thou desire my slumbers should be broken, while shadows like to thee do mock my sight?") The poet is hesitant to open up his inner heart to the Guide. Instead of doing what he was asked to do, he accuses the Guide of trying to spy on him ("is it thy spirit that thou send'st from thee"). He thinks that the Guide is jealous and wants to find out shameful things about the poet's behaviour ("to find out shames and idle hours in me, the scope and tenure of thy jealousy"). Then he starts to brag about the supposed superiority of his love ("O no, thy love though much, is not so great"). The poet says that it is not the

Guide's love for him, but his love for the Guide that keeps him awake at nights ("it is my love that keeps mine eye awake, mine own true love that doth my rest defeat, to play the watch-man ever for thy sake"). In the last two lines the poet spells out the true cause of his unhappiness. The poet cannot correctly perform his exercise because his mind is wondering where and with whom the Guide spends his time ("for thee watch I, whilst thou dost wake elsewhere, from me far off, with others all too near"). It is the poet's jealousy that does not allow him to perform correctly his meditation. As long as he is driven by such selfish emotion he will not be able to move further along the path.

It was such an imaginary jealousy that derailed the evolutionary process in "The Winter's Tale". Here is King Leontes' outburst of jealousy[61]:

> "Too hot, too hot!
> To mingle friendship far is mingling bloods.
> I have tremor cordis on me: my heart dances;
> But not for joy; not joy."

---

[61] See "Hermione's plan" (Shakespeare for the Seeker, Volume 3, Chapter 6.1).

SONNET LXII

Sin of self-love possesseth all mine eye
And all my soul, and all my every part;
And for this sin there is no remedy,
It is so grounded inward in my heart.
Me thinks no face so gracious is as mine,
No shape so true, no truth of such account,
And for myself mine own worth do define,
As I all other in all worths surmount.
But when my glass shows me myself indeed
Beated and chopp'd with tanned antiquity,
Mine own self love quite contrary I read
Self, so self loving were iniquity,
    'Tis thee (myself) that for myself I praise,
    Painting my age with beauty of thy days.

Now we may observe how the methodology implemented by the Guide starts to bring slowly its fruits. The poet discovers that his self-love prevents him from moving forward. The poet admits that it was his selfishness that led him to the ignorant reaction described in the previous Sonnet. The poet's self-love took control over everything what he sees, over his soul and every part of him ("sin of self-love possesseth all mine eye and all my soul, and all my every part"). The poet confesses that it is not so easy to get rid of it, so deeply it is rooted in his heart ("and for this sin there is no remedy, it is so grounded inward in my heart"). Then he lists the features that have made him to think so highly about himself: "no face so gracious is as mine", "no shape so true", and "as I all other in all worths surmount". In other words, in the poet's own estimation he surpasses everybody else. Then he notices that his own image in the mirror contradicts such a description ("but when my glass shows me myself indeed beated and chopp'd with tanned antiquity"). And he realizes that it is a great error to love himself so much ("mine own self love quite contrary I read self, so self loving were iniquity"). Then, the poet skilfully turns his observation into a self-satisfying excuse. He claims that in reality his self-admiration is just a proof of his love of the Guide ("it is thee, myself, that for myself I praise painting my age with beauty of thy days"). The poet's conclusion is another sign of his arrogance and ignorance.

Olivia in "Twelfth Night" also recognized such signs of self-love in Malvolio[62]:

> "Oh, you are sick of self-love, Malvolio, and taste with a distempered appetite."

---

[62] See "Malvolio" (Shakespeare for the Seeker, Volume 4, Chapter 7.1).

SONNET LXIII

Against my love shall be as I am now
With time's injurious hand crushed and o'erworn,
When hours have drained his blood and fild his brow
With lines and wrinkles, when his youthful morn
Hath travelled on to Age's steepy night,
And all those beauties whereof now he's King
Are vanishing, or vanished out of sight,
Stealing away the treasure of his Spring.
For such a time do I now fortify
Against confounding Age's cruel knife,
That he shall never cut from memory
My sweet love's beauty, though my lover's life.
    His beauty shall in these black lines be seen,
    And they shall live, and he in them still green.

The poet underlines the distinction between the Guide's external or mortal form and his inner essence. The poet is preparing himself for the fact that his Guide's external beauty is going to be worn out ("against my love shall be as I am now, with time's injurious hand crushed and o'erworn"). The injurious time is going to sap the Guide's vigour and cover his face with lines and wrinkles ("when hours have drained his blood and fild his brow with lines and wrinkles"). His youth will be swallowed by old age ("when his youthful morn hath travelled on to age's steepy night"). Then the Guide's beautiful companions, who are robbing him of his youth, will abandon him ("and all those beauties whereof now he's king are vanishing, or vanished out of sight, stealing away the treasure of his spring"). The poet realizes that the Guide's external appearance is not immortal. Therefore, he decides to prepare himself for such a time when his Guide will depart ("for such a time do I now fortify, against confounding age's cruel knife"). He intends to preserve his friend's beauty even if the cruel knife of time takes away his life ("that he shall never cut from memory my sweet love's beauty, though my lover's life"). The Guide's inner essence will be preserved and live in the poet's verses ("his beauty shall in these black lines be seen"). In this way, the Guide's essence will be made available to the future generations ("and they shall live, and he in them still green"). Previously, the poet alluded to such a functionality of his verses. We may notice that the poet's understanding of the role of his poetry has changed. Instead of the Guide's mortal features, the poet emphasises the preservation of the Guide's inner essence.

Similarly, Horatio was asked to preserve Hamlet's experiences by recording his story[63]:

> "O good Horatio, what a wounded name,
> Things standing thus unknown, shall live behind me!
> If thou didst ever hold me in thy heart
> Absent thee from felicity awhile,
> And in this harsh world draw thy breath in pain,
> To tell my story."

---

[63] See "The fencing match" (Shakespeare for the Seeker, Volume 4, Chapter 7.3).

SONNET LXIV

When I have seen by time's fell hand defaced
The rich proud cost of outworn buried age,
When sometime lofty towers I see down-razed,
And brass eternal slave to mortal rage.
When I have seen the hungry Ocean gain
Advantage on the Kingdom of the shore,
And the firm soil win of the watery main,
Increasing store with loss, and loss with store.
When I have seen such interchange of state,
Or state itself confounded, to decay,
Ruin hath taught me thus to ruminate
That Time will come and take my love away.
    This thought is as a death which cannot choose
    But weep to have, that which it fears to lose.

Once again, the poet returns to his contemplation of the destructivity of time. He recalls seeing time defacing ancient sepulchres, lofty towers, and monuments ("when I have seen by time's fell hand defaced the rich proud cost of outworn buried age, when sometime lofty towers I see down-razed, and brass eternal slave to mortal rage"). He has also seen the ocean ruining kingdoms, followed by the land taking back its territory from the ocean ("when I have seen the hungry ocean gain advantage on the kingdom of the shore, and the firm soil win of the watery main"). It is a process of gains from losses, and losses of gains ("increasing store with loss, and loss with store"). The same process applies to the cyclical formations and falls of countries ("when I have seen such interchange of state, or state itself confounded, to decay"). The poet realizes that the same unavoidable law of destructivity applies to his beloved Guide ("ruin hath taught me thus to ruminate that time will come and take my love away"). And this very thought is as painful as death itself ("this thought is as a death"). Despite his previous claim of being able to preserve the Guide's inner essence, the poet is horrified by the thought of his friend's death. His only reaction is to weep in fear of losing his friend ("this thought is as a death which cannot choose but weep to have, that which it fears to lose").

Time's destructive powers were also described by Prospero in "The Tempest", when he woke up from his fancies[64]:

> "And, like the baseless fabric of this vision,
> The cloud-capp'd towers, the gorgeous palaces,
> The solemn temples, the great globe itself,
> Ye all which it inherit, shall dissolve
> And, like this insubstantial pageant faded,
> Leave not a rack behind."

---

[64] See "Prospero's challenges" (Shakespeare for the Seeker, Volume 4, Chapter 8.1).

SONNET LXV

Since brass, nor stone, nor earth, nor boundless sea,
But sad mortality o'er-sways their power,
How with this rage shall beauty hold a plea,
Whose action is no stronger than a flower?
O how shall summer's honey breath hold out,
Against the wrackful siege of battering days,
When rocks impregnable are not so stout,
Nor gates of steel so strong but time decays?
O fearful meditation, where, alack,
Shall time's best Jewel from time's chest lie hid?
Or what strong hand can hold his swift foot back,
Or who his spoil of beauty can forbid?
    O none, unless this miracle have might,
    That in black ink my love may still shine bright.

This is the continuation of the poet's meditation on the destructivity of time. The poet realizes that brass, stone, earth, and sea are not capable of withstanding mortality ("since brass, nor stone, nor earth, nor boundless sea, but sad mortality o'er-sways their power"). How, he asks, a gentle beauty, which is no stronger than a flower, may defend itself against the rage of mortality ("how with this rage shall beauty hold a plea, whose action is no stronger than a flower"). And how the Guide's sweet breath shall hold out against injurious time, when neither rocks nor iron gates are strong enough to resist its destructivity ("how shall summer's honey breath hold out, against the wrackful siege of battering days, when rocks impregnable are not so stout, nor gates of steel so strong but time decays"). This is a frightening meditation ("O fearful meditation"). Where, asks the poet, time's most precious jewel may be hidden from time itself? ("where, alack, shall time's best jewel from time's chest lie hid?") Who will be able to stop time or save from him the Guide's beauty ("or what strong hand can hold his swift foot back, or who his spoil of beauty can forbid?") The poet concludes by expressing his hope that, by a miracle, his verses may preserve the Guide's radiance ("O none, unless this miracle have might, that in black ink my love may still shine bright").

An episode with Hermione's statue in "The Winter's Tale" is an example of such a "miracle" that was implemented through objective art. Here is Paulina instructing Leontes how to approach his "resurrected" wife[65]:

> "Start not; her actions shall be holy as
> You hear my spell is lawful: do not shun her
> Until you see her die again; for then
> You kill her double. Nay, present your hand:
> When she was young you woo'd her; now in age
> Is she become the suitor?"

---

[65] See "Final steps" (Shakespeare for the Seeker, Volume 3, Chapter 6.1).

SONNET LXVI

Tired with all these for restful death I cry,
As to behold desert a beggar born,
And needy Nothing trimm'd in jollity,
And purest faith unhappily forsworn,
And gilded honour shamefully misplaced,
And maiden virtue rudely strumpeted,
And right perfection wrongfully disgraced,
And strength by limping sway disabled,
And art made tongue-tied by authority,
And Folly (Doctor-like) controlling skill,
And simple-Truth miscalled Simplicity,
And captive-good attending Captain ill.
    Tired with all these, from these would I be gone;
    Save that to die, I leave my love alone.

It seems that the poet's lofty thoughts described in the previous Sonnets did not help him overcome his longing for his friend. As a result, he is getting depressed. He implies that only restful death would free him from his miserable state ("tired with all these for restful death I cry"). He compares his situation to all sort of human miseries, i.e., a worthy person who is without means ("to behold desert a beggar born"), a worthless one who is given plenty ("needy nothing trimm'd in jollity"), a sincere one who is outsmarted ("purest faith unhappily forsworn"), an unfit one who is honoured ("gilded honour shamefully misplaced"), an innocent one who is abused ("maiden virtue rudely strumpeted"), a honest one who is disgraced ("right perfection wrongfully disgraced"), a skilful one who is disabled ("strength by limping sway disabled"), a creative one who is censored ("art made tongue-tied by authority"), a useless sophist who is promoted ("folly, doctor-like, controlling skill"), a straightforward one who is considered to be foolish ("simple truth miscalled simplicity"), and a good one who is forced to serve wickedness ("captive good attending captain ill"). Tired with all of these, the poet would like to be gone ("tired with all these, from these would I be gone"). But the poet misses one important thing in his reckoning. Namely, most of these ills are a reflection of his actions and his doing. This becomes apparent in the last line of the Sonnet, which says: "save that to die, I leave my love alone". He is still strongly attached to worldly pleasures. His love is maculated by his earthly attachments.

Hamlet was faced with a similar situation when he was trying to figure out how to escape from his depression[66]:

> "Thus conscience does make cowards of us all;
> And thus the native hue of resolution
> Is sicklied o'er with the pale cast of thought,
> And enterprises of great pith and moment
> With this regard their currents turn awry,
> And lose the name of action."

It seems that the poet arrived at such a state that he needs the Guide's encouragement. Otherwise he may get lost in his idle contemplation. In the following four Sonnets the Guide delivers such an encouragement.

---

[66] See "To be or not to be" (Shakespeare for the Seeker, Volume 4, Chapter 7.3)

The Guide's fifth counsel (Sonnets 67 - 70)

SONNET LXVII

Ah wherefore with infection should he live,
And with his presence grace impiety,
That sin by him advantage should achieve,
And lace itself with his society?
Why should false painting imitate his cheek,
And steal dead seeming of his living hue?
Why should poor beauty indirectly seek,
Roses of shadow, since his Rose is true?
Why should he live, now nature bankrupt is,
Beggared of blood to blush through lively veins,
For she hath no exchequer now but his,
And proud of many, lives upon his gains?
    O him she stores, to show what wealth she had,
    In days long since, before these last so bad.

The Guide, like a Chorus, addresses the readers and explains what the poet's role and his potentiality are. In the previous Sonnet the poet referred to his death as an escape from corrupted life. Yet, the poet was not ready for it. In the Guide's vocabulary to "live" means the state of "not to be", i.e., ordinary life that is driven by worldly pleasures; "death" is the state of "to be", i.e., an elevated spiritual condition allowing for fulfilling one's evolutionary function. This part of the spiritual process is encompassed by the formula "to die before dying".

The Guide asks why the poet should "live" while he is infected with all of those vices of ordinary life ("wherefore with infection should he live?") The poet's ordinary life would serve only as an artificial gilding of the wickedness of meaningless activities ("with his presence grace impiety, that sin by him advantage should achieve, and lace itself with his society?") The Guide compares such gilding to using a make-up to cover some natural defects ("why should false painting imitate his cheek, and steal dead seeming of his living hue?") And why should the poet use make-up to imitate beauty, when his inner being is true beauty? ("Why should poor beauty indirectly seek, roses of shadow, since his rose is true?") Therefore, why should the poet waste his life when Nature is bankrupt and she needs fresh blood to keep her alive? ("Why should he live, now nature bankrupt is, beggared of blood to blush through lively veins"). The poet is the only treasure in Nature's coffers, and she needs him badly to preserve herself ("for she hath no exchequer now but his, and proud of many, lives upon his gains"). This is why Nature needs to keep this unique treasure to show the future generations how prosperous she is, when these present days will turn into misery ("him she stores, to show what wealth she had, in days long since, before these last so bad").

The poet's role in the evolutionary process is equivalent to the role of friends indicated in "Timon of Athens". Here is Timon's description of the roles and function of the "friends"[67]:

> "O you gods, think I, what need we have any
> friends, if we should ne'er have need of 'em? they
> were the most needless creatures living, should we
> ne'er have use for 'em, and would most resemble
> sweet instruments hung up in cases that keep their
> sounds to themselves."

---

[67] See "Friends" (Shakespeare for the Seeker, Volume 2, Chapter 4.3)

SONNET LXVIII

Thus is his cheek the map of days out-worn,
When beauty lived and died as flowers do now,
Before these bastard signs of fair were born,
Or durst inhabit on a living brow:
Before the golden tresses of the dead,
The right of sepulchres, were shorn away,
To live a second life on second head,
Ere beauty's dead fleece made another gay:
In him those holy antique hours are seen,
Without all ornament, itself and true,
Making no summer of another's green,
Robbing no old to dress his beauty new,
    And him as for a map doth Nature store,
    To show false Art what beauty was of yore.

The Guide continues his explanation to the readers of why is it so important that the poet's inner beauty be preserved. The Guide says that the poet is a sample of the inner beauty that was bestowed on mankind in antiquity ("thus is his cheek the map of days out-worn"). In those ancient times, however, beauty was misused ("when beauty lived and died as flowers do now"). Since those times only false beauty is left ("before these bastard signs of fair were born, or durst inhabit on a living brow"). Such false beauty ("these bastard signs of fair") is a reference to the various occults and dogmatic approaches that were becoming quite abundant in Europe at that time ("to live a second life on second head"). The Guide compares them to wigs made from the hair of dead people ("before the golden tresses of the dead, ... were shorn away"). The evolutionary functionality of these ancient concepts and ideas ("false Art") is dead ("the right of sepulchres"). It is only through the poet that it may be possible to regain the evolutionary potentiality that was lost a long time ago ("In him those holy antique hours are seen, without all ornament, itself and true, making no summer of another's green"). The poet is the first among ordinary men who is capable of fulfilling man's evolutionary potential ("robbing no old to dress his beauty new"). The Guide concludes his explanation saying that this is why Nature needs to preserve the poet as a paragon of true humanity ("and him as for a map doth Nature store, to show false Art what beauty was of yore").

In "Pericles, Prince of Tyre" there is a reference to the corruption of the evolutionary process that occurred in antiquity[68]:

> "But custom what they did begin
> Was with long use account no sin."

---

[68] See "Corruption of the transmission" (Shakespeare for the Seeker, Volume 2, Chapter 4.3).

SONNET LXIX

Those parts of thee that the world's eye doth view,
Want nothing that the thought of hearts can mend:
All tongues (the voice of souls) give thee that end,
Uttering bare truth, even so as foes Commend.
Their outward thus with outward praise is crown'd;
But those same tongues that give thee so thine own,
In other accents do this praise confound
By seeing farther than the eye hath shown.
They look into the beauty of thy mind,
And that in guess they measure by thy deeds,
Then churls their thoughts (although their eyes were kind)
To thy fair flower add the rank smell of weeds,
    But why thy odour matcheth not thy show,
    The solye is this, that thou dost common grow.

Now the Guide addresses the poet. He comments on the poet's previously written verses. The Guide says that the external form of the verses is perfect; there is nothing that may be improved ("those parts of thee that the world's eye doth view want nothing that the thought of hearts can mend"). Everybody, even the poet's enemies, agree with such an appraisal of the poet's writings ("all tongues, the voice of souls, give thee that end, uttering bare truth, even so as foes commend"). And this outward form of the his verses has earned him public praise ("their outward thus with outward praise is crown'd"). Yet, the same people who praise the poet's writings will change their opinion once they have grasped their inner meaning ("but those same tongues that give thee so thine own, in other accents do this praise confound by seeing farther than the eye hath shown"). Then they will be able to see the true value of the poet's message ("they look into the beauty of thy mind, and that in guess they measure by thy deeds"). Although at first they judged the poet kindly, afterwards their harsh thoughts will tell them that his verses contain some uncomfortable truth ("then churls their thoughts, although their eyes were kind, to thy fair flower add the rank smell of weeds"). And the Guide concludes that the poet is surrounded by fools and this is the reason why they raise objections against his verses ("but why thy odour matcheth not thy show, the solye is this, that thou dost common grow").

Peter Quincy's introduction to "Pyramus and Thisby" in "A Midsummer Night's Dream" alluded to such an uncomfortable inner content embedded within a seemingly confused form[69]:

> "We do not come as minding to contest you,
> Our true intent is. All for your delight
> We are not here. That you should here repent you,
> The actors are at hand and by their show
> You shall know all that you are like to know."

---

[69] See "Pyramus and Thisby" (Shakespeare for the Seeker, Volume 4, Chapter 8.3).

SONNET LXX

That thou art blamed shall not be thy defect,
For slander's mark was ever yet the fair;
The ornament of beauty is suspect,
A Crow that flies in heaven's sweetest air.
So thou be good, slander doth but approve,
Their worth the greater, being wooed of time,
For Canker vice the sweetest buds doth love,
And thou present'st a pure unstained prime.
Thou hast passed by the ambush of young days,
Either not assailed, or victor being charged,
Yet this thy praise cannot be so thy praise,
To tie up envy, evermore enlarged,
    If some suspect of ill masked not thy show,
    Then thou alone kingdoms of hearts shouldst owe.

The Guide continues his explanation of the merits of the poet's verses. He says that any slanderous reaction to his poetry is only proof of its true value ("that thou art blamed shall not be thy defect"). Because true beauty always attracts some form of wickedness ("for slander's mark was ever yet the fair, the ornament of beauty is suspect"). It is like a crow that pollutes the sweet air of the sky ("a crow that flies in heaven's sweetest air"). The Guide encourages the poet to keep doing what he does, and that he better get used to slander ("so thou be good, slander doth but approve"). The poet should be prepared that slanders against him will intensify with the passing of time ("their worth the greater, being wooed of time"). Because slanderers are like a worm, which prefers to devour the sweetest buds ("for Canker vice the sweetest buds doth love"). Right now the poet has arrived at his zenith, therefore he is the most attractive target for them ("and thou present'st a pure unstained prime"). The Guide says that the poet has managed to escape the usual temptations of his youth either by ignoring or resisting them ("thou hast passed by the ambush of young days, either not assailed, or victor being charged"). Then the Guide warns the poet that his praise will not stop the envious from slandering him even more ("yet this thy praise cannot be so thy praise, to tie up envy, evermore enlarged"). If the poet's verses were not marred by the suspicions of the ignorant, then he alone would be able to offer true happiness to many men ("if some suspect of ill masked not thy show, then thou alone kingdoms of hearts shouldst owe").

Shakespeare in his plays often indicates the destructivity of envy. Here is Montague's comment in "Romeo and Juliet" on Romeo being affected by an envious worm:[70]

> "As is the bud bit with an envious worm,
> Ere he can spread his sweet leaves to the air,
> Or dedicate his beauty to the sun."

---

[70] See "Romeo" (Shakespeare for the Seeker, Volume 3, Chapter 6.6).

Detachment (Sonnets 71 - 72)

SONNET LXXI

No Longer mourn for me when I am dead,
Then you shall hear the surly sullen bell
Give warning to the world that I am fled
From this vile world with vilest worms to dwell:
Nay if you read this line, remember not,
The hand that writ it, for I love you so,
That I in your sweet thoughts would be forgot,
If thinking on me then should make you woe.
O if (I say) you look upon this verse,
When I (perhaps) compounded am with clay,
Do not so much as my poor name rehearse;
But let your love even with my life decay.
    Lest the wise world should look into your moan,
    And mock you with me after I am gone.

The Guide encouraged the poet to continue what he was doing. It should be emphasized that the poet does not understand fully the process. He is still driven by his emotions and sentiments of ordinary attachments. The current stage of the process is a preparation for the poet's "dying before dying". This is the only way that the poet may fulfil his potentiality and discharge his role (see Sonnet 67). The poet alluded to such a transition when we heard from him last time, i.e., in Sonnet 66.

The poet appeals to the Guide to not mourn for him when he hears the funeral bells announcing his death and his departure from this world ("no longer mourn for me when I am dead, then you shall hear the surly sullen bell give warning to the world that I am fled from this vile world"). At that time the poet will be gone from this corrupted world and his body dwelling with horrid worms ("with vilest worms to dwell"). The poet asks the Guide that, when he reads these words, he should not remember who wrote them ("if you read this line, remember not, the hand that writ it"). The poet loves him so much that he prefers to be forgotten than making his friend feeling sad ("for I love you so, that I in your sweet thoughts would be forgot, if thinking on me then should make you woe"). And the Guide should not remember the poet's name either, but let die his love when the poet's body is dissolved in the earth ("if, I say, you look upon this verse, when I, perhaps, compounded am with clay, do not so much as my poor name rehearse, but let your love even with my life decay"). Otherwise, the wise of this world would have the right to mock the Guide, because he himself was not able to distance himself from emotional attachments ("lest the wise world should look into your moan, and mock you with me after I am gone").

In his comment to Claudio in "Measure for Measure", Duke Vincentio had this to say about dying before dying[71]:

> "What's yet in this
> That bears the name of life? Yet in this life
> Lie hid moe thousand deaths: yet death we fear,
> That makes these odds all even."

---

[71] See "Claudio and Isabella" (Shakespeare for the Seeker, Volume 4, Chapter 7.2).

SONNET LXXII

O lest the world should task you to recite,
What merit lived in me that you should love
After my death (dear love) forget me quite,
For you in me can nothing worthy prove.
Unless you would devise some virtuous lie,
To do more for me than mine own desert,
And hang more praise upon deceased I,
Than niggard truth would willingly impart:
O lest your true love may seem false in this,
That you for love speak well of me untrue,
My name be buried where my body is,
And live no more to shame nor me, nor you.
    For I am shamed by that which I bring forth,
    And so should you, to love things nothing worth.

The poet continues with his preparation for death. He asks the Guide to forget about his love, otherwise he might be asked to explain its merit ("O lest the world should task you to recite, what merit lived in me that you should love after my death, dear love, forget me quite"). The poet insists that there is nothing of value in him ("for you in me can nothing worthy prove"). Therefore, the Guide would have to lie to make his friend look better than he is and give him more praise than he deserves ("unless you would devise some virtuous lie, to do more for me than mine own desert, and hang more praise upon deceased I, than niggard truth would willingly impart"). By doing that the Guide would show that his love was false ("O lest your true love may seem false in this, that you for love speak well of me untrue"). Let his name and his body be buried, asks the poet, so he will shame neither himself nor his friend ("my name be buried where my body is, and live no more to shame nor me, nor you"). The poet feels ashamed at how little he was able to achieve ("for I am shamed by that which I bring forth"). And his shame also stains the Guide for loving someone so worthless ("and so should you, to love things nothing worth"). It is the first time that we hear some signs of humility in the poet's voice.

Helena in "All's Well That Ends Well" declared a similar worthlessness of her love of Bertram[72]:

> " 'Twere all one
> That I should love a bright particular star
> And think to wed it, he is so above me:
> In his bright radiance and collateral light
> Must I be comforted, not in his sphere.
> The ambition in my love thus plagues itself:
> The hind that would be mated by the lion
> Must die for love."

---

[72] See "Developmental mismatch" (Shakespeare for the Seeker, Volume 2, Chapter 5.1).

The Guide's sixth counsel (Sonnets 73 - 74)

SONNET LXXIII

That time of year thou mayst in me behold,
When yellow leaves, or none, or few do hang
Upon those boughs which shake against the cold,
Bare ruin'd choirs, where late the sweet birds sang.
In me thou seest the twilight of such day,
As after Sun-set fadeth in the West,
Which by and by black night doth take away,
Death's second self that seals up all in rest.
In me thou see'st the glowing of such fire,
That on the ashes of his youth doth lie,
As the death-bed, whereon it must expire,
Consumed with that which it was nourish'd by.
    This thou perceivest, which makes thy love more strong,
    To love that well, which thou must leave ere long.

A developmental cycle consists of the seven stages. The Guide's sixth counsel is an introduction to the poet's sixth stage of his journey. There is no linear progression within a cycle. There will be "intervals" or "gaps". These gaps are the most challenging stages of the process. The Sonnet is a preparation for such a gap. In this respect, the Sonnet parallels "Titus Andronicus" within Shakespeare's Roman plays, "Macbeth" within the Celtic plays, "Richard III" within the History plays, "Romeo and Juliet" within the Italian plays, "All's Well That Ends Well" within the French plays, and "Hamlet" within the Bohemian plays.

In this Sonnet the Guide instructs the poet that, at a certain time, he should keep the Guide particularly firmly in his mind ("that time of year thou mayst in me behold"). This will help the poet to deal with the coming departure of the Guide. The time of such an experience will be marked in the same way as the coming of winter. The coming of the winter is indicated by the yellow leafs and the bare branches on which the birds used to sing ("when yellow leaves, or none, or few do hang upon those boughs which shake against the cold, bare ruin'd choirs, where late the sweet birds sang"). By keeping the Guide in his mind, the poet will notice the twilight, such as that which appears in the west after sunset ("in me thou seest the twilight of such day, as after sunset fadeth in the west"). Then the twilight will be taken away by black night, which like death, will put all in eternal rest ("which by and by black night doth take away, death's second self that seals up all in rest"). At such a time the poet will be able to see a glowing fire within the ashes of his previous attachments ("in me thou see'st the glowing of such fire, that on the ashes of his youth doth lie"). The ashes are a death-bed for the poet's false-self, which will be diminished when its fuel is burnt out ("as the death-bed, whereon it must expire, consumed with that which it was nourish'd by"). When the poet perceives these signs, he will be able to experience true love ("this thou perceivest, which makes thy love more strong"). At that moment the poet will be able to leave behind his worldly pleasures ("to love that well, which thou must leave ere long").

The Guide's counsel is an echo of the symbolical rebirth or the renewal that is represented by the mythological Phoenix. A similar description is contained in the Soothsayer's vision inserted at the conclusion of "Cymbeline". According to the Soothsayer, the sight of the vanishing eagle foretold the "rebirth" of Cymbeline's Britain[73]:

> "For the Roman eagle,
> From south to west on wing soaring aloft,
> Lessen'd herself, and in the beams o' the sun
> So vanish'd: which foreshow'd our princely eagle,
> The imperial Caesar, should again unite
> His favour with the radiant Cymbeline,
> Which shines here in the west."

---

[73] See "Renewal" (Shakespeare for the Seeker, Volume 1, Chapter 3.2).

SONNET LXXIV

But be contented when that fell arrest,
With out all bail shall carry me away,
My life hath in this line some interest,
Which for memorial still with thee shall stay.
When thou reviewest this, thou dost review,
The very part was consecrate to thee,
The earth can have but earth, which is his due,
My spirit is thine, the better part of me,
So then thou hast but lost the dregs of life,
The prey of worms, my body being dead,
The coward conquest of a wretch's knife,
Too base of thee to be remembered,
    The worth of that, is that which it contains,
    And that is this, and this with thee remains.

The Guide continues with the poet's preparation for the "gap". The Guide advises the poet that he should not be discouraged when he will be physically separated from him ("but be contented when that fell arrest, with out all bail shall carry me away"). The Guide's presence will be preserved by this very statement, which the poet has to remember ("my life hath in this line some interest, which for memorial still with thee shall stay"). Each time the poet recalls this line, he will be able to be in the presence of the immortal part of his Guide ("when thou reviewest this, thou dost review, the very part was consecrate to thee"). The earth can keep only the mortal part, but the poet can have access to the Guide's essence, i.e., his immortal part ("the earth can have but earth, which is his due, my spirit is thine, the better part of me"). So, the poet is going to be separated from a useless residue, which may serve only as food for worms ("so then thou hast but lost the dregs of life, the prey of worms, my body being dead"). The body is the only bounty of wretched death, and is not worthy to be remembered ("the coward conquest of a wretch's knife, too base of thee to be remembered"). The important thing is that which is contained in this counsel ("the worth of that, is that which it contains, and that is this"). And as long as the poet remembers this counsel, the Guide's essence will remain with him ("and this with thee remains").

Duke Vincentio in "Measure for Measure" was also preparing Claudio for "dying before dying"[74]:

> "Thou'rt by no means valiant;
> For thou dost fear the soft and tender fork
> Of a poor worm. Thy best of rest is sleep,
> And that thou oft provokest; yet grossly fear'st
> Thy death, which is no more."

---

[74] See "Claudio and Isabella" (Shakespeare for the Seeker, Volume 4, Chapter 7.2).

Impermanency (Sonnets 75 - 76)

SONNET LXXV

So are you to my thoughts as food to life,
Or as sweet season'd showers are to the ground;
And for the peace of you I hold such strife,
As 'twixt a miser and his wealth is found.
Now proud as an enjoyer, and anon
Doubting the filching age will steal his treasure,
Now counting best to be with you alone,
Then better'd that the world may see my pleasure,
Some-time all full with feasting on your sight,
And by and by clean starved for a look,
Possessing or pursuing no delight
Save what is had, or must from you be took.
    Thus do I pine and surfeit day by day,
    Or gluttoning on all, or all away.

This Sonnet describes the poet's reaction to the Guide's previous counsel. The poet has understood that the Guide's essence is as important to him as rain is needed for the garden. However, the poet's approach to the Guide's essence is the same as a miser treats his hidden treasure ("and for the peace of you I hold such strife, as 'twixt a miser and his wealth is found"). One moment he enjoys happily his treasure, and the next he is frightened that someone may steal it ("now proud as an enjoyer, and anon doubting the filching age will steal his treasure"). The same happens to the poet. One moment he thinks it is best to be alone with the Guide, but then he would like to show off his happiness to others ("now counting best to be with you alone, then better'd that the world may see my pleasure"). The poet has previously had a similar experience (see Sonnet 52). Now, however, his description reveals deeper aspects of his encounters with the Guide. Sometimes he feels over-saturated with the Guide's presence ("some-time all full with feasting on your sight"). Later on, he is longing for it. The poet realizes that neither having nor pursuing does him anything good ("and by and by clean starved for a look, possessing or pursuing no delight"). What matters is what the poet experienced or took from these encounters ("save what is had, or must from you be took"). The poet feels that he has not mastered these encounters yet. Therefore he suffers because he is disturbed by the impermanency of his inner states ("thus do I pine and surfeit day by day"). He is either disturbed by too strong an impact, or he is distraught by the lack of it ("or gluttoning on all, or all away").

Pericles in "Pericles, Prince of Tyre" went through a similar experience. Pericles compared it to being like a tennis-ball that the water and the wind play with[75]:

> "A man whom both the waters and the wind,
> In that vast tennis-court, have made the ball
> For them to play upon."

---

[75] See "Inspirational vision" (Shakespeare for the Seeker, Volume 2, Chapter 4.1).

SONNET LXXVI

Why is my verse so barren of new pride?
So far from variation or quick change?
Why with the time do I not glance aside
To new found methods, and to compounds strange?
Why write I still all one, ever the same,
And keep invention in a noted weed,
That every word doth almost tell my name,
Showing their birth, and where they did proceed?
O know sweet love I always write of you,
And you and love are still my argument:
So all my best is dressing old words new,
Spending again what is already spent:
    For as the Sun is daily new and old,
    So is my love still telling what is told.

The path that Shakespeare outlines in the Sonnets is a long and a difficult one. It is an old path, in the sense that it has been indicated to man a long time ago. Since the arrival of man on this planet, this path has been trod by many. Therefore, the path is well known. This is why the poet does not intend to introduce any innovations in his poetry ("why is my verse so barren of new pride, so far from variation or quick change"). Neither is he introducing new methods nor styles ("why with the time do I not glance aside to new found methods, and to compounds strange"). He writes about the same subject and in the same style, so it is obvious where his inspiration is coming from ("why write I still all one, ever the same, and keep invention in a noted weed, that every word doth almost tell my name, showing their birth, and where they did proceed"). Namely, the poet is always writing about love and about his Guide ("O know sweet love I always write of you, and you and love are still my argument"). The best the poet can do is to use new phrases to tell what has already been told ("so all my best is dressing old words new, spending again what is already spent"). He intends to retell his story, again and again, just like the sun that rises and sets every day ("for as the sun is daily new and old"). The poet's love for the Guide keeps him repeating what has already been told ("so is my love still telling what is told"). In other words, the object of the poet's love is constant. However, the poet is still not able to keep permanency of his inner states.

When Ferdinand met Miranda in "The Tempest", he was in a state similar to the poet's[76]. To demonstrate his constancy he had to practise patience by working as a log-man:

> "Hear my soul speak:
> The very instant that I saw you, did
> My heart fly to your service; there resides,
> To make me slave to it; and for your sake
> Am I this patient log-man."

---

[76] See "Process" (Shakespeare for the Seeker, Volume 4, Chapter 8.1).

The Guide's seventh counsel (Sonnet 77)

SONNET LXXVII

Thy glass will show thee how thy beauties wear,
Thy dial how thy precious minutes waste,
The vacant leaves thy mind's imprint will bear,
And of this book, this learning mayst thou taste.
The wrinkles which thy glass will truly show,
Of mouthed graves will give thee memory,
Thou by thy dial's shady stealth mayst know,
Time's thievish progress to eternity.
Look what thy memory can not contain,
Commit to these waste blanks, and thou shalt find
Those children nursed, deliver'd from thy brain,
To take a new acquaintance of thy mind.
    These offices, so oft as thou wilt look,
    Shall profit thee, and much enrich thy book.

The poet's comment about his writings prompts the Guide to provide him with further instructions. He indicates that the poet has to wait till he improves his inner states. Only then will he be able to record correctly the Guide's teaching. In other words, the poet is still not ready yet.

As time passes and the poet gets older ("thy glass will show thee how thy beauties wear"), the poet's intellect faculty will be gradually purified, so it will be better prepared to record the Guide's teaching ("the vacant leaves thy mind's imprint will bear, and of this book, this learning mayst thou taste"). The ordinary intellect is useful only to remember about the unstoppable passing of time ("the wrinkles which thy glass will truly show, of mouthed graves will give thee memory, thou by thy dial's shady stealth mayst know, time's thievish progress to eternity"). But the Guide's teaching cannot be confined to such an inferior faculty ("look what thy memory can not contain"). Instead, the teaching, to which the poet is exposed to, may be properly recorded in the subtle layers of his intellect which are still inactive ("commit to these waste blanks"). The Guide's words are like a nourishment that will activate them ("and thou shalt find those children nursed, deliver'd from thy brain, to take a new acquaintance of thy mind"). As in the first counsel, the Guide refers to the subtle faculties as "those children nursed, deliver'd from thy brain". It is through "those children" that the poet may enrich his inner being and be able to enrich his skills ("these offices, so oft as thou wilt look, shall profit thee, and much enrich thy book").

King Richard II also compared the activation of the subtle levels of the mind to begetting children[77]:

> "My brain I'll prove the female to my soul,
> My soul the father; and these two beget
> A generation of still-breeding thoughts,
> And these same thoughts people this little world."

---

[77] See "Preliminary realization" (Shakespeare for the Seeker, Volume 1, Chapter 1).

Jealousy (Sonnets 78 - 81)

SONNET LXXVIII

So oft have I invoked thee for my Muse,
And found such fair assistance in my verse,
As every *Alien* pen hath got my use,
And under thee their poesy disperse.
Thine eyes, that taught the dumb on high to sing,
And heavy ignorance aloft to fly,
Have added feathers to the learned's wing,
And given grace a double Majesty.
Yet be most proud of that which I compile,
Whose influence is thine, and born of thee,
In others' works thou dost but mend the style,
And Arts with thy sweet graces graced be.
    But thou art all my art, and dost advance
    As high as learning, my rude ignorance.

The poet has been inspired by the Guide, whom he considers as his Muse ("so oft have I invoked thee for my Muse, and found such fair assistance in my verse"). The Guide has also told the poet that he should look at some previously written poetry as a template for his writings ("as every *Alien* pen hath got my use and under thee their poesy disperse"). As indicated in the previous Sonnets, the Guide is the source of the poet's inspiration and his learning ("thine eyes, that taught the dumb on high to sing and heavy ignorance aloft to fly"). In other words, the Guide's actions have provided the content for the poet's verses ("have added feathers to the learned's wing, and given grace a double majesty"). This is why, claims the poet, the Guide should be proud of his effect and his influence on the poet's writings ("yet be most proud of that which I compile, whose influence is thine, and born of thee"). Yet the Guide has criticized the poet's works. At the same time he has made only a few adjustments to the works of those other poets ("in others' works thou dost but mend the style, and arts with thy sweet graces graced be"). So the poet becomes jealous of the other poets.

And he insists that his writing is superior because it was the Guide who inspired it ("but thou art all my art, and dost advance as high as learning, my rude ignorance").

Jealousy makes the poet vulnerable, because it blinds his perception. For example, Borachio in "Much Ado About Nothing" was able to interfere with Claudio's planned wedding with Hero because of Claudio's unjustified jealousy[78]:

> "and there shall appear such seeming truth
> of Hero's disloyalty that jealousy shall be called
> assurance and all the preparation overthrown."

---

[78] See "Villain" (Shakespeare for the Seeker, Volume 3, Chapter 6.6).

SONNET LXXIX

Whilst I alone did call upon thy aid,
My verse alone had all thy gentle grace,
But now my gracious numbers are decayed,
And my sick Muse doth give another place.
I grant (sweet love) thy lovely argument
Deserves the travail of a worthier pen,
Yet what of thee thy Poet doth invent,
He robs thee of, and pays it thee again,
He lends thee virtue, and he stole that word,
From thy behaviour, beauty doth he give
And found it in thy cheek: he can afford
No praise to thee, but what in thee doth live.
    Then thank him not for that which he doth say,
    Since what he owes thee, thou thyself dost pay.

This Sonnet focuses on another aspect of the poet's inner imperfections. Let's recall that by now the poet communicates with his Guide during his meditation. During such encounters the Guide deliberately incites certain reactions to unmask the poet's inner inadequacies. By monitoring his own reactions, the poet may identify his weaknesses. These weaknesses are not perceptible in his ordinary state. In this particular case, the Guide induces jealousy, which manifests itself as the poet's desire for the exclusivity of his friend's attention. Previously, the poet had the full attention of his Guide ("whilst I alone did call upon thy aid, my verse alone had all thy gentle grace"). Now, the poet blames the Guide for losing his inspiration, because the Guide is preoccupied with someone else ("but now my gracious numbers are decayed, and my sick Muse doth give another place"). The poet admits that it would require a better writer than himself to express adequately the Guide's teaching ("I grant, sweet love, thy lovely argument deserves the travail of a worthier pen"). The poet argues that the other writer is not any better; he just gets ideas from the Guide and then gives them back to him ("yet what of thee thy Poet doth invent, he robs thee of, and pays it thee again"). There is nothing more in the other poet's writing, says our poet, except what he learned from the Guide's actions and what he saw in his face ("he lends thee virtue, and he stole that word, from thy behaviour, beauty doth he give and found it in thy cheek"). He is incapable of inventing anything more than what he can see in the Guide ("can afford no praise to thee, but what in thee doth live"). Therefore, the Guide should not give the other poet too much credit for something that he took from him ("then thank him not for that which he doth say, since what he owes thee, thou thyself dost pay").

The poet has entirely missed the point. By emphasizing the other writer's work, the Guide indicates that the poet should pay attention to and use it as a template for his own writing. By doing that, the poet would find an explanation of his present state. All of that, however, is lost on the poet. Instead, he keeps arguing and bargaining for the guide's attention.

Lady Macbeth was also bargaining for her husband's attention. Here is a sample of her persuasive skills[79]:

> "I have given suck, and know
> How tender 'tis to love the babe that milks me:
> I would, while it was smiling in my face,
> Have pluck'd my nipple from his boneless gums,
> And dash'd the brains out, had I so sworn as you
> Have done to this."

---

[79] See "Scotland: 11th century AD" (Shakespeare for the Seeker, Volume 1, Chapter 3.3).

SONNET LXXX

O how I faint when I of you do write,
Knowing a better spirit doth use your name,
And in the praise thereof spends all his might,
To make me tongue-tied speaking of your fame.
But since your worth (wide as the Ocean is)
The humble as the proudest sail doth bear,
My saucy bark (inferior far to his)
On your broad main doth wilfully appear.
Your shallowest help will hold me up afloat,
Whilst he upon your soundless deep doth ride,
Or (being wrecked) I am a worthless boat,
He of tall building, and of goodly pride.
    Then if he thrive and I be cast away,
    The worst was this, my love was my decay.

The poet is discouraged when he realizes that the other writer's praises of the Guide are more adequate than his own ("O how I faint when I of you do write, knowing a better spirit doth use your name"). The poet is intimidated by the other writer's talent and skills ("and in the praise thereof spends all his might, to make me tongue-tied speaking of your fame"). It may be presumed that it was the other writer who introduced the imagery of the ocean to represent the guide's love ("but since your worth wide as the ocean is"). The poet adapts this imaginary to describe himself as a humble bark, which is much inferior to the other ship ("the humble as the proudest sail doth bear, my saucy bark, inferior far to his, on your broad main doth wilfully appear"). The other writer is able to sail over the Guide's infinitive love, while the poet hopes that his poems will keep him floating over shallowest regions ("your shallowest help will hold me up afloat, whilst he upon your soundless deep doth ride"). Even if the poet ends up being wrecked, nothing will be lost, because he is like a worthless boat ("being wrecked, I am a worthless boat"). The poet may sink, but the other writer will continue to float like a mighty and majestic ship ("he of tall building, and of goodly pride").

Again, the poet misses the point, i.e., the fact that they both, he and his presumed rival, are being carried by the Guide's love. And it does not really matter if the other writer thrives or not ("then if he thrive and I be cast away"). What the poet considers to be the worst case, in reality would be the best outcome, i.e., to immerse himself completely in the Guide's love ("the worst was this, my love was my decay"). Only through such a complete immersion would it be possible for him to reach his destination. The imaginary of the poet's immersion in the Guide's love is a further sign of the operation of the purified aspect of the heart. (This particular subtle faculty is indicated by the colour red.)

Here is Benedick's meditation in "Much Ado About Nothing" on the same theme[80], i.e., "to be truly turned over and over ... in love":

> "But in loving, Leander the good
> swimmer, Troilus the first employer of panders, and
> a whole bookfull of these quondam carpet-mangers,
> whose names yet run smoothly in the even road of a
> blank verse, why, they were never so truly turned
> over and over as my poor self in love."

---

[80] See "Conclusion" (Shakespeare for the Seeker, Volume 3, Chapter 6.3).

SONNET LXXXI

Or I shall live your Epitaph to make,
Or you survive when I in earth am rotten,
From hence your memory death cannot take,
Although in me each part will be forgotten.
Your name from hence immortal life shall have,
Though I (once gone) to all the world must die,
The earth can yield me but a common grave,
When you entombed in men's eyes shall lie,
Your monument shall be my gentle verse,
Which eyes not yet created shall o'er-read,
And tongues to be, your being shall rehearse,
When all the breathers of this world are dead,
    You still shall live (such virtue hath my Pen)
    Where breath most breathes, even in the mouths of men.

The poet revisits his meditation on death. But his current understanding is much deeper than his previous rendering, when his inner state was visibly maculated by his earthly attachments (e.g., see Sonnet 66). Now the poet considers two possibilities, either he will live to write the Guide's epitaph, or the Guide will survive him ("I shall live your Epitaph to make, or you survive when I in earth am rotten"). If the poet dies first, the Guide will be preserved within the poet's verses ("from hence your memory death cannot take"). So, even though the poet's body will be rotting in his grave, the Guide's name will live eternally ("although in me each part will be forgotten, your name from hence immortal life shall have"). But the poet will be forgotten ("though I, once gone, to all the world must die, the earth can yield me but a common grave"). Whereas when the Guide dies to ordinary men's eyes, the poet's verses will be his monument ("when you entombed in men's eyes shall lie, your monument shall be my gentle verse"). His verses will be read over and over again by the future generations ("which eyes not yet created shall o'er-read, and tongues to be"). In this way the Guide's essence will be preserved when all those who are now living will be dead ("your being shall rehearse, when all the breathers of this world are dead").

The poet claims that his pen has such power that it will hold the Guide's teaching as long as there are people ("you still shall live, such virtue hath my pen, where breath most breathes, even in the mouths of men"). The poet's conclusion was predicted by the Guide in his fourth counsel, when he stated that the poet's praise "shall still find room, even in the eyes of all posterity" (see Sonnet 55). Similarly, Timon of Athens wrote his own epitaph in which he passed his instruction[81]:

> "Here lie I, Timon; who, alive, all living men did hate:
> Pass by and curse thy fill, but pass and stay not here thy gait."

Timon advised Athenians that they should "pass by and curse thy fill" of their current state. They should not stay there; they should move forwards. Because Timon's "gold" will not remain there; it will be transferred to another place.

...

The important thing is that by immersing himself in the Guide's love (Sonnet 80), the poet has overcome his jealousy. It looks that he has recognized the template that was indicated to him by the Guide (Sonnets 78, 79) and learned from it the true nature of the inner states. This is why he was able to arrive at a spiritually constructive conclusion.

The Sonnet 81 concludes the poet's response to the Guide's seven counsels. The seven counsels mark the seven stages of the first developmental cycle. At the time of his initiation, the poet's level corresponded to that of a spiritual kindergarten. During the following phase he was at the stage of a spiritual teenager. Now the

---

[81] See "Conclusion" (Shakespeare for the Seeker, Volume 2, Chapter 4.3).

Guide may bring him onto the next turn of the evolutionary spiral, i.e., the stage of a mature man. In accordance with the developmental methodology, some of the previous stages, i.e., those which have not been completely developed - will have to be repeated. At the same time, the poet will have to go through a set of new and more challenging experiences. The following Sonnet is the Guide's eighth counsel that introduces the poet to these new challenges.

The Guide's eighth counsel (Sonnet 82)

SONNET LXXXII

I grant thou wert not married to my Muse
And therefore mayst without attaint o'erlook
The dedicated words which writers use
Of their fair subject, blessing every book.
Thou art as fair in knowledge as in hue,
Finding thy worth a limit past my praise,
And therefore art enforced to seek anew
Some fresher stamp of the time bettering days
And do so love, yet when they have devised
What strained touches Rhetoric can lend,
Thou truly fair, wert truly sympathized
In true plain words, by thy true telling friend.
  And their gross painting might be better used
  Where cheeks need blood, in thee it is abused.

In this Sonnet the Guide introduces the poet to the second cycle of his journey.

Ideally, the new stage would be the continuation of the last stage of the previous cycle. However, because of human imperfections and errors, there can be delays and interruptions in the process. This is why the first stage of a new cycle may be overlapped with certain intermediate stages of the previous cycle. Such an overlap would indicate, in this case, that the poet must be exposed several times to the same evolutionary impact before he is able to assimilate it effectively. In other words, multiple exposures serve as multi-layered "coatings" that may be required for the completion of the process. The same methodology was implemented in Western Europe in the four evolutionary branches of the modern cycle. These branches are illustrated in Shakespeare's English, French, Italian, and Bohemian plays.

It seems that the poet has stopped writing. So, his current stage is overlapped with that described previously in Sonnet 23, i.e., the first stage of the previous cycle. At that time he was overwhelmed with his task. Now the poet is asked to use his newly acquired knowledge and his partially activated subtle faculties ("hue") to overcome the previously encountered limitations ("thou art as fair in knowledge as in hue"). In other words, the poet is expected to act as an adult and use his new skills to perform the required task. His task is to record correctly the Guide's teaching. The Guide says, however, that the poet does not need to be restricted to the Guide's counsels ("I grant thou wert not married to my Muse"). The poet is encouraged to look at other concepts and doctrines described by other writers ("and therefore mayst without attaint o'erlook the dedicated words which writers use of their fair subject, blessing every book"). But he should keep in mind, warns the Guide, that he has acquired new skills, which would be difficult to overestimate ("finding thy worth a limit past my praise"). Therefore, the poet should use his new skills to extract the relevant information from those texts ("and therefore art enforced to seek anew some fresher stamp of the time bettering days"). The poet should exercise flexibility, but should remember that his new skills are much more effective than any elaborate but dogmatic rhetoric ("and do so love, yet when they have devised what strained touches rhetoric can lend, thou truly fair, wert truly sympathized in true plain words"). Any embellishing or gilding of truth is only like a desperate attempt at bringing to life something that is already dead ("and their gross painting might be better used where cheeks need blood"). In the case of the poet, he would abuse his skills if he was implementing such unnecessary sophistry ("in thee it is abused").

A similar approach of simplicity and flexibility was advocated by Hamlet in the stage directions he gave to the players[82]:

---

[82] See "The players' performance" (Shakespeare for the Seeker, Volume 4, Chapter 7.3).

"Suit the action to the word, the
word to the action; with this special o'erstep not
the modesty of nature: for any thing so overdone is
from the purpose of playing, whose end, both at the
first and now, was and is, to hold, as 'twere, the
mirror up to nature; to show virtue her own feature,
scorn her own image, and the very age and body of
the time his form and pressure."

Self-deception (Sonnets 83 - 93)

SONNET LXXXIII

And therefore to your fair no painting set,
I found, or thought I found, you did exceed
The barren tender of a Poet's debt:
And therefore have I slept in your report,
That you yourself being extant well might show,
How far a modern quill doth come too short,
Speaking of worth, what worth in you doth grow,
This silence for my sin you did impute,
Which shall be most my glory, being dumb;
For I impair not beauty being mute,
When others would give life, and bring a tomb.
    There lives more life in one of your fair eyes
    Than both your Poets can in praise devise.

This is the poet's response to the Guide's latest counsel given in the previous Sonnet. The Guide has advised him to avoid in his poems any artificial embellishment or unnecessary sophistry. The poet denies that he has ever considered beautifying the Guide with any embellishments ("and therefore to your fair no painting set, I found, or thought I found"). Quite to the contrary, the poet knew that the Guide was better than anything that any poet could describe ("you did exceed the barren tender of a poet's debt"). The poet admits that he has been negligent in his task, because he did not write at all. He claims that the Guide's presence is so much superior to anything that any poet could describe ("and therefore have I slept in your report, that you yourself being extant well might show, how far a modern quill doth come too short, speaking of worth, what worth in you doth grow"). Yet, the poet implies that the Guide scorned him unjustly, because his silence was the greatest way of expressing his admiration ("this silence for my sin you did impute, which shall be most my glory, being dumb"). By remaining silent, the poet does not mar his friend's beauty ("for I impair not beauty being mute"). While others would kill it by trying to do it ("when others would give life, and bring a tomb"). The poet concludes that there is more life in one of the Guide's eye, then he himself and the other poet could ever create ("there lives more life in one of your fair eyes than both your poets can in praise devise").

The poet misses the main point of the Guide's counsel, which indicates that he should perform a specific task. Now is the right time for him to write about the Guide and to record his teaching. This is the poet's specific function. By remaining silent the poet ignores his responsibility.

Olivia in "Twelfth Night" demonstrated a similar attitude with respect to her "beauty"[83]. Instead of using it in a constructive manner, she intended to keep it idly as an inventory:

> "I will give
> out divers schedules of my beauty: it shall be
> inventoried, and every particle and utensil
> labelled to my will: as, item, two lips,
> indifferent red; item, two grey eyes, with lids to
> them; item, one neck, one chin, and so forth."

This is why Cesario scorned her, telling her she was just too proud of herself.

---

[83] See "Cruel maid" (Shakespeare for the Seeker, Volume 4, Chapter 7.1).

SONNET LXXXIV

Who is it that says most, which can say more,
Than this rich praise, that you alone, are you,
In whose confine immured is the store,
Which should example where your equal grew,
Lean penury within that Pen doth dwell,
That to his subject lends not some small glory,
But he that writes of you, if he can tell,
That you are you, so dignifies his story.
Let him but copy what in you is writ,
Not making worse what nature made so clear.
And such a counter-part shall fame his wit,
Making his style admired every where.
 You to your beauteous blessings add a curse,
 Being fond on praise, which makes your praises worse.

The poet continues to defend his silence. He says that his Guide is an exemplar of human perfection. Which writer, asks the poet, can say anything more to praise him than just saying that he is he ("who is it that says most, which can say more than this rich praise, that you alone, are you"). All beauty is stored in him, says the poet, so that there's nothing to compare him to but to himself ("in whose confine immured is the store, which should example where your equal grew"). Even a bad poet would greatly dignify his writing by saying simply that he is he ("lean penury within that pen doth dwell, that to his subject lends not some small glory, but he that writes of you, if he can tell, that you are you"). Any poet who would be able to describe him accurately, presenting him no worse than what nature made so clearly, would become famous and his poetry would be admired everywhere ("not making worse what nature made so clear, ... shall fame his wit, making his style admired every where"). The poet concludes saying that the Guide does a disservice to himself by demanding to be praised ("you to your beauteous blessings add a curse, being fond on praise, which makes your praises worse").

The poet has been asked to write about his friend. He mistakenly assumes that the Guide, like Olivia (quoted in the previous Sonnet), is just fond of the poet's admiration. Valentine in "Two Gentlemen of Verona" was also quite puzzled when his beloved Sylvia asked him to write a love letter to her unidentified lover. Here is Speed's explanation of Sylvia's purpose[84]:

> "He being her pupil, to become her tutor.
> O excellent device! was there ever heard a better,
> That my master, being scribe, to himself should write the letter?"

Valentine did not realize that the letter he was writing was addressed to himself.

---

[84] See "Advanced structure" (Shakespeare for the Seeker, Volume 3, Chapter 6.7).

SONNET LXXXV

My tongue-tied Muse in manners holds her still,
While comments of your praise richly compiled,
Reserve their Character with golden quill,
And precious phrase by all the Muses filed.
I think good thoughts, whilst other write good words,
And like unletter'd clerk still cry Amen,
To every Hymn that able spirit affords,
In polish'd form of well-refined pen.
Hearing you praised, I say 'tis so, 'tis true,
And to the most of praise add some-thing more,
But that is in my thought, whose love to you
(Though words come hind-most) holds his rank before,
    Then others, for the breath of words respect,
    Me for my dumb thoughts, speaking in effect.

The poet continues his bragging about the superiority of his silent praises of the Guide.

His poetry is silent, says the poet ("my tongue-tied Muse in manners holds her still"), while others are praising the Guide by painting him with a golden pen and rich phrases inspired by all the muses ("reserve their character with golden quill, and precious phrase by all the Muses filed"). He says that his praise of the Guide takes the form of good thoughts about the Guide ("I think good thoughts"), while other poets write just words ("whilst other write good words"). In this context, the poet compares himself to an illiterate parish clerk who cries "amen" to every hymn he hears ("and like unletter'd clerk still cry Amen, to every Hymn that able spirit affords"). When he hears the Guide being praised, says the poet, he confirms that it is right, that it is true. But then he adds a little more to their praises of the Guide ("and to the most of praise add some-thing more"). What he adds is only in his thoughts. But in his mind he knows he loves him the most, though he speaks the least ("whose love to you, though words come hind-most, holds his rank before"). The poet appeals to the Guide to respect others for their words, but he himself should be acknowledged for speaking silently ("then others, for the breath of words respect, me for my dumb thoughts, speaking in effect").

The poet's argument parallels that of Prince of Aragon in "The Merchant of Venice", who also considered himself better than others[85]:

> "I will not choose what many men desire,
> Because I will not jump with common spirits
> And rank me with the barbarous multitudes."

This is why he ended up as a double fool:

> "With one fool's head I came to woo,
> But I go away with two."

---

[85] See "Trials" (Shakespeare for the Seeker, Volume 3, Chapter 6.4).

SONNET LXXXVI

Was it the proud full sail of his great verse,
Bound for the prize of (all too precious) you,
That did my ripe thoughts in my brain inhearse,
Making their tomb the womb wherein they grew?
Was it his spirit, by spirits taught to write,
Above a mortal pitch, that struck me dead?
No, neither he, nor his compeers by night
Giving him aid, my verse astonished.
He nor that affable familiar ghost
Which nightly gulls him with intelligence,
As victors of my silence cannot boast,
I was not sick of any fear from thence.
    But when your countenance fill'd up his line,
    Then lack'd I matter, that enfeebled mine.

In the previous Sonnet, the poet was boasting about the superiority of his thoughts over the other writers' words. Now, he admits that a beautiful verse written by the alien poet, whom he mentioned previously in Sonnets 78 - 81, stopped his thoughts before he was able to formulate them ("did my ripe thoughts in my brain inhearse, making their tomb the womb wherein they grew"). He describes the verse as "the proud full sail of his great verse, bound for the prize of you". Wasn't the other poet's spirit, asks the poet, that silenced his thoughts? ("was it his spirit, by spirits taught to write, above a mortal pitch, that struck me dead?") No, it was neither him nor his ghostly companions that astonished the poet so much ("neither he, nor his compeers by night giving him aid, my verse astonished"). Neither was his rival's friendly ghost, which spies on him at nights ("nor that affable familiar ghost which nightly gulls him with intelligence"). He is not afraid of them ("I was not sick of any fear from thence"). But it was the fact that the Guide looked favourably on the other poet's writing. It was the poet's jealousy that enfeebled him ("but when your countenance fill'd up his line, then lack'd I matter; that enfeebled mine").

The important thing to notice is that during the first cycle there was no interaction between the poet and the other writer. Now, however, through a second exposure to the other writer's works, the poet has established an invisible but tangible link with him and the other poet's companions, whom he calls "his compeers". The poet does not realize that the other writer and his companions are the Guides from the past. They form the evolutionary transmission chain. This is why the Guide has asked him to study their poems and he would make only some minor adjustments in their writings (see Sonnet 78). During the first cycle, the poet was able to discern the fact that they were all encompassed within the Guide's essence (see Sonnet 31). The present experience indicates that the poet has arrived at a stage that allows him to break through the limitations of time. This means that his subtle faculties have been further developed. But the poet's emotional attachments prevent him from noticing it.

Count Claudio in "Much Ado About Nothing" was silenced in a similar manner, when he allowed jealousy to veil his perception[86]. Here is Beatrice's account of that moment:

> "The count is neither sad, nor sick, nor merry, nor
> well; but civil count, civil as an orange, and
> something of that jealous complexion."

---

[86] See "Villain" (Shakespeare for the Seeker, Volume 3, Chapter 6.3).

SONNET LXXXVII

Farewell thou art too dear for my possessing,
And like enough thou know'st thy estimate,
The Charter of thy worth gives thee releasing:
My bonds in thee are all determinate.
For how do I hold thee but by thy granting,
And for that riches where is my deserving?
The cause of this fair gift in me is wanting,
And so my patent back again is swerving.
Thy self thou gavest, thy own worth then not knowing,
Or me to whom thou gav'st it, else mistaking,
So thy great gift upon misprision growing,
Comes home again, on better judgement making.
    Thus have I had thee as a dream doth flatter,
    In sleep a King, but waking no such matter.

The previous cycle of the process ended-up with the poet overcoming his jealousy. Now we may see that it was only a temporary victory, as he is again affected by it. As previously, jealousy drives him towards separation from his Guide. The poet decides to say goodbye to his friend and tries to justify his decision.

The poet declares that the Guide is too worthy for him ("thou art too dear for my possessing"), and he knows very well his own value ("and like enough thou know'st thy estimate"). Because his great value, the Guide has the right to abandon the poet ("the charter of thy worth gives thee releasing"). So, declares the poet, the Guide has severed the ties that bound him to the poet ("my bonds in thee are all determinate"). The poet says that the Guide's presence was given to him by the Guide ("for how do I hold thee but by thy granting"). And he does not think that he deserves such a valuable gift ("and for that riches where is my deserving"). He thinks that he is lacking that which is needed to be able to keep such a treasure ("the cause of this fair gift in me is wanting"). So he gives back his right to possess this treasure ("and so my patent back again is swerving"). He arrogantly assumes that the Guide made an error by giving this gift to him. He says that either the Guide underestimated his own worth, or he overestimated the poet's ability ("thy self thou gavest, thy own worth then not knowing, or me to whom thou gav'st it, else mistaking"). And because of the error, now the gift is returned back to the owner ("so thy great gift upon misprision growing, comes home again, on better judgement making"). The poet concludes that all that happened was like a dream ("thus have I had thee as a dream doth flatter"). When he was sleeping he thought that he was a king. And now, when he wakes up, he finds that it was not the case ("in sleep a king, but waking no such matter"). The poet does not realize that separation is a stage of the process through which he is now guided. It was indicated to him by the Guide in Sonnet 73. Only through experiencing separation will he be able to move forward.

Claudio in "Much Ado About Nothing" also separated himself from Hero. In that way he was able to remove an inner veil that was blinding him from seeing her true beauty. Here is the moment of his awakening[87]:

> "Sweet Hero! now thy image doth appear
> In the rare semblance that I loved it first."

---

[87] See "Invisible assistant" (Shakespeare for the Seeker, Volume 3, Chapter 6.3).

SONNET LXXXVIII

When thou shalt be disposed to set me light,
And place my merit in the eye of scorn,
Upon thy side, against myself I'll fight,
And prove thee virtuous, though thou art forsworn:
With mine own weakness being best acquainted,
Upon thy part I can set down a story
Of faults concealed, wherein I am attainted:
That thou in losing me, shalt win much glory:
And I by this will be a gainer too,
For bending all my loving thoughts on thee,
The injuries that to myself I do,
Doing thee vantage, double-vantage me.
    Such is my love, to thee I so belong,
    That for thy right, myself will bear all wrong.

The poet still treats his relationship with the Guide in an ordinary way. His present meditation is just a form of bargaining with the Guide for his attention. He does not know that he has to free himself from such conventional thinking and doing before he can be reunited with his Guide.

In his imagination, the poet considers various scenarios that might occur in the future and he tries to work out his response. For example, he imagines that the Guide may be inclined to belittle him and make him the object of other people's scorn ("when thou shalt be disposed to set me light, and place my merit in the eye of scorn"). In such a case, the poet would side with the Guide and he would agree with him ("upon thy side, against myself I'll fight"). In this way, thinks the poet, he would demonstrate that the Guide is virtuous, even when the Guide is lying about him ("and prove thee virtuous, though thou art forsworn"). The poet ignorantly assumes that he knows his own weaknesses better than anyone else ("with mine own weakness being best acquainted"). Therefore, he can tell a story about his hidden faults and make others believe him ("upon thy part I can set down a story of faults concealed, wherein I am attainted; that thou in losing me, shalt win much glory"). So, continues the poet, he will gain by directing all his loving thoughts on the Guide ("and I by this will be a gainer too, for bending all my loving thoughts on thee"). At the same time, by blaming himself he will also be helping the Guide. Therefore he will double his gains ("doing thee vantage, double-vantage me"). The poet declares that he loves the Guide so much, that for his sake he will take every wrong upon himself ("such is my love, to thee I so belong, that for thy right, myself will bear all wrong").

Petruchio[88] in "The Taming of the Shrew" adopted a similar strategy while preparing himself for his first encounter with Katharina:

> "Say that she rail; why then I'll tell her plain
> She sings as sweetly as a nightingale:
> Say that she frown, I'll say she looks as clear
> As morning roses newly wash'd with dew:
> Say she be mute and will not speak a word;
> Then I'll commend her volubility,
> And say she uttereth piercing eloquence:
> If she do bid me pack, I'll give her thanks,
> As though she bid me stay by her a week:
> If she deny to wed, I'll crave the day
> When I shall ask the banns and when be married."

---

[88] See "Taming school" (Shakespeare for the Seeker, Volume 3, Chapter 6.5).

SONNET LXXXIX

Say that thou didst forsake me for some fault,
And I will comment upon that offence,
Speak of my lameness, and I straight will halt:
Against thy reasons making no defence.
Thou canst not (love) disgrace me half so ill,
To set a form upon desired change,
As I'll myself disgrace; knowing thy will,
I will acquaintance strangle and look strange:
Be absent from thy walks and in my tongue,
Thy sweet beloved name no more shall dwell,
Lest I (too much profane) should do it wrong:
And haply of our old acquaintance tell.
 For thee, against my self I'll vow debate,
 For I must ne'er love him whom thou dost hate.

The poet continues with the analysis of his imaginary situation. He tries to prepare himself for any supposed accusation by the Guide. If the Guide names any fault of his, then the poet will further expand upon such accusation ("say that thou didst forsake me for some fault, and I will comment upon that offence"). For example, if the Guide speaks of the poet's lameness, he will start to limp ("speak of my lameness, and I straight will halt: against thy reasons making no defence"). The poet says that the Guide cannot disgrace him half as badly as he will do himself as soon as he knows what the Guide's will is ("thou canst not, love, disgrace me half so ill, to set a form upon desired change, as I'll myself disgrace; knowing thy will"). He will pretend that he does not know the Guide at all, and will start to act as a stranger ("I will acquaintance strangle and look strange"). He will avoid meeting him and talking about him ("be absent from thy walks; and in my tongue"). He will not even mention the Guide's name for fear of disgracing it by implying his association with him ("thy sweet beloved name no more shall dwell, lest I, too much profane, should do it wrong: and haply of our old acquaintance tell"). For the Guide's sake the poet is willing to vow to be his own enemy, because he cannot care about someone who is hated by the Guide ("for thee, against my self I'll vow debate, for I must ne'er love him whom thou dost hate").

Romeo[89] went through a similar experience when his outward form (i.e., his name) was an issue. Here is Romeo's comment to Juliet:

> "By a name
> I know not how to tell thee who I am:
> My name, dear saint, is hateful to myself,
> Because it is an enemy to thee;
> Had I it written, I would tear the word."

---

[89] See "Romeo" (Shakespeare for the Seeker, Volume 3, Chapter 6.6).

SONNET XC

Then hate me when thou wilt, if ever, now,
Now while the world is bent my deeds to cross,
Join with the spite of fortune, make me bow,
And do not drop in for an after loss:
Ah do not, when my heart hath 'scaped this sorrow,
Come in the rearward of a conquered woe,
Give not a windy night a rainy morrow,
To linger out a purposed over-throw.
If thou wilt leave me, do not leave me last,
When other petty griefs have done their spite,
But in the onset come, so shall I taste
At first the very worst of fortune's might.
> And other strains of woe, which now seem woe,
> Compared with loss of thee, will not seem so.

The poet becomes more and more distraught because of the Guide's absence. He sinks further into a state of imaginary rejection. His present state is driven by fear and grief. In his fearful fantasy he assumes that the Guide might hate him ("then hate me when thou wilt"). So, asks the poet, if the Guide hates him he should hate him now, i.e., when the world is determined to frustrate everything he tries to do ("now, while the world is bent my deeds to cross"). He asks the Guide to add to his misfortune and make him collapse under it ("join with the spite of fortune, make me bow"). The Guide should not wait to slap him after he has already endured the blow ("do not, when my heart hath 'scaped this sorrow"). Nor should he let him think that he has avoided the sorrow, only to come later and turn bad into worst ("give not a windy night a rainy morrow, to linger out a purposed over-throw"). If the Guide is going to leave him, says the poet, he should not wait until the end, i.e., after other little sorrows have done their damage ("if thou wilt leave me, do not leave me last, when other petty griefs have done their spite"). Instead, the Guide should leave him now, so the poet may experience the worst misfortune first ("but in the onset come, so shall I taste at first the very worst of fortune's might"). Then other sorrows, which seem painful now, won't seem so bad when compared with the loss of the Guide ("and other strains of woe, which now seem woe, compared with loss of thee, will not seem so").

Similarly in "Cymbeline", Imogen's perception of reality was distracted by her fears and imagination when she mistook the headless body of Cloten for Posthumus, her beloved husband[90]:

> "A headless man! The garments of Posthumus!
> I know the shape of's leg: this is his hand;
> His foot Mercurial; his Martial thigh;
> The brawns of Hercules."

---

[90] See "Imperfections" (Shakespeare for the Seeker, Volume 1, Chapter 3.2).

SONNET XCI

Some glory in their birth, some in their skill,
Some in their wealth, some in their body's force,
Some in their garments though new-fangled ill:
Some in their Hawks and Hounds, some in their Horse.
And every humour hath his adjunct pleasure,
Wherein it finds, a joy above the rest,
But these particulars are not my measure,
All these I better in one general best.
Thy love is better than high birth to me,
Richer than wealth, prouder than garments' cost,
Of more delight than Hawks and Horses be:
And having thee, of all men's pride I boast.
    Wretched in this alone, that thou mayst take,
    All this away, and me most wretched make.

The poet tries to describe the nature of his attraction and attachment to the Guide. We may note that his present assessment is more refined than his emotional outburst described at the beginning of his journey. He says that some people pay much attention to their social status, some to their skills, or wealth, or strength, or even to trendy but ridiculous clothes ("their garments though new-fangled ill"). Some are proud of their hawks, or hounds, or horses. Above all, however, they enjoy the particular pleasures that complement their character ("and every humour hath his adjunct pleasure, wherein it finds, a joy above the rest"). The poet states, however, that such pleasures are not part of his happiness ("but these particulars are not my measure"). There is something else that he values most ("all these I better in one general best"). Namely, the Guide's love is something that is much more valuable than high status, wealth, expensive clothes, hawks, or horses. And by having it, he feels like the richest man ("and having thee, of all men's pride I boast"). At the same time, by losing it, he may become the most miserable among all men ("all this away, and me most wretched make").

The poet concludes that he is not interested in mundane things. At that time, however, he does not realize yet that he is the victim of a less obvious but nevertheless obscuring desire. Namely, he is driven by desire for his Guide's love.

Helena's approach in "All's Well That Ends Well" is an example of the attitude that was free from such selfish desire. Helena's beloved Count of Rousillon left France and went to wars in Italy. In this way he was able to escape from Helena. Helena, therefore, decided to remove herself from France, so the Count could return and be safe at home[91]:

> "No, come thou home, Rousillon,
> Whence honour but of danger wins a scar,
> As oft it loses all: I will be gone;
> My being here it is that holds thee hence:
> Shall I stay here to do't? no, no, although
> The air of paradise did fan the house
> And angels officed all: I will be gone,
> That pitiful rumour may report my flight,
> To consolate thine ear."

---

[91] See "Pilgrimage" (Shakespeare for the Seeker, Volume 2, Chapter 5.1).

SONNET XCII

But do thy worst to steal thyself away,
For term of life thou art assured mine,
And life no longer than thy love will stay,
For it depends upon that love of thine.
Then need I not to fear the worst of wrongs,
When in the least of them my life hath end,
I see, a better state to me belongs
Than that which on thy humour doth depend.
Thou canst not vex me with inconstant mind,
Since that my life on thy revolt doth lie,
Oh what a happy title do I find,
Happy to have thy love, happy to die!
    But what's so blessed fair that fears no blot,
    Thou mayst be false, and yet I know it not.

The poet starts slowly to get to the bottom of his present situation. In other word, the purpose of the Guide's absence starts to produce the needed result. The poet recognizes that he is strongly affected by his inconstant moods. He blames the Guide for it, without realizing that his moods are the reflections of his inner inadequacies.

The poet bitterly appeals to the Guide to do the worst, i.e., to go ahead and leave him ("but do thy worst to steal thyself away"). The poet implies that he will live as long as the Guide loves him ("and life no longer than thy love will stay"). Therefore, the poet does not have to fear the worst of the Guide's wrongs. Because his life will end as a result of the Guide's smallest of injuries ("then need I not to fear the worst of wrongs, when in the least of them my life hath end"). The poet starts to realize that there is a better state within his reach, which does not depend on the Guide's seemingly changing moods ("I see a better state to me belongs than that which on thy humour doth depend"). He says that the Guide will not be able to vex him with his inconstant mind ("thou canst not vex me with inconstant mind"). Therefore, he will be happy if he has the Guide's love; and if he cannot have it, he will be happy to die ("O what a happy title do I find, happy to have thy love, happy to die"). So he finds himself in a truly perfect situation in which there is no room for worries ("but what's so blessed fair that fears no blot"). The Guide might be unfaithful, but the poet does not need to know it ("thou mayst be false, and yet I know it not").

King Henry V, on the other hand, described himself as a fellow of "uncoined constancy". Here is an excerpt from his wooing of Princess Katharine[92]:

> "And while thou
> livest, dear Kate, take a fellow of plain and
> uncoined constancy; for he perforce must do thee
> right, because he hath not the gift to woo in other
> places: for these fellows of infinite tongue, that
> can rhyme themselves into ladies' favours, they do
> always reason themselves out again."

---

[92] See "Partial reformation" (Shakespeare for the Seeker, Volume 1, Chapter 1).

SONNET XCIII

So shall I live, supposing thou art true,
Like a deceived husband, so love's face,
May still seem love to me, though altered new:
Thy looks with me, thy heart in other place.
For there can live no hatred in thine eye,
Therefore in that I cannot know thy change,
In many's looks, the false heart's history
Is writ in moods and frowns and wrinkles strange.
But heaven in thy creation did decree,
That in thy face sweet love should ever dwell,
Whate'er thy thoughts, or thy heart's workings be,
Thy looks should nothing thence, but sweetness tell.
    How like Eve's apple doth thy beauty grow,
    If thy sweet virtue answer not thy show.

The poet compares his situation to that of a deceived husband ("so shall I live, supposing thou art true, like a deceived husband"). Because he can see love on the Guide's face, but this love is for someone else ("so love's face may still seem love to me, though altered new"). The poet accuses the Guide of having his heart somewhere else, while his attitude towards him remains the same ("thy looks with me, thy heart in other place"). There never can be any hatred in the Guide's eyes, so it is impossible to notice a change of his heart ("for there can live no hatred in thine eye, therefore in that I cannot know thy change"). Usually unfaithfulness is expressed through people's looks, moods, frowns, and grimaces ("in many's looks, the false heart's history is writ in moods, and frowns, and wrinkles strange"). But when heaven created the Guide, it decided that his face will always be expressing sweet love ("but heaven in thy creation did decree, that in thy face sweet love should ever dwell"). There is nothing else in his face but love ("thy looks should nothing thence, but sweetness tell"). And the poet concludes that the Guide's beauty is as misleading as Eve's apple, because his appearance does not reflect his intent ("how like Eve's apple doth thy beauty grow, if thy sweet virtue answer not thy show").

By looking at Cressida's appearance, Ulysses in "Troilus and Cressida" was able to detect her "wanton spirit"[93]:

> "Her wanton spirits look out
> At every joint and motive of her body."

---

[93] See "Idolatry" (Shakespeare for the Seeker, Volume 2, Chapter 4.2).

The Guide's ninth counsel (Sonnets 94 - 99)

SONNET XCIV

They that have power to hurt, and will do none,
That do not do the thing, they most do show,
Who moving others, are themselves as stone,
Unmoved, cold, and to temptation slow:
They rightly do inherit heaven's graces,
And husband nature's riches from expense,
They are the Lords and owners of their faces,
Others, but stewards of their excellence:
The summer's flower is to the summer sweet,
Though to itself, it only live and die,
But if that flower with base infection meet,
The basest weed out-braves his dignity:
    For sweetest things turn sourest by their deeds,
    Lilies that fester, smell far worse than weeds.

The poet's conclusion from the previous Sonnet prompts the Guide to deliver his next counsel, which may help the poet to clarify his confusion. The Guide explains the nature of those who are charged with the task of guiding humanity. Such men and women have power to hurt others, but choose not to do so ("they that have power to hurt, and will do none"). They do not act in the way that others expect them to do ("that do not do the thing, they most do show"). They are able to influence others, but themselves are unswayable ("who moving others, are themselves as stone"). They are inheritors and carriers of the entire spectrum of evolutionary energy ("they rightly do inherit heaven's graces"). They are charged with preserving nature's greatest treasures ("and husband nature's riches from expense"). They are in full control of their moods ("they are the lords and owners of their faces"). Others are like ornaments of their perfection ("others, but stewards of their excellence"). They contribute to their perfection in the same way as flowers add the sweetness to the summer; they live and then die ("the summer's flower is to the summer sweet, though to itself, it only live and die"). But when such a flower is infected, it becomes worse than weed ("but if that flower with base infection meet, the basest weed outbraves his dignity"). Because when misused, the sweetest things become the sourest, like rotten lilies that smell worse than weeds ("for sweetest things turn sourest by their deeds; lilies that fester, smell far worse than weeds").

This last sentence is a warning to the poet, because he faces the danger of misusing his gifts and turning himself into a rotten lily.

Marcellus, one of the watchmen in "Hamlet", recognized that Denmark was infected by such misuse of its potential[94]:

"Something is rotten in the state of Denmark."

---

[94] See "Elsinore" (Shakespeare for the Seeker, Volume 4, Chapter 7.3).

SONNET XCV

How sweet and lovely dost thou make the shame,
Which like a canker in the fragrant Rose,
Doth spot the beauty of thy budding name?
Oh in what sweets dost thou thy sins enclose!
That tongue that tells the story of thy days,
(Making lascivious comments on thy sport)
Cannot dispraise, but in a kind of praise,
Naming thy name, blesses an ill report.
Oh what a mansion have those vices got,
Which for their habitation chose out thee,
Where beauty's veil doth cover every blot,
And all things turns to fair, that eyes can see!
    Take heed (dear heart) of this large privilege,
    The hardest knife ill used doth lose his edge.

The Guide continues his counsel by pointing out that the poet's behaviour is like a fragrant rosebud that has been infected by a worm ("thou make the shame, which like a canker in the fragrant Rose). The Guide says that the poet's good look is but a cover-up for his vices ("in what sweets dost thou thy sins enclose"). Then the Guide gives us a hint about the poet's life prior to his encounter with him ("that tongue that tells the story of thy days"). It looks that the poet was engaged in a rather lustful and liberal way of living ("making lascivious comments on thy sport"). But because of the poet's fame, his vices became covered-up by people's praises ("cannot dispraise, but in a kind of praise"). In other words, the poet's fame made his misdeeds look good ("naming thy name, blesses an ill report"). And the Guide exclaims: "what a mansion have those vices got, which for their habitation chose out thee". The poet is like a house, whose external beauty conceals every fault and all things appear to be good ("where beauty's veil doth cover every blot and all things turns to fair that eyes can see!"). The Guide warns the poet: be careful, because you may lose your privileged position ("take heed, dear heart, of this large privilege"). Because if misused, even the best knife will quickly lose its sharpness ("the hardest knife ill used doth lose his edge").

Ophelia in "Hamlet" gave a similar counsel to her brother, when he was preaching to her about chastity[95]:

> "But, good my brother,
> Do not, as some ungracious pastors do,
> Show me the steep and thorny way to heaven;
> Whiles, like a puff'd and reckless libertine,
> Himself the primrose path of dalliance treads,
> And recks not his own rede."

---

[95] See "Evolutionary impulse" (Shakespeare for the Seeker, Volume 4, Chapter 7.3).

SONNET XCVI

Some say thy fault is youth, some wantonness,
Some say thy grace is youth and gentle sport,
Both grace and faults are lov'd of more and less:
Thou mak'st faults graces, that to thee resort:
As on the finger of a throned Queen,
The basest Jewel will be well esteem'd:
So are those errors that in thee are seen,
To truths translated, and for true things deem'd.
How many Lambs might the stern Wolf betray,
If like a Lamb he could his looks translate.
How many gazers mightst thou lead away,
If thou wouldst use the strength of all thy state?
    But do not so, I love thee in such sort,
    As thou being mine, mine is thy good report.

The Guide continues to point out the poet's shortcomings. He says that some people blame the poet's youth for his bad behaviour, others say that the problem is his lust ("some say thy fault is youth, some wantonness"). Yet others admire both, the poet's youth and his licentiousness ("some say thy grace is youth and gentle sport"). The poet himself turns his faults into glory and indulges in them ("thou mak'st faults graces, that to thee resort"). This is like a worthless ring that is admired by many because a queen is wearing it ("as on the finger of a throned queen, the basest jewel will be well esteem'd"). In the same way people look at the poet's faults ("so are those errors that in thee are seen"). Truth is corrupted and bad things are treated as virtues ("to truths translated, and for true things deem'd"). How many lambs, asks the Guide, could a wolf deceive if he could make himself look like a lamb; and how many of his admirers is the poet going to lead astray ("how many gazers mightst thou lead away"). But do not so, he tells the poet, because the Guide's love is of such kind that his functionality depends on the poet's behaviour ("I love thee in such sort, as thou being mine,

mine is thy good report").

The Shepherd in "The Winter's Tale" was also worried that his sheep would be led astray by the wolf[96]:

> "They have scared away two of my
> best sheep, which I fear the wolf will sooner find
> than the master."

---

[96] See "Shakespeare's symbols" (Shakespeare for the Seeker, Volume 3, Chapter 6.1).

SONNET XCVII

How like a Winter hath my absence been
From thee, the pleasure of the fleeting year?
What freezings have I felt, what dark days seen?
What old December's bareness everywhere?
And yet this time removed was summer's time,
The teeming Autumn big with rich increase,
Bearing the wanton burden of the prime,
Like widow'd wombs after their Lords' decease:
Yet this abundant issue seemed to me,
But hope of Orphans, and un-fathered fruit,
For Summer and his pleasures wait on thee,
And thou away, the very birds are mute.
    Or if they sing, 'tis with so dull a cheer,
    That leaves look pale, dreading the Winter's near.

The Guide explains the nature of his absence. He warned the poet about it in his sixth counsel (Sonnet 73 -74). The Guide's presence was like a fathering spring, which planted a new seed. Afterwards he was watching and waiting for the appearance of a fruit. The growth of the poet's inner being is such a fruit. The fruits grow during summer and they are harvested in autumn. The Guide's absence was like summer ("and yet this time removed was summer's time"). Now it is spiritual autumn, therefore the Guide expects to see the fruit of his previous efforts ("the teeming autumn big with rich increase, bearing the wanton burden of the prime, like widow'd wombs after their lords' decease"). Instead, the Guide feels like it is winter ("how like a winter hath my absence been from thee, the pleasure of the fleeting year?") It is cold, the days are dark, and everything around is as barren as in December ("what freezings have I felt, what dark days seen? what old December's bareness everywhere?") Because for the Guide the natural growth is like un-fathered fruits ("yet this abundant issue seemed to me, but hope of orphans, and un-fathered fruit"). Their appearance is meaningless; they grow by themselves. What matters is the growth of the Rose, i.e., the poet's inner being. Summer is still waiting for the arrival of the Rose; but he is not there yet ("for summer and his pleasures wait on thee, and thou away"). As long as the Rose is not there, the birds remain silent ("and thou away, the very birds are mute"). Even if they sing, they do it so grimly that even the leaves loose their colours, dreading the approaching winter ("or if they sing, 'tis with so dull a cheer, that leaves look pale, dreading the winter's near"). In other words, the Guide indicates that the poet has missed a spiritual season, i.e., an opportunity for inner growth.

A fearful note associated with the misuse of spring was inserted into a song at the conclusion of "Love's Labour's Lost"[97]:

> "When daisies pied and violets blue
> And lady-smocks all silver-white
> And cuckoo-buds of yellow hue
> Do paint the meadows with delight,
> The cuckoo then, on every tree,
> Mocks married men; for thus sings he, Cuckoo;
> Cuckoo, cuckoo: O word of fear,
> Unpleasing to a married ear!"

---

[97] See "Conclusion" (Shakespeare for the Seeker, Volume 2, Chapter 5.3).

SONNET XCVIII

From you have I been absent in the spring,
When proud pied April (dressed in all his trim)
Hath put a spirit of youth in every thing:
That heavy *Saturn* laughed and leapt with him.
Yet nor the lays of birds, nor the sweet smell
Of different flowers in odour and in hue,
Could make me any summer's story tell:
Or from their proud lap pluck them where they grew:
Nor did I wonder at the Lilly's white,
Nor praise the deep vermilion in the Rose,
They were but sweet, but figures of delight:
Drawn after you, you pattern of all those.
 Yet seemed it Winter still, and you away,
 As with your shadow I with these did play.

It looks like the poet has missed an entire spiritual year. In the previous Sonnet, the Guide told us that the poet missed summer and autumn; the winter was approaching. Now he tells us that the winter has passed and it is spring again. Yet, there are no signs of the Rose.

The Guide was absent since the spring ("from you have I been absent in the spring"). Then April arrived, dressed in a multicoloured robe ("when proud pied April, dressed in all his trim"). He rejuvenated everything; even Saturn, the god of old age, laughed and danced with him ("hath put a spirit of youth in every thing that heavy Saturn laughed and leapt with him"). Yet none of these, neither singing birds nor sweet smelling flowers could satisfy the Guide's expectation ("yet nor the lays of birds, nor the sweet smell of different flowers in odour and in hue, could make me any summer's story tell"). None of those, therefore, could make him admire the whiteness of the Lily or the redness of the Rose ("nor did I wonder at the lily's white, nor praise the deep vermilion in the rose"). These were only but the symbols of the poet's still unfulfilled potentialities ("they were but sweet, but figures of delight: drawn after you, you pattern of all those"). The poet was not there; it still felt like winter time ("yet seemed it winter still, and you away"). The Guide was still waiting for the poet ("as with your shadow I with these did play").

Helena[98] in "All's Well That Ends Well" followed a similar seasonal schedule:

> "But with the word the time will bring on summer,
> When briers shall have leaves as well as thorns,
> And be as sweet as sharp. We must away;
> Our wagon is prepared, and time revives us:
> All's well that ends well; still the fine's the crown;
> Whate'er the course, the end is the renown."

---

[98] See "Pilgrimage" (Shakespeare for the Seeker, Volume 2, Chapter 5.1).

SONNET XCIX

The forward violet thus did I chide,
Sweet thief whence didst thou steal thy sweet that smells
If not from my love's breath, the purple pride,
Which on thy soft cheek for complexion dwells?
In my love's veins thou hast too grossly dy'd,
The Lilly I condemned for thy hand,
And buds of marjoram had stol'n thy hair,
The Roses fearfully on thorns did stand,
One blushing shame, another white despair:
A third nor red, nor white, had stol'n of both,
And to his robbery had annexed thy breath,
But for his theft, in pride of all his growth
A vengeful canker eat him up to death.
    More flowers I noted, yet I none could see,
    But sweet, or colour it had stol'n from thee.

The Guide is still waiting for the poet to wake up from his spiritual indolence. The Guide describes various signs of spring, which should help the poet awake from his lethargy. The Guide sends him speechless images of the spring, i.e., the reminders of his initiation. He tells how he scolded the presumptuous violet for stealing the poet's sweet scent ("the forward violet thus did I chide: sweet thief, whence didst thou steal thy sweet that smells, if not from my love's breath"); and for being so proud of its imperial colour on its petals, which was stolen from the poet's veins ("the purple pride, which on thy soft cheek for complexion dwells, in my love's veins thou hast too grossly dy'd"). The Guide condemned the lily for stealing its whiteness from the poet's hand ("the lilly I condemned for thy hand") and the marjoram buds for taking away the poet's curly hair ("and buds of marjoram had stol'n thy hair"). The Guide's references to the roses are symbolic indications of the impacts to which the poet was previously exposed. Namely, the blushing and pale roses are guilty of stealing the poet's redness and whiteness ("the roses fearfully on thorns did stand, one blushing shame, another white despair"). The third rose, which is neither red nor white, was accused by the Guide of the theft of both colours from the poet's completion, and of the robbery of the poet's sweet breath ("a third nor red, nor white, had stol'n of both, and to his robbery had annexed thy breath"). But the third rose has already been punished, because it was eaten by a vengeful worm ("but for his theft, in pride of all his growth a vengeful canker eat him up to death"). The Guide concludes that he has noticed more flowers. All of them reflected the poet's still unfulfilled potentiality ("more flowers I noted, yet I none could see, but sweet, or colour it had stol'n from thee").

The Guide uses a colour code to specify the impulses of evolutionary energy to which the poet was exposed during the first cycle of the process. Namely, he makes references to three impulses, which are symbolically indicated by yellow (Sonnet 24), white (Sonnets 40 - 43), and red (Sonnets 46, 80). These are three out of the four colours of the spectrum of evolutionary energy that were indicated by Moth in "Love's Labour's Lost" (see the analysis of Sonnet 37). Moth alluded to another meaning of white and red, which is also used by the Guide[99]:

> "If she be made of white and red,
> Her faults will ne'er be known,
> For blushing cheeks by faults are bred
> And fears by pale white shown."

The Guide tells us that the poet, like Don Adriano in "Love's Labour's Lost", was not able to adsorb these impulses effectively enough. Therefore, their effect has been corrupted. This is why the red rose is "blushing shame" and the white rose is pale in "despair". Then the Guide explains what the reason of the poet's failure was. It looks like the poet's behaviour was such that it

---

[99] See "Technical background" (Shakespeare for the Seeker, Volume 2, Chapter 5.3).

caused shame and fear. This behaviour is compared to a vengeful canker, which ate the third rose to its death. This very similar to the situation of Romeo, who like the fresh bud was bitten by an envious worm (see the analysis of Sonnet 70):

> "As is the bud bit with an envious worm,
> Ere he can spread his sweet leaves to the air,
> Or dedicate his beauty to the sun."

The yellow colour can also be used to mark envy or jealousy (see Beatrice's comment in the analysis of Sonnet 86). In other words, it is the poet's jealousy that prevents him from making progress. It was jealousy that interfered with the operation of the subtle faculties. This is symbolically marked by the third rose, i.e., by the yellow rose, which "a vengeful canker eat him up to death".

Another important thing to notice is the fact that the poet has not yet been exposed to the fourth, i.e., black impulse. The colour black is associated with a purified aspect of the intellect faculty. It seems that this aspect is the dominating feature of the poet's potentiality. Therefore, the methodology implemented by the Guide is focussed on the development of this particular subtle faculty. But this faculty can only be activated when the previously administered impulses have been absorbed, at least partially.

This is the last opportunity for the poet to wake up. Shakespeare emphasizes this by adding an extra line, i.e., 15th line, to this Sonnet. All other Sonnets have 14 lines, i.e., three four-line stanzas with a final couplet.

Awakening (Sonnets 100 - 103)

SONNET C

Where art thou Muse that thou forget'st so long,
To speak of that which gives thee all thy might?
Spend'st thou thy fury on some worthless song,
Darkening thy power to lend base subjects light,
Return forgetful Muse, and straight redeem,
In gentle numbers time so idly spent,
Sing to the ear that doth thy lays esteem,
And gives thy pen both skill and argument.
Rise resty Muse, my love's sweet face survey,
If time have any wrinkle graven there,
If any, be a *Satire* to decay,
And make time's spoils despised every where,
    Give my love fame faster than time wastes life,
    So thou prevent'st his scythe, and crooked knife.

Finally, the poet understands the Guide's message. The poet's awakening is marked by the revival of his poetical inspiration: his Muse is back. But now he blames his Muse for his own negligence. He asks where she has been that she has forgotten for so long to inspire him and talk about the Guide who is the source of all her power ("where art thou Muse that thou forget'st so long, to speak of that which gives thee all thy might"). Has she, asks the poet, used her talents on some worthless poems, abusing her power by making useless things to look brighter ("spend'st thou thy fury on some worthless song, darkening thy power to lend base subjects light"). The poet asks his Muse to compensate for the wasted time by inspiring him to write his verses ("return forgetful Muse, and straight redeem, in gentle numbers time so idly spent"). Please give me inspiration, says the poet, so I may have enough skills and reason to compose my poems ("sing to the ear that doth thy lays esteem, and gives thy pen both skill and argument"). Wake up sleepy Muse, continues the poet, and examine the face of my beloved and look for any traces of aging ("rise resty Muse, my love's sweet face survey, if time have any wrinkle graven there"). If you spot any, then produce a nasty satire on aging and make everybody despise time's destructive powers ("if any, be a satire to decay, and make time's spoils despised every where"). Allow me, asks the poet, to make my Guide's fame grow faster than time's destructivity, so you may protect him against time's cruelty ("give my love fame faster than time wastes life, so thou prevent'st his scythe, and crooked knife").

Duke Orsino in "Twelfth Night" experienced a similar awakening when he discovered that all the time his true love was just next to him[100]:

> "Your master quits you; and for your service done him,
> So much against the mettle of your sex,
> So far beneath your soft and tender breeding,
> And since you call'd me master for so long,
> Here is my hand: you shall from this time be
> Your master's mistress."

---

[100] See "Union" (Shakespeare for the Seeker, Volume 4, Chapter 7.1).

SONNET CI

O truant Muse what shall be thy amends,
For thy neglect of truth in beauty dyed?
Both truth and beauty on my love depends:
So dost thou too, and therein dignified:
Make answer Muse, wilt thou not haply say,
Truth needs no colour, with his colour fixed,
Beauty no pencil, beauty's truth to lay:
But best is best, if never intermixed.
Because he needs no praise, wilt thou be dumb?
Excuse not silence so, for't lies in thee,
To make him much out-live a gilded tomb:
And to be praised of ages yet to be.
    Then do thy office Muse; I teach thee how,
    To make him seem long hence, as he shows now.

The poet continues to blame his Muse and demands that she should amend her errors. Previously he claimed that his silence was the greatest way of praising the Guide (see Sonnets 83 - 85). Now he realizes that he was wrong. So he reverses his previous arguments and scorns his Muse for neglecting the truth that resides in beauty ("O truant Muse what shall be thy amends, for thy neglect of truth in beauty dyed"). Both truth and beauty depend on the Guide's love ("both truth and beauty on my love depends"). His Muse also depends on and is dignified by his love ("so dost thou too, and therein dignified"). Are you going to tell me again, asks the poet, that truth does not need embellishment because its beauty is constant and perfect, therefore it should not be mixed with inferior things? ("Truth needs no colour, with his colour fixed, beauty no pencil, beauty's truth to lay; but best is best, if never intermixed"). So, are you going to be silent because my beloved does not need praise? ("Because he needs no praise, wilt thou be dumb?") No, says the poet, do not give me such excuses ("excuse not silence so"). And he charges his Muse with the task that he himself was charged with by the Guide, i.e., to make the Guide live longer than his decorated tomb ("for't lies in thee, to make him much outlive a gilded tomb"). Therefore do your job, requests the poet, and I will tell you how. So in the future the Guide will manifest himself in the same manner as he does now ("then do thy office Muse; I teach thee how, to make him seem long hence, as he shows now").

Montague in "Romeo and Juliet" also attempted to preserve Juliet's beauty. He decided to build a golden statue[101]:

> "For I will raise her statue in pure gold;
> That while Verona by that name is known,
> There shall no figure at such rate be set
> As that of true and faithful Juliet."

---

[101] See "Rebuke" (Shakespeare for the Seeker, Volume 3, Chapter 6.6).

SONNET CII

My love is strengthened though more weak in seeming
I love not less, though less the show appear,
That love is merchandized, whose rich esteeming,
The owner's tongue doth publish every where.
Our love was new, and then but in the spring,
When I was wont to greet it with my lays,
As *Philomel* in summer's front doth sing,
And stops his pipe in growth of riper days:
Not that the summer is less pleasant now
Than when her mournful hymns did hush the night,
But that wild music burthens every bough,
And sweets grown common lose their dear delight,
    Therefore like her, I some-time hold my tongue:
    Because I would not dull you with my song.

In his most recent counsel the Guide indicated that the poet had been asleep during the previous summer (Sonnet 98). Now we hear the poet's excuses of why he remained idle during that time. The poet claims that his love was strengthened, although outwardly it may not seem so ("my love is strengthened, though more weak in seeming"). He does not love less, but he shows it less ("I love not less, though less the show appear"). He argues that by showing off how he loves, he would be turning his love into commodity ("that love is merchandized, whose rich esteeming, the owner's tongue doth publish every where"). He admits that at the beginning his love was still immature and he used to write poems about it. It was spring ("our love was new, and then but in the spring, when I was wont to greet it with my lays"). And he compares himself to the nightingale that sang at the beginning of the spring, but ceased to sing at the time of harvest ("as Philomel in summer's front doth sing: and stops his pipe in growth of riper days"). It is not because the summer is less pleasant than the spring, when the nightingale silenced the dark night with her sad tunes ("not that the summer is less pleasant now than when her mournful hymns did hush the night"). It is because the entire environment has been saturated with her inspiring music. And as sweet things become common so they loose their delight ("but that wild music burthens every bough, and sweets grown common lose their dear delight). Therefore like the nightingale, the poet keeps silence to not bore the Guide with his verses ("therefore like her, I sometime hold my tongue, because I would not dull you with my song"). The main point of the poet's explanation is the fact that he does what he thinks is right, and not what he has been asked to do.

Clown in "Othello" scorned Cassio's musicians for not doing what they were asked to do, i.e., to play "music that may not be heard"[102]:

> "If you have any music that may not be heard, to't again: but, as they say to hear music the general does not greatly care."

---

[102] See "Developmental techniques" (Shakespeare for the Seeker, Volume 3, Chapter 6.2).

SONNET CIII

Alack what poverty my Muse brings forth,
That having such a scope to show her pride,
The argument all bare is of more worth
Than when it hath my added praise beside.
Oh blame me not if I no more can write!
Look in your glass and there appears a face,
That over-goes my blunt invention quite,
Dulling my lines, and doing me disgrace.
Were it not sinful then, striving to mend,
To mar the subject that before was well,
For to no other pass my verses tend,
Than of your graces and your gifts to tell.
    And more, much more than in my verse can sit,
    Your own glass shows you, when you look in it.

The poet continues the debate with his Muse. After a brief awakened period, he starts to fall back into his previous sleepy state.

How limited is my Muse, says the poet ("what poverty my Muse brings forth"), that despite having such a great topic to praise ("that having such a scope to show her pride") she argues that her praise would only lessen the Guide's value ("the argument all bare is of more worth than when it hath my added praise beside"). I should not be blamed, argues the poet, for not being able to write! He tells the Guide to look in a mirror at the reflection of his face. It is the beauty of the Guide's face that overwhelms and disgraces the poet's skills, making his verses sound dull ("dulling my lines, and doing me disgrace"). Wouldn't be disgraceful to tarnish the image by trying to improve it? ("Were it not sinful then, striving to mend, to mar the subject that before was well"). The only purpose of the poet's writing is to describe the Guide's beauty and his perfection ("for to no other pass my verses tend, than of your graces and your gifts to tell"). The Guide's reflection in a mirror can show much more than the poet's verses ("and more, much more than in my verse can sit, your own glass shows you, when you look in it").

Hamlet also run into trouble because he was not able to discern the difference between an image and the true value of his father. Here is his argument posed to Gertrude[103], his mother:

> "Look here, upon this picture, and on this,
> The counterfeit presentment of two brothers.
> See, what a grace was seated on this brow;
> Hyperion's curls; the front of Jove himself;
> An eye like Mars, to threaten and command;
> A station like the herald Mercury
> New-lighted on a heaven-kissing hill;
> A combination and a form indeed,
> Where every god did seem to set his seal,
> To give the world assurance of a man:
> This was your husband."

Let's remember that the poet's Muse reappeared as the result of the Guide's action. Therefore, his Muse carries and delivers the Guide's "music that may not be heard". The poet's debate is a sign of his lack of understanding of the Muse's role. In other words, the poet has fallen into his third "wintry season". It is at such moments that the Guide's intervention is needed.

---

[103] See "Ophelia's prophesies" (Shakespeare for the Seeker, Volume 4, Chapter 7.3)

The Guide's tenth counsel (Sonnet 104)

SONNET CIV

To me fair friend you never can be old,
For as you were when first your eye I ey'd,
Such seems your beauty still: Three Winters cold,
Have from the forests shook three summers' pride,
Three beauteous springs to yellow *Autumn* turned,
In process of the seasons have I seen,
Three April perfumes in three hot Junes burned,
Since first I saw you fresh, which yet are green.
Ah yet doth beauty like a Dial hand,
Steal from his figure, and no pace perceived,
So your sweet hue, which methinks still doth stand
Hath motion, and mine eye may be deceived.
    For fear of which, hear this thou age unbred,
    Ere you were born was beauty's summer dead.

Once again the Guide interrupts the poet's debate and delivers his next counsel. The counsel is addressed not only to the poet, but also to the present and future generations of readers. The Guide tells the poet that he should remember that his inner beauty can never be exhausted ("to me fair friend you never can be old"). But it can degenerate if not cultivated correctly. And this is the Guide's concern, because the poet's beauty has not grown since the first time he met him ("for as you were when first your eye I ey'd, such seems your beauty still"). In the meantime, three cold winters passed and shook the leaves off three proud summers ("three winters cold, have from the forests shook three summers' pride"). And three beautiful springs turned into yellow autumns ("three beauteous springs to yellow autumn turned"). In other words, the poet missed three spiritual seasons. During that time the Guide saw three springs' perfumes burnt during three hot summers ("in process of the seasons have I seen, three April perfumes in three hot Junes burned"). Yet, says the Guide, despite having been given these three opportunities, the poet still remains as immature as he was when he saw him for the first time ("since first I saw you fresh, which yet are green"). These three opportunities are a symbolic reference to the three impulses, or thee colours of the roses, to which the poet was exposed. The Guide emphasizes that there is a time limit within which the poet's beauty may grow ("so your sweet hue, which methinks still doth stand, hath motion). Because beauty's potential is like the hand of a clock, which steals away from hour to hour with no perceived movements ("yet doth beauty like a dial-hand, steal from his figure, and no pace perceived"). So it is with the poet's potentiality, which the Guide compares to sweet colours and which, he is afraid, may be lost ("so your sweet hue, which methinks still doth stand, hath motion, and mine eye may be deceived"). Fearing this, the Guide announces to all future generations of mankind ("for fear of which, hear this thou age unbred"): before the birth of this poet, true beauty remained in its latent state ("ere you were born was beauty's summer dead"). In other words, it is the first time that this particular evolutionary potentiality is within the reach of ordinary men.

Duke Orsino in "Twelfth Night" made a reference to such beauty when he for the first time saw Olivia[104]:

> "O, when mine eyes did see Olivia first,
> Methought she purged the air of pestilence!"

---

[104] See "Cruel maid" (Shakespeare for the Seeker, Volume 4, Chapter 7.1).

Wonderment (Sonnets 105 - 107)

SONNET CV

Let not my love be called Idolatry,
Nor my beloved as an Idol show,
Since all alike my songs and praises be
To one, of one, still such, and ever so.
Kind is my love today, tomorrow kind,
Still constant in a wondrous excellence,
Therefore my verse to constancy confined,
One thing expressing, leaves out difference.
Fair, kind, and true, is all my argument,
Fair, kind, and true, varying to other words,
And in this change is my invention spent,
Three themes is one, which wandrous scope affords.
 Fair, kind and true, here often lived alone.
 Which three till now, never kept seat in one.

Once again, the poet is back on the right track. He is composing new poems about the Guide. He declares that, despite the fact that all his poems are addressed to one person and are about one person, his love should not be called idolatry nor his beloved should be looked at as an idol ("since all alike my songs and praises be to one, of one, still such, and ever so"). The poet also claims that his love is and always will be constant ("kind is my love today, tomorrow kind, still constant in a wondrous excellence"). Therefore, his poems will also be an expression of the constancy of his love ("therefore my verse to constancy confined, one thing expressing, leaves out difference"). He describes his love as fair, kind, and true ("fair, kind, and true, is all my argument, fair, kind, and true, varying to other words"). He writes about fair, kind, and true in various ways, and this is the subject to which he dedicates his creativity ("and in this change is my invention spent, three themes is one, which wandrous scope affords"). Let's recall that the theme of the unity of trinity was indicated to the poet by the

Guide in his first counsel (see Sonnet 8). The poet concludes that never before fair, kind, and true were united in one person ("fair, kind and true, here often lived alone, which three till now, never kept seat in one"). It is the first time that the poet, i.e., an ordinary man, has arrived at a stage where he is capable of recognizing the unity of trinity within the Guide's essence, i.e., a sample of human perfection.

Shakespeare uses an evolutionary triad to illustrate the operational functionality of the "unity of trinity". The triad consists of an aspiring aspect, a guiding aspect, and an element of evolutionary energy (see the Introduction). In this Sonnet, the three parts of the triad are referred to as fair, kind and true, respectively. However, only when all these three parts are correctly aligned and harmonized, can they start to operate correctly and discharge their evolutionary functionality. Such a balanced and harmonious triad is a functional representation of the unity of trinity. The poet has recognized such a perfectly functioning triad within the Guide's essence. Now it is up to the poet himself to emulate such a triad within his inner self.

As mentioned in the discussion of Sonnet 15, Octavius Caesar, Octavia, and Mark Antony represented such an advanced triad. Octavius Caesar initiated and directed its operation. The first step of the preparation required Mark Antony to marry Octavia. Octavia, Octavius' sister, represented an element of evolutionary energy. The marriage provided the needed structure for the constructive absorption of evolutionary energy. In Octavius' words, Octavia was "a great part of myself":

> "You take from me a great part of myself;
> Use me well in 't. Sister, prove such a wife
> As my thoughts make thee, and as my farthest band
> Shall pass on thy approof."

However, Mark Antony's incomprehension of the importance of

the triad led to its disintegration and the collapse of the Roman evolutionary cycle[105].

---

[105] See "Meeting of the triumvirs" (Shakespeare for the Seeker, Volume 1, Chapter 2.3).

SONNET CVI

When in the Chronicle of wasted time,
I see descriptions of the fairest wights,
And beauty making beautiful old rhyme,
In praise of Ladies dead, and lovely Knights,
Then, in the blazon of sweet beauty's best,
Of hand, of foot, of lip, of eye, of brow,
I see their antique Pen would have expressed,
Even such a beauty as you master now.
So all their praises are but prophecies
Of this our time, all you prefiguring,
And for they looked but with divining eyes,
They had not skill enough your worth to sing:
    For we which now behold these present days,
    Have eyes to wonder, but lack tongues to praise.

The poet expands further on his concluding couplet of the previous Sonnet.

The poet says that when he looks at the ancient descriptions of great people and reads the poems written in praise of beautiful ladies and lovely knights of the past ("I see descriptions of the fairest wights, and beauty making beautiful old rhyme"), he realizes that all of them were an attempt at presenting the qualities that are now manifested by the Guide ("I see their antique pen would have expressed even such a beauty as you master now"). Those ancient poems are a catalogue of such beauty, i.e., they include the description of hands, feet, lips, eyes, foreheads. The poet says that those writers were prophesying our time ("so all their praises are but prophecies of this our time"). They were divinely inspired and were foretelling the appearance of a perfect exemplar of humanity ("all you prefiguring, and for they looked but with divining eyes"). At that time, however, they were not capable of recognizing true beauty ("they had not skill enough your worth to sing"). It is only now that humanity has been granted the privilege to recognize such beauty ("for we which now behold these present days, have eyes to wonder"). Although the poet is able to recognize it, he lacks the skills to describe this wonder adequately ("but lack tongues to praise").

According to Bassanio in "The Merchant of Venice", Portia of Belmont was the manifestation of such a beauty that was the object of many quests in ancient times[106]:

> "Nor is the wide world ignorant of her worth,
> For the four winds blow in from every coast
> Renowned suitors, and her sunny locks
> Hang on her temples like a golden fleece;
> Which makes her seat of Belmont Colchos' strand,
> And many Jasons come in quest of her."

---

[106] See "Pilgrimage" (Shakespeare for the Seeker, Volume 3, Chapter 6.4).

SONNET CVII

Not mine own fears, nor the prophetic soul,
Of the wide world, dreaming on things to come,
Can yet the lease of my true love control,
Supposed as forfeit to a confined doom.
The mortal Moon hath her eclipse endured,
And the sad Augurs mock their own presage,
Incertainties now crown them-selves assured,
And peace proclaims Olives of endless age.
Now with the drops of this most balmy time,
My love looks fresh, and death to me subscribes,
Since spite of him I'll live in this poor rhyme,
While he insults o'er dull and speechless tribes.
    And thou in this shalt find thy monument,
    When tyrants' crests and tombs of brass are spent.

It looks like the poet has regained self-confidence. He announces that neither his fears nor some dark predictions can affect his idealistic love ("not mine own fears, nor the prophetic soul of the wide world, dreaming on things to come, can yet the lease of my true love control, supposed as forfeit to a confined doom"). The deadly Moon has been eclipsed ("the mortal moon hath her eclipse endured"), and even the fortune-tellers disregard their own gloomy predictions ("the sad augurs mock their own presage"). Uncertainties have been resolved and peace has firmly been established ("and peace proclaims olives of endless age"). The blessed drops of regenerating time have refreshed the poet's love ("now with the drops of this most balmy time, my love looks fresh"). Even death has renounced its rights ("and death to me subscribes"). The poet will live on in his verses, while death will triumph only over the ignorant and the faithless ("while he insults o'er dull and speechless tribes"). The poet's rhymes will be the Guide's everlasting monument ("thou in this shalt find thy monument"), when people of this world will be gone and forgotten ("when tyrants' crests and tombs of brass are spent").

Here is Pauline in "The Winter's Tale" inviting her guests to witness the resurrection of Queen Hermione, who was preserved in a monument[107]:

> "If you can behold it,
> I'll make the statue move indeed, descend
> And take you by the hand; but then you'll think -
> Which I protest against - I am assisted
> By wicked powers."

---

[107] See "Final steps" (Shakespeare for the Seeker, Volume 3, Chapter 6.1).

The Guide's eleventh counsel (Sonnet 108)

SONNET CVIII

What's in the brain that Ink may character,
Which hath not figured to thee my true spirit,
What's new to speak, what now to register,
That may express my love, or thy dear merit?
Nothing sweet boy, but yet like prayers divine,
I must each day say over the very same,
Counting no old thing old, thou mine, I thine,
Even as when first I hallowed thy fair name.
So that eternal love in love's fresh case,
Weighs not the dust and injury of age,
Nor gives to necessary wrinkles place,
But makes antiquity for aye his page,
    Finding the first conceit of love there bred,
    Where time and outward form would show it dead.

It is time for the Guide's next counsel. The Guide reconfirms his love for the poet and reminds him about his still unfulfilled task.

What else could the Guide say about himself in addition to what he has already transmitted to the poet's mind? ("What's in the brain that ink may character, which hath not figured to thee my true spirit"). There is nothing else he can emphasize that would reconfirm his love and the poet's potentiality ("what's new to speak, what now to register, that may express my love, or thy dear merit"). There's nothing else but, like saying prayers, the Guide has to repeat the same thing over and over every again ("but yet like prayers divine, I must each day say over the very same"). The Guide reminds the poet that the things he told him previously are still valid ("counting no old thing old, thou mine, I thine"). This has not changed since he first time he praised the poet's inner beauty ("even as when first I hallowed thy fair name"). When renewed, true love does not show any traces of age and passing of time ("so that eternal love in love's fresh case, weighs not the dust and injury of age, nor gives to necessary wrinkles place"). Instead, it uses the past as its servant ("but makes antiquity for aye his page"). It was in antiquity, says the Guide, that true love was born; it has survived till today, despite the fact that time and love's outward form are gone ("finding the first conceit of love there bred, where time and outward form would show it dead"). Such an assurance expressed by the Guide is a preparation for the poet's next experience, i.e., rebuke. The poet will be subjected to rebuke in the following Sonnets.

It was such an eternal love that Thaisa recognized in Prince Pericles[108]:

> "To me he seems like diamond to glass."

---

[108] See "Inspirational vision" (Shakespeare for the Seeker, Volume 2, Chapter 4.1).

Rebuke (Sonnets 109 - 125)

SONNET CIX

O never say that I was false of heart,
Though absence seemed my flame to qualify,
As easy might I from my self depart,
As from my soul which in thy breast doth lie:
That is my home of love, if I have ranged,
Like him that travels I return again,
Just to the time, not with the time exchanged,
So that myself bring water for my stain,
Never believe though in my nature reigned
All frailties that besiege all kinds of blood,
That it could so preposterously be stained,
To leave for nothing all thy sum of good:
    For nothing this wide Universe I call,
    Save thou my Rose, in it thou art my all.

As usual the poet argues and excuses himself for any faults pointed out to him by the Guide. Now we find out that it was the poet's unfaithfulness that caused the long periods of winter, i.e., the Guide's absence. The poet says that although his disappearances might suggest so, he never was false in his love ("never say that I was false of heart, though absence seemed my flame to qualify"). He states that he could not separate his soul from the Guide's breath anymore than he could detach himself from his own self ("as easy might I from my self depart as from my soul which in thy breast doth lie"). He says that the Guide is his love's home ("that is my home of love"). Even if the poet is away, he is like a traveller who always returns home on time ("like him that travels I return again, just to the time, not with the time exchanged"). So his absence is excused ("so that myself bring water for my stain"). He asks the Guide never to believe that the weaknesses of his hot blood could stain his inner self ("never believe though in my nature reigned all frailties that besiege all kinds of blood, that it could so preposterously be stained"). He would never, he claims, leave something so valuable and look for something worthless ("to leave for nothing all thy sum of good"). He says that by worthless he means the entire universe, except the Guide himself, whom he calls his rose. The Guide represents everything to him ("for nothing this wide universe I call, save thou my rose, in it thou art my all"). By addressing the Guide as "my Rose", the poet indicates that he has recognized the Rose's beauty, i.e., the Guide's inner essence.

The Duke of Vienna in "Measure for Measure" made a similar plea when he was explaining his reasons for pursuing Isabella[109]:

> "No, holy father; throw away that thought;
> Believe not that the dribbling dart of love
> Can pierce a complete bosom. Why I desire thee
> To give me secret harbour, hath a purpose
> More grave and wrinkled than the aims and ends
> Of burning youth."

---

[109] See "Claudio and Isabella" (Shakespeare for the Seeker, Volume 4, Chapter 7.2).

SONNET CX

Alas 'tis true, I have gone here and there,
And made my self a motley to the view,
Gored mine own thoughts, sold cheap what is most dear,
Made old offences of affections new.
Most true it is, that I have looked on truth
Askance and strangely: But by all above,
These blenches gave my heart another youth,
And worse essays proved thee my best of love,
Now all is done, have what shall have no end,
Mine appetite I never more will grind
On newer proof, to try an older friend,
A god in love, to whom I am confined.
    Then give me welcome, next my heaven the best,
    Even to thy pure and most most loving breast.

The poet continues his confession by admitting the various violations of trust that he committed in the past. The Guide acts as a mirror of the poet's inner self. Therefore, the poet's previous accusations of the Guide were just a reflection of the poet's transgressions. These breaches were the cause of the Guide's absences. They served as rebuke of the poet's transgressions. Presently, the Guide is still absent. But this time, the poet responds in a more constructive manner to this most recent rebuke.

The poet admits that he has gone here and there, and made himself a fool ("I have gone here and there, and made my self a motley to the view"). He betrayed his own beliefs and sold cheaply that which is the most precious gift ("gored mine own thoughts, sold cheap what is most dear"). He committed usual sensual offences ("made old offences of affections new"). And it is true, he admits, that he treated the Guide's counsels with doubt and contempt ("most true it is, that I have looked on truth askance and strangely"). But now he swears by heaven that those breaches have cleansed him ("but by all above, these blenches gave my heart another youth"). And those disrespectful adventures proved to him that the Guide is his true love ("and worse essays proved thee my best of love"). The poet declares that he is done with all of that. Now he has arrived at the point which will have no end ("now all is done, have what shall have no end"). The poet declares that he will no longer put his friend's values to the test by whetting his appetite on new things ("mine appetite I never more will grind on newer proof, to try an older friend"). The Guide is his god of love to whom he is entirely committed ("a god in love, to whom I am confined"). The poet begs to be admitted again into the Guide's company, which is the next best thing to heaven ("then give me welcome, next my heaven the best, even to thy pure and most most loving breast").

The poet's declaration "most most loving breast" is similar to Bertram's surprising pronouncement in the final scene of "All's Well That Ends Well" [110]:

"I'll love her dearly, ever, ever dearly."

---

[110] See "Modulation of beauty" (Shakespeare for the Seeker, Volume 2, Chapter 5.1).

SONNET CXI

O for my sake do you wish fortune chide
The guilty goddess of my harmful deeds,
That did not better for my life provide,
Than public means which public manners breeds.
Thence comes it that my name receives a brand,
And almost thence my nature is subdued
To what it works in, like the Dyer's hand,
Pity me then, and wish I were renewed,
Whilst like a willing patient I will drink,
Potions of Eisell 'gainst my strong infection,
No bitterness that I will bitter think,
Nor double penance to correct correction.
    Pity me then dear friend, and I assure ye,
    Even that your pity is enough to cure me.

The poet implies that the Guide does not approve the way in which he earns his living ("for my sake do you wish fortune chide, the guilty goddess of my harmful deeds, that did not better for my life provide, than public means which public manners breeds"). It looks like the poet compromised his values and that his name was tainted with bad publicity ("thence comes it that my name receives a brand"). Because of this, his very nature has almost been stained, like a dyer's hand ("and almost thence my nature is subdued to what it works in, like the dyer's hand"). He asks the Guide to take pity on him; he hopes to be able to erase the stains ("pity me then, and wish I were renewed"). In the meantime, he will drink bitter medicine to cure himself from this infection ("whilst like a willing patient I will drink, potions of eisell 'gainst my strong infection"). No matter how bitter the medicine is, he will not complain ("no bitterness that I will bitter think"). He will accept the double penance to correct his errors ("nor double penance, to correct correction"). The poet assures the Guide that his pity alone is enough to cure him ("I assure ye, even that your pity is enough to cure me").

Similarly, Friar Laurence in "Two Gentlemen of Verona" was trying to erase his previous errors by secluding himself in a forest[111]:

> " 'Tis true; for Friar Laurence met them both,
> As he in penance wander'd through the forest."

---

[111] See "Evolutionary sequence" (Shakespeare for the Seeker, Volume 3, Chapter 6.7).

SONNET CXII

Your love and pity doth the impression fill,
Which vulgar scandal stamped upon my brow,
For what care I who calls me well or ill,
So you o'er-green my bad, my good allow?
You are my All the world, and I must strive,
To know my shames and praises from your tongue,
None else to me, nor I to none alive,
That my steeled sense or changes right or wrong,
In so profound *Abysm* I throw all care
Of others' voices, that my Adder's sense,
To critic and to flatterer stopped are:
Mark how with my neglect I do dispense.
    You are so strongly in my purpose bred,
    That all the world besides methinks y'are dead.

This is the continuation of the poet's protestations from the previous Sonnet. If the Guide grants his pity, which the poet has asked for, then this will be enough to make up for the damage the poet has done to his reputation ("your love and pity doth the impression fill, which vulgar scandal stamped upon my brow"). The poet does not care who calls him good or bad as long as the Guide forgives him his errors and acknowledges his merits ("for what care I who calls me well or ill, so you o'er-green my bad, my good allow"). The Guide is the poet's entire world, and the poet will strive to learn from him what is good and what is bad ("you are my all the world, and I must strive, to know my shames and praises from your tongue"). No one else opinion is of any account anymore; only the Guide has the power to affect the poet's stubbornness and to reverse his understanding of what is right and what is wrong ("none else to me, nor I to none alive, that my steeled sense or changes right or wrong"). The poet declares that he will disregard his concerns for the outside world and he will ignore his critics and flatterers ("in so profound abysm I throw all care of others' voices, that my adder's sense, to critic and to flatterer stopped are"). The poet asks the Guide to observe how determined he is in his resolution ("mark how with my neglect I do dispense"). The poet concludes that the Guide is so completely ingrained in his soul, that there is nothing left of him for the rest of the world ("you are so strongly in my purpose bred, that all the world besides methinks y'are dead"). The poet's constructive response to the rebuke will open a new range of experiences.

Here is Petruchio declaring, though a bit humorously, a similar resolution in his description of Katharina[112]:

> "She is my goods, my chattels; she is my house,
> My household stuff, my field, my barn,
> My horse, my ox, my ass, my any thing."

---

[112] See "Taming school" (Shakespeare for the Seeker, Volume 3, Chapter 6.5).

SONNET CXIII

Since I left you, mine eye is in my mind,
And that which governs me to go about,
Doth part his function, and is partly blind,
Seems seeing, but effectually is out:
For it no form delivers to the heart
Of bird, of flower, or shape which it doth lack,
Of his quick objects hath the mind no part,
Nor his own vision holds what it doth catch:
For if it see the rud'st or gentlest sight,
The most sweet-favour or deformed'st creature,
The mountain, or the sea, the day, or night:
The Crow, or Dove, it shapes them to your feature.
    Incapable of more replete, with you,
    My most true mind thus maketh mine untrue.

The poet describes his recent experiences that are associated with the operation of the subtle faculty of the intellect. The activation of this particular faculty was triggered by the poet's exposure to the White Lady during the first cycle of the process (see Sonnet 40). The poet started to exercise this faculty by meditating on the Guide's image (see Sonnet 43). Now the poet gives more details about its operation.

The poet calls this subtle faculty "my eye in my mind" ("since I left you, mine eye is in my mind, and that which governs me to go about"). Previously he could use this subtle faculty to communicate with his inner heart (see Sonnet 46). Now he finds out that the eye of his mind can register only certain images. So, the poet thinks that this faculty is partially blind ("doth part his function, and is partly blind, seems seeing, but effectually is out"). It is blind because it is lacking the ability to hold or deliver images of physical forms or shapes ("for it no form delivers to the heart of bird, of flower, or shape which it doth lack"). In other words, this new faculty does not register images of mortal things ("of his quick objects hath the mind no part, nor his own vision holds what it doth catch"). Neither is the new faculty capable of differentiating between rude and gentle sights. Any sight that it catches, whether it is an image of a rough or a delicate sight, a pleasant or an ugly-looking creature, a mountain or the sea, the day or the night, the crow or the dove, it shapes them all in such a way that they take the image of the Guide ("for if it see the rud'st or gentlest sight … it shapes them to your feature"). The poet concludes that this new subtle faculty has been completely saturated with the Guide's image ("incapable of more replete, with you"). And this is the reason why this faculty overrides his ordinary perception ("my most true mind thus maketh mine untrue").

The poet's experience indicates that the subtle faculty of the intellect reaches into invisible, i.e., immortal world. This is why this faculty does not register any mortal forms. The entry into the invisible world allows to experience the unity of all multiplicity of mortal forms, such as beauty, ugliness, rudeness, gentleness, etc., etc. All those multiplicities converge within the Guide's essence. This is why it is possible, through immersion in the Guide's essence, to arrive at such a state where all those multiplicities disappear and form unity.

Desdemona in "Othello" also made a reference to such an experience[113]:

"I saw Othello's visage in his mind."

---

[113] See "Desdemona" (Shakespeare for the Seeker, Volume 3, Chapter 6.2).

SONNET CXIV

Or whether doth my mind being crowned with you
Drink up the monarch's plague this flattery?
Or whether shall I say mine eye saith true,
And that your love taught it this *Alchemy*?
To make of monsters, and things indigest,
Such cherubins as your sweet self resemble,
Creating every bad a perfect best
As fast as objects to his beams assemble:
Oh 'tis the first, 'tis flattery in my seeing,
And my great mind most kingly drinks it up,
Mine eye well knows what with his gust is 'greeing,
And to his palate doth prepare the cup.
    If it be poisoned, 'tis the lesser sin,
    That mine eye loves it and doth first begin.

The poet continues to describe his experiences due to his newly activated subtle faculty of the intellect. He tries now to verify the truthfulness of these experiences.

As in Sonnet 113, "mine eye" refers to "my great mind" or the poet's inner mind, i.e., the subtle faculty of the intellect. The poet is wondering whether the experiences described in the previous Sonnet are a form of flattery ("or whether doth my mind being crowned with you drink up the monarch's plague this flattery?") Or these experiences are true images registered by his inner mind ("or whether shall I say mine eye saith true"). He suspects that this faculty might be affected by the alchemy of the Guide's love. Because only alchemy would be capable of transmuting beastly things into angelic ones, which resemble the Guide's perfection ("that your love taught it this Alchemy to make of monsters, and things indigest, such cherubins as your sweet self resemble"). If this is the case, then such transmutations seem to be taking place instantaneously ("creating every bad a perfect best as fast as objects to his beams assemble"). He concludes, however, that this is rather the first case, i.e., his inner mind indulges in flattery ("Oh 'tis the first, 'tis flattery in my seeing, and my great mind most kingly drinks it up"). Because the poet's inner mind knows very well what would delight him, it offers him a dose of flattery ("mine eye well knows what with his gust is 'greeing, and to his palate doth prepare the cup if it be poisoned"). In such a case accepting such flattery would be a lesser error, because it is induced by the poet's faculty and not by the Guide's love ("it is the lesser sin, that mine eye loves it and doth first begin").

Again, it is of no importance what the poet thinks about his experiences. What matters is the true nature of the experiences and their effect on the poet's inner self. In addition to providing an explanation of the unity of multiplicities, this experience also indicates the origin of time. Namely, the origin of time is the same as the origin of the multiplicities of forms, i.e., the transition from the invisible world into the ordinary world. It is at this transition that the everlasting presence diverges instantaneously into past, present, and future. ("as fast as objects to his beams assemble"). The poet alluded to such a motionless transition in Sonnet 51 ("then should I spur though mounted on the wind, in winged speed no motion shall I know"). This means that when immersing within the Guide's essence, the distinction between past, presence, and future disappears. This experience points out that through the development of the subtle faculties it is possible to avoid the cruelty of time. The fact that the poet is able to experience it, but is not able to understand, indicates that he still misses the link that would allow him to translate correctly his experiences from the inner to the ordinary intellect ("my most true mind thus maketh mine untrue").

Posthumus in "Cymbeline" faced a similar situation when he awaked from his visionary dream and found beside him a richly decorated book with a written oracle in it[114]:

> "A book? O rare one!
> Be not, as is our fangled world, a garment
> Nobler than that it covers: let thy effects
> So follow, to be most unlike our courtiers,
> As good as promise."

Posthumus doubted whether the oracle was genuine.

---

[114] See "Techniques" (Shakespeare for the Seeker, Volume 1, Chapter 3.2).

SONNET CXV

Those lines that I before have writ do lie,
Even those that said I could not love you dearer,
Yet then my judgment knew no reason why,
My most full flame should afterwards burn clearer.
But reckoning time, whose million'd accidents
Creep in 'twixt vows, and change decrees of Kings,
Tan sacred beauty, blunt the sharp'st intents,
Divert strong minds to the course of altering things:
Alas why fearing of time's tyranny,
Might I not then say now I love you best,
When I was certain o'er in-certainty,
Crowning the present, doubting of the rest:
    Love is a Babe, then might I not say so
    To give full growth to that which still doth grow.

The Guide leads the poet through a process that focuses on the simultaneous activation of the subtle faculties of the intellect and the heart. The previous two Sonnets illustrate the poet's experiences related to a subtle layer of the intellect. In this Sonnet, the poet describes his experiences triggered by a purified aspect of the heart faculty (the "red faculty"). The poet discovers another dimension of love.

The poet says that he was lying in the poem, which he wrote previously ("those lines that I before have writ do lie"). He was lying even when he wrote that it was impossible to love more deeply than his loving of the Guide ("even those that said I could not love you dearer"). At that time he did not know the reason of love, because the flame of his love was still burning his imperfections ("yet then my judgment knew no reason why my most full flame should afterwards burn clearer"). Previously, the poet alluded to such "purging fire" in Sonnet 45.

It is the passage of time with millions of unpredictable events that destroys many things, such as breaking promises, changing the verdicts of kings, darken sacred beauty, weakening the most determined intentions, or diverting the most confident minds towards uncertainly ("but reckoning time, whose million accidents creep in betwixt vows, and change decrees of kings, tan sacred beauty, blunt the sharpest intents, divert strong minds to the course of altering things"). Why then should not the poet have said that he loved the most ("might I not then say now I love you best"). At that time he was still ignorant of his own inconstancy ("when I was certain o'er in-certainty"). By making such statements, he was simply cherishing the present and ignoring the past and the future ("crowning the present, doubting of the rest"). The poet concludes that love is like a growing child, therefore it was obvious that he could not know what full grown love is like ("love is a babe, then might I not say so to give full growth to that which still doth grow").

Benedick[115] in "Much Ado About Nothing" went through a similar realization:

> "A man loves the meat
> in his youth that he cannot endure in his age.
> Shall quips and sentences and these paper bullets of
> the brain awe a man from the career of his humour?"

---

[115] See "Assimilation of creative energy" (Shakespeare for the Seeker, Volume 3, Chapter 6.3).

SONNET CXVI

Let me not to the marriage of true minds
Admit impediments, love is not love
Which alters when it alteration finds,
Or bends with the remover to remove.
O no, it is an ever fixed mark
That looks on tempests and is never shaken;
It is the star to every wandering bark,
Whose worth's unknown, although his height be taken.
Love's not Time's fool, though rosy lips and cheeks
Within his bending sickle's compass come,
Love alters not with his brief hours and weeks,
But bears it out even to the edge of doom:
    If this be error and upon me proved,
    I never writ, nor no man ever loved.

The poet further expounds on the nature of love. We can see that the poet's intuitive feelings have greatly been improved. Now he does not wish to interfere with the union of true minds, i.e., the evolutionary process leading to the unity of the higher states of mind ("let me not to the marriage of true minds admit impediments"). Such unity may be realized only in the presence of the unitive energy of love. This is why he says that love is no love if it is affected by any changes, or becomes inconstant because of the beloved's absence ("love is not love which alters when it alteration finds, or bends with the remover to remove"). Love is like a fixed mark that is unshaken by tempests ("it is an ever fixed mark that looks on tempests and is never shaken"). Love is like a guiding star for every wandering ship ("it is the star to every wandering bark"); it is perceptible but its worth is beyond any measure ("whose worth's unknown, although his height be taken"). Love is not at the mercy of time, though time devours beautiful faces ("love's not time's fool, though rosy lips and cheeks within his bending sickle's compass come"). Love is not measured by hours and weeks, but endures till the last day ("love alters not with his brief hours and weeks, but bears it out even to the edge of doom"). The poet concludes that if his claim is not true or is proven wrong, then he never wrote a word, and no man ever loved ("if this be error and upon me proved, I never writ, nor no man ever loved").

King Henry V had this to say about the effect of time on his love of Princess Katharine[116]:

> "But, in faith,
> Kate, the elder I wax, the better I shall appear:
> my comfort is, that old age, that ill layer up of
> beauty, can do no more, spoil upon my face: thou
> hast me, if thou hast me, at the worst; and thou
> shalt wear me, if thou wear me, better and better."

---

[116] See "Dawn of perfection" (Shakespeare for the Seeker, Volume 1, Chapter 1).

SONNET CXVII

Accuse me thus, that I have scanted all,
Wherein I should your great deserts repay,
Forgot upon your dearest love to call,
Whereto all bonds do tie me day by day,
That I have frequent been with unknown minds,
And given to time your own dear-purchased right,
That I have hoisted sail to all the winds
Which should transport me farthest from your sight.
Book both my wilfulness and errors down,
And on just proof surmise, accumulate,
Bring me within the level of your frown,
But shoot not at me in your wakened hate:
    Since my appeal says I did strive to prove
    The constancy and virtue of your love.

Despite his claims and experiences, the poet is not able to sustain his inner states. He goes back to his previous presumptions about the Guide's supposed accusations ("accuse me thus, that I have scanted all, wherein I should your great deserts repay"). The Guide's frowning, hate, etc., are just the poet's imagination and are a marker of his inconstancy. The poet presumes that the Guide might accuse him of neglecting his meditation, which he was supposed to do every day ("forgot upon your dearest love to call, whereto all bonds do tie me day by day"). He also feels guilty for wasting his time on meaningless ideas instead of studying the Guide's counsels ("that I have frequent been with unknown minds, and given to time your own dear-purchased right"). The poet admits that he has not been able to follow his priority and that be allowed himself to be driven astray from the straight course ("that I have hoisted sail to all the winds which should transport me farthest from your sight"). He assumes that his actions and errors have caused the Guide's anger ("book both my wilfulness and errors down, and on just proof surmise accumulate, bring me within the level of your frown"). Then the poet desperately calls upon the Guide to not hate him for his mistakes ("but shoot not at me in your wakened hate"). He concludes with a sheepish argument that all of his acts were driven by his desire to test the constancy of the Guide's love and virtues ("since my appeal says I did strive to prove the constancy and virtue of your love").

Here is Imogen[117] in "Cymbeline" explaining in what manner Posthumus can keep himself on the straight course:

> "I ... have charged him,
> At the sixth hour of morn, at noon, at midnight,
> To encounter me with orisons, for then
> I am in heaven for him."

---

[117] See "Imperfections" (Shakespeare for the Seeker, Volume 1, Chapter 3.2).

SONNET CXVIII

Like as to make our appetites more keen
With eager compounds we our palate urge,
As to prevent our maladies unseen,
We sicken to shun sickness when we purge.
Even so being full of your ne'er cloying sweetness,
To bitter sauces did I frame my feeding;
And sick of welfare, found a kind of meetness,
To be diseased ere that there was true needing.
Thus policy in love to anticipate
The ills that were, not grew to faults assured,
And brought to medicine a healthful state
Which rank of goodness would by ill be cured.
    But thence I learn and find the lesson true,
    Drugs poison him that so fell sick of you.

The poet continues with his flawed justification of his inconstant behaviour. He argues that his straying off from the path was useful. It was like having an appetizer to sharpen the appetite ("like as to make our appetites more keen with eager compounds we our palate urge"), or taking a laxative to avoid sickness later on ("as to prevent our maladies unseen, we sicken to shun sickness when we purge"). The poet compares his behaviour to switching from sickly-sweetness to a bitter but healthier diet ("being full of your ne'er cloying sweetness, to bitter sauces did I frame my feeding"). The poet admits that because of feeling tired of his good fortune, he wanted to experience some illness, before actually becoming sick ("and sick of welfare, found a kind of meetness, to be diseased ere that there was true needing"). It was this strategy of prevention against eventual disease that led him to administer medicine to a healthy state ("thus policy in love to anticipate the ills that were, not grew to faults assured, and brought to medicine a healthful state"). In this way the poet's boredom, which was caused by his good fortune, could be cured ("which, rank of goodness, would by ill be cured"). Since then, however, he has learnt his lesson ("but thence I learn and find the lesson true"). Namely, the medicine will poison him who is already sick with love for the Guide ("drugs poison him that so fell sick of you").

A similarly fictitious medicine was prescribed by Cardinal Pandulph[118] in in "King John":

"And falsehood falsehood cures."

---

[118] See "The Two Noble Kinsmen" (Shakespeare for the Seeker, Volume 4, Chapter 8.3).

SONNET CXIX

What potions have I drunk of *Siren* tears
Distilled from Lymbecks foul as hell within,
Applying fears to hopes, and hopes to fears,
Still losing when I saw myself to win?
What wretched errors hath my heart committed,
Whilst it hath thought itself so blessed never?
How have mine eyes out of their Spheres been fitted
In the distraction of this madding fever?
O benefit of ill, now I find true
That better is, by evil still made better.
And ruined love when it is built anew
Grows fairer than at first, more strong, far greater.
    So I return rebuked to my content,
    And gain by ill thrice more than I have spent.

The poet continues with his justification of the errors that he made in the past. He looks at his actions as an accidental mix of errors and good deeds. He has not understood yet that he is guided through a very well defined set of experiences. And it does not really matter what he thinks about his motivation, excuses, or outcomes. The important thing is the specific sequence of his experiences and their timing.

So, the poet wonders what poison he drank that made him lose when he thought that he was winning ("still losing when I saw myself to win"). He thinks that it must be some distilled hellish siren's tears that promised him hope to overcome his fears ("have I drunk of siren tears distilled from limbecks foul as hell within, applying fears to hopes, and hopes to fears"). What inspiration it was, he asks himself, which led him to committing such grave errors at the time when he thought he had never been more blessed ("what wretched errors hath my heart committed, whilst it hath thought itself so blessed never"). It must be the delirium of this frenetic fever that distracted his vision ("how have mine eyes out of their spheres been fitted in the distraction of this madding fever"). Yet how strange it is, wonders the poet, that such evil can bring benefit ("O benefit of ill"). Now the poet can see that through evil certain things can be made even better ("now I find true that better is, by evil still made better"). And when old love is ruined and then rebuilt anew, it may grow more beautiful, stronger, and greater ("and ruined love when it is built anew grows fairer than at first, more strong, far greater"). So, having been rebuked for his mistakes, the poet realizes that he gained much more than he lost ("so I return rebuked to my content, and gain by ill thrice more than I have spent").

Here is Hecate's distilled potion recipe that induced in Macbeth a sense of false security[119]:

> "And that distill'd by magic sleights
> Shall raise such artificial sprites
> As by the strength of their illusion
> Shall draw him on to his confusion:
> He shall spurn fate, scorn death, and bear
> He hopes 'bove wisdom, grace and fear:
> And you all know, security
> Is mortals' chiefest enemy."

---

[119] See "Scotland: 11th century AD" (Shakespeare for the Seeker, Volume 1, Chapter 3.3).

SONNET CXX

That you were once unkind be-friends me now,
And for that sorrow, which I then did feel,
Needs must I under my transgression bow,
Unless my Nerves were brass or hammered steel.
For if you were by my unkindness shaken
As I by yours, you've passed a hell of Time,
And I a tyrant have no leisure taken
To weigh how once I suffered in your crime.
O that our night of woe might have remembered
My deepest sense, how hard true sorrow hits,
And soon to you, as you to me then tendered
The humble salve, which wounded bosoms fits!
    But that your trespass now becomes a fee,
    Mine ransoms yours, and yours must ransom me.

We start to see more clearly the developmental methodology implemented by the Guide. Let's recall, that the Guide acts as a mirror of the poet's inner self. To be developmentally effective, the poet's reflections in this mirror are advanced into the future. In this way the poet is prepared for his experiences ahead of time. In this Sonnet the poet refers to the Guide's withdrawal during the wintry seasons described in Sonnet 104. The Guide's disappearance was the result of the poet's trespasses to which he refers in this Sonnet. We have to keep in mind that the poet has not understood yet the Guide's teaching techniques. Therefore, he does not recognize himself in the Guide's actions. But he recognizes their beneficial effect.

The poet says that the fact that the Guide was once cruel to him, helps him now ("that you were once unkind be-friends me now"). He admits that he would have to be made of hardened steel or brass not to bow down under the incurred pain ("and for that sorrow, which I then did feel, needs must I under my transgression bow, unless my nerves were brass or hammered steel"). If the Guide felt the same way about the poet's trespasses, he must have also passed through horrible times ("for if you were by my unkindness shaken as I by yours, you've passed a hell of time"). The poet feels guilty that, like a cruel tyrant, he has not taken into consideration the pain that he himself once suffered ("and I a tyrant have no leisure taken to weigh how once I suffered in your crime"). He wishes that at the time of his negligence he remembered how difficult it was when he was stricken by sorrows ("O that our night of woe might have remembered my deepest sense, how hard true sorrow hits"). The poet asks for forgiveness for not offering right away his explanations and apology ("and soon to you, as you to me then tendered the humble salve, which wounded bosoms fits"). Yet, once again, the poet misses the point. Instead of learning a lesson, he ends up bargaining with the Guide. Now he claims that his transgression cancels out the Guide's offence, and by the same token, the Guide's supposed trespass must cancel out his wrongdoing ("but that your trespass now becomes a fee, mine ransoms yours, and yours must ransom me").

Posthumus' experiences in "Cymbeline" also included travel into the future, i.e., from 1st century Britain to 16th century Italy. In Italy he was exposed to the idea of the chivalric worship of true beauty[120]:

> "It was much like an argument that fell out last
> night, where each of us fell in praise of our
> country mistresses."

This experience helped Posthumus recover from his spiritual blindness.

---

[120] See "Celtic connection" (Shakespeare for the Seeker, Volume 3, Chapter 6.4).

SONNET CXXI

'Tis better to be vile than vile esteemed,
When not to be, receives reproach of being,
And the just pleasure lost, which is so deemed,
Not by our feeling, but by others' seeing.
For why should others' false adulterate eyes
Give salutation to my sportive blood?
Or on my frailties why are frailer spies;
Which in their wills count bad what I think good?
No, I am that I am, and they that level
At my abuses, reckon up their own,
I may be straight though they them-selves be bevel
By their rank thoughts, my deeds must not be shown
    Unless this general evil they maintain,
    All men are bad and in their badness reign.

The poet analyses the objectivity of the evaluation of one's actions. His skilful argumentation leads him to the conclusion that he himself is not guilty of any offence. Although seemingly convincing, such skilful arguments are just side effects of his progress. They allow him to identify flaws of his previous assumptions.

The poet says that it is better to be bad than to be accused of being such ("it is better to be vile than vile esteemed"). If one is not bad but is reproved by others for being evil, he loses the satisfaction of feeling good about himself ("when not to be, receives reproach of being, and the just pleasure lost, which is so deemed"). And such satisfaction is lost not because of one's feeling, but through the judgement of others ("not by our feeling, but by others' seeing"). Therefore, such false and corrupted opinions should not be used to justify the poet's indulgences ("for why should others' false adulterate eyes give salutation to my sportive blood"). By the same token, those who are prone to corruption are not qualified to denounce the poet's weaknesses ("or on my frailties why are frailer spies"). They consider those things as bad, but in reality they are beneficial to the poet ("which in their wills count bad what I think good"). The poet states that he is what he is. And those, who accuse him of deception, are simply revealing their own shortcomings ("and they that level at my abuses, reckon up their own"). The poet claims that he is honest, but that the others are corrupted ("I may be straight though they them-selves be bevel"). His actions cannot be evaluated by the false criteria used by the others ("by their rank thoughts, my deeds must not be shown"). Because by applying such false criteria, all people would be evil and stuck in their deception ("unless this general evil they maintain, all men are bad and in their badness reign").

This is why Iago in "Othello" did not want to disclosure who he really was[121]:

"I am not what I am."

---

[121] See "Iago - the whisperer" (Shakespeare for the Seeker, Volume 3, Chapter 6.2).

SONNET CXXII

Thy gift, thy tables, are within my brain
Full charactered with lasting memory,
Which shall above that idle rank remain
Beyond all date even to eternity.
Or at the least, so long as brain and heart
Have faculty by nature to subsist,
Till each to razed oblivion yield his part
Of thee, thy record never can be missed:
That poor retention could not so much hold,
Nor need I tallies thy dear love to score,
Therefore to give them from me was I bold,
To trust those tables that receive thee more,
    To keep an adjunct to remember thee,
    Were to import forgetfulness in me.

The poet continues excusing his various offences. In this way, we are finding more about his breaches of the discipline of the path. This time he skilfully defends himself against giving away a notebook containing the Guide's counsels ("thy gift, thy tables"). The Guide had mentioned such a notebook in Sonnet 16; he referred to it as his "barren rhyme". The poet claims that he did not need to keep it, because he was able to commit the counsels to his memory, which is more efficient than a notebook ("are within my brain full charactered with lasting memory, which shall above that idle rank remain beyond all date even to eternity"). They will be preserved as long as the faculties of the intellect and the heart exist ("so long as brain and heart have faculty by nature to subsist"). The Guide's counsels, therefore, will be preserved till the poet's faculties pass into oblivion ("till each to razed oblivion yield his part of thee, thy record never can be missed"). The poet insists that that little notebook could not hold as much as his faculties would, and he does not need to keep a written record of how much the Guide loves him ("that poor retention could not so much hold, nor need I tallies thy dear love to score"). Therefore, he gave away the notebook, trusting that his faculties would serve the purpose more effectively ("therefore to give them from me was I bold, to trust those tables that receive thee more"). Again, he sheepishly concludes that by giving away the notebook, he demonstrated that he did not rely on an intermediary to remember the Guide ("to keep an adjunct to remember thee, were to import forgetfulness in me").

When giving away the notebook, the poet ignored one of the previous counsels. In that counsel the poet was advised that his ordinary intellect and memory were not sufficient yet to hold the impact of the Guide's teaching (see Sonnet 77). Therefore, the Guide gave him the notebook, which the poet was supposed to read over and over again. A similar instruction was included in Shakespeare's First Folio. Shakespeare's colleagues advised the readers to "Read him, therefore, and again, and again".

Similarly, Cassio did not perceive the importance of Othello's "gift", i.e., a handkerchief that he found in his room. He carelessly passed the handkerchief to Bianca. Here are Othello's comments about Cassio's mistake[122]:

> "He had my handkerchief."
>
> "That's not so good now."

---

[122] See "Developmental techniques" (Shakespeare for the Seeker, Volume 3, Chapter 6.2).

SONNET CXXIII

No! Time, thou shalt not boast that I do change,
Thy pyramids built up with newer might
To me are nothing novel, nothing strange,
They are but dressings of a former sight:
Our dates are brief, and therefore we admire,
What thou dost foist upon us that is old,
And rather make them born to our desire,
Than think that we before have heard them told:
Thy registers and thee I both defy,
Not wondering at the present, nor the past,
For thy records, and what we see doth lie,
Made more or less by thy continual haste:
    This I do vow and this shall ever be,
    I will be true despite thy scythe and thee.

For the third time the poet returns to his meditation on the destructivity of time. Previously the poet attempted to deal with the cruelty of time in Sonnets 19 and 60. The possibility of overcoming time's destructivity was introduced to him by the Guide in his first counsel (Sonnet 12). At first, the poet's approach was pretty naïve (Sonnet 19). During the first cycle his understanding was improved and the poet's undertook more practical strategy. Namely, he decided to conquer time by the power of his verses. Now, we may observe how the poet's understanding went through a further refinement.

The poet's present argumentation is more refined than his previous protestations about time. He arrives at the conclusion that he may overcome time destructivity by being true to himself. The poet starts to recognize that he himself has to change first before he may discharge his task. In this way we may see how the experiences, to which he has been exposed, have allowed him to refine his understanding and thinking. Such refinement is the result of the activation of the subtle faculty of the intellect.

He claims that time is not going to make him change his faithfulness ("time, thou shalt not boast that I do change"). Everything around us is just a record of time's destructivity. New monuments are simply replicas of what existed before; there is nothing novel or impressive about them ("thy pyramids built up with newer might to me are nothing novel, nothing strange, they are but dressings of a former sight"). Our lives are short, therefore we admire old things which time tricks us with ("our dates are brief, and therefore we admire what thou dost foist upon us that is old"). Time replicates them anew to fool us, rather than having us recognize in them the same old staff ("and rather make them born to our desire, than think that we before have heard them told"). The poet says that he defies time and its history ("thy registers and thee I both defy"). He is not interested in the present nor in the past, because history and all what we see around is a form of deception ("not wondering at the present, nor the past, for thy records, and what we see doth lie"). All these are the result of time's continuous rashness ("made more or less by thy continual haste"). The poet makes the vow to be true to himself despite time's destructive power ("this I do vow and this shall ever be, I will be true despite thy scythe and thee").

The poet's conclusion is consistent with his previous experience described in Sonnet 114. At that time he was not able to understand it, because he was still missing a link that would allow him to translate correctly his experiences from the inner to the ordinary intellect. Now he realizes that he needs to work on himself first before he is able to overcome time's destructive power.

Here is Pericles' comment about time's deceptive power[123]:

---

[123] See "Inspirational vision" (Shakespeare for the Seeker, Volume 2, Chapter 4.1).

"Time's the king of men;
He's both their parent, and he is their grave.
And gives them what he will, not what they crave."

SONNET CXXIV

If my dear love were but the child of state,
It might for fortune's bastard be unfathered,
As subject to time's love, or to time's hate,
Weeds among weeds, or flowers with flowers gathered.
No it was builded far from accident,
It suffers not in smiling pomp, nor falls
Under the blow of thralled discontent,
Whereto th' inviting time our fashion calls;
It fears not policy that *Heretic*,
Which works on leases of short numbered hours,
But all alone stands hugely politic,
That it nor grows with heat, nor drowns with showers.
    To this I witness call the fools of time,
    Which die for goodness, who have lived for crime.

The poet's more effective approach to the destructivity of time, which is described in the previous Sonnet, has been the result of the activation of a reformed faculty of the intellect. In this Sonnet we may discern the operation of a subtle faculty of the heart. This subtle faculty of the heart allows to perceive another dimension of love. Previously, the poet described his understanding of love in Sonnet 115. At that time he concluded that love was like a growing child. Such an understanding of love was introduced by the Guide in his initial counsel.

Now the poet announces that his love is independent of all worldly influences. He says that if his love was accidental, it might be considered to be just fortune's bastard ("if my dear love were but the child of state, it might for fortune's bastard be unfathered"). Such accidental love, like hate, would be dependent on time, i.e., rejected as worthless or quickly exploited ("as subject to time's love, or to time's hate, weeds among weeds, or flowers with flowers gathered"). The poet's love was planned, designed, and developed ("it was builded far from accident"). This is why it is independent of deceitful displays and bitter displeasures, which are so common these days ("it suffers not in smiling pomp, nor falls under the blow of thralled discontent, whereto the inviting time our fashion calls"). The poet's love is not afraid of short-lived scheming, but stands alone immensely prudent ("it fears not policy that heretic, which works on leases of short numbered hours, but all alone stands hugely politic"). This means that it does not need pleasure to grow, nor is reduced by misfortune ("that it nor grows with heat, nor drowns with showers"). To confirm his claims, the poet calls as his witnesses all those fools who dedicated their lives to supposed goodness, but in reality their departure from this world was the only constructive contribution to that cause ("to this I witness call the fools of time, which die for goodness, who have lived for crime").

Romeo, for example, allowed himself to be influenced by bitter displeasure and, as a result, ended-up as fortune-fool[124]:

"O, I am fortune's fool!"

---

[124] See "Villain" (Shakespeare for the Seeker, Volume 3, Chapter 6.6).

SONNET CXXV

Were't ought to me I bore the canopy,
With my extern the outward honouring,
Or laid great bases for eternity,
Which proves more short than waste or ruining?
Have I not seen dwellers on form and favour
Lose all, and more by paying too much rent
For compound sweet; Forgoing simple savour,
Pitiful thrivers in their gazing spent.
No, let me be obsequious in thy heart,
And take thou my oblation, poor but free,
Which is not mixed with seconds, knows no art,
But mutual render only me for thee.
    Hence, thou suborned *Informer*, a true soul
    When most impeached, stands least in thy control.

After finding the means to deal with the destructivity of time and experiencing a new dimension of love, the poet is able to identify his greatest enemy. This is his corrupted self, whom he calls Informer. It was this Informer that was interfering with the poet's progress.

The poet declares that he does not care about the public display of honours or monuments, which are subjected to destruction and downfall ("were't ought to me I bore the canopy, with my extern the outward honouring, or laid great bases for eternity, which proves more short than waste or ruining"). He says he has seen the downfalls of pitiful overachievers who relied on rewards and favours, and who overspent on sophisticated pleasures ("have I not seen dwellers on form and favour lose all, and more by paying too much rent for compound sweet; forgoing simple savour, pitiful thrivers, in their gazing spent"). The poet declares that he will be obedient and faithful to the Guide ("no, let me be obsequious in thy heart"). This is a free-given gift, which does not have any attachments and does not contain second-rated things ("and take thou my oblation, poor but free, which is not mixed with seconds, knows no art"). The poet surrenders to the Guide ("but mutual render, only me for thee"). And he declares that he will not be influenced by the Informer. Because when condemned, a true soul is not anymore in the Informer's power ("hence, thou suborned *Informer*, a true soul when most impeached, stands least in thy control"). Such surrender is a sign that the poet has arrived onto the next stage of his journey. Now it is time for the Guide to introduce him to the next challenge.

Mercutio in "Romeo and Juliet" was also able to identify such an Informer, who was responsible for Verona's problems. It was Queen Mab, who[125]:

> "Sometime she gallops o'er a courtier's nose,
> And then dreams he of smelling out a suit;
> And sometime comes she with a tithe-pig's tail
> Tickling a parson's nose as a' lies asleep."

---

[125] See "Villain" (Shakespeare for the Seeker, Volume 3, Chapter 6.6).

The Guide's twelfth counsel (Sonnet 126)

SONNET CXXVI

O thou, my lovely Boy who in thy power,
Dost hold time's fickle glass, his sickle, hour:
Who hast by waning grown, and therein showest,
Thy lovers withering, as thy sweet self growest.
If Nature (sovereign mistress over wrack)
As thou goest onwards still will pluck thee back,
She keeps thee to this purpose, that her skill.
May time disgrace, and wretched minutes kill.
Yet fear her O thou minion of her pleasure,
She may detain, but not still keep her treasure!
Her *Audite* (though delayed) answered must be,
And her *Quietus* is to render thee.
(   )
(   )

The Guide acknowledges that the poet has made substantial progress and he is now capable of holding time in check ("O thou, my lovely Boy who in thy power dost hold time's fickle glass, his sickle, hour"). This particular progress was marked by the poet's experiences described in Sonnet 114.

According to the Guide, the poet's inner beauty has grown ("thy sweet self growest"). The poet has grown through the process of dying gradually to his worldly pleasures ("who hast by waning grown, and therein showest, thy lovers withering"). The Guide advises him that Nature, which has the overall control over mortal forms ("sovereign mistress over wrack"), may slow down the passing of time as long as he keeps making the right efforts ("as thou goest onwards still will pluck thee back). By keeping time in check, Nature helps the poet to move forward along the path ("she keeps thee to this purpose, that her skill, may time disgrace, and wretched minutes kill"). The Guide warns the poet, however, that he should not be distracted by Nature's worldly pleasures ("yet fear her, thou minion of her pleasure"). The poet's time for completing his journey is limited. Nature may slow down the passing of time, but she cannot keep the poet's mortal form forever ("she may detain, but not still keep her treasure"). Even if she delays time, at the end she has to provide an account of her handling of the poet's mortal form ("her audit, though delayed, answered must be"). And to settle down her account, she has to hand him over ("and her quietus is to render thee"). This warning is a repeat of the Guide's first counsel, which he delivered in Sonnet 4.

The poet was able to identify and come to terms with worldly attractions. Now, he is ready for exposure to more subtle challenges. The Guide's reference to "her pleasure" is a warning about the upcoming challenges. He does not specify these challenges. This is why the Sonnet is missing the concluding couplet. Instead, there are only two empty brackets. In this way the Guide indicates that now it is up to the poet to recognize these challenges and to deal with them accordingly by using his newly developed skills.

The upcoming challenges are disclosed in the next Sonnet. The poet will be exposed to an evolutionary impulse, which is symbolically represented by the Black Lady. At first, the Guide will unveil the Lady's beauty just for a brief moment. (He implemented a similar approach with the appearance of the White Lady during the first cycle.) Such an unveiling will allow to identify any remaining traces of the poet's inner impurities. Afterwards, the poet will be able to continue his journey only if he manages to complete the process of "dying before dying". He has to "die" before Nature's is called upon to return her loan.

Helena in "All's Well That Ends Well" also left an "unfinished" sentence to indicate the challenges that Bertram was going to be faced with[126]:

> "The court's a learning place, and he is one -..."

The readers may complete the sentence by adding "that needs to learn".

---

[126] See "Reformation" (Shakespeare for the Seeker, Volume 2, Chapter 5.1).

Unveiling (Sonnets 127 - 128)

SONNET CXXVII

In the old age black was not counted fair,
Or if it were, it bore not beauty's name:
But now is black beauty's successive heir,
And beauty slandered with a bastard shame,
For since each hand hath put on Nature's power,
Fairing the foul with Art's false borrowed face,
Sweet beauty hath no name no holy bower,
But is profaned, if not lives in disgrace.
Therefore my Mistress' eyes are Raven black,
Her eyes so suited, and they mourners seem,
At such who not born fair no beauty lack,
Sland'ring Creation with a false esteem,
    Yet so they mourn becoming of their woe,
    That every tongue says beauty should look so.

Shakespeare's Sonnets, and his plays, illustrate the spiritual process leading to the development of the inner being or the angelic soul. The inner structure of the inner being consists of four subtle faculties. A colour code is used to mark these four subtle faculties, i.e., yellow, red, white, and black (see Sonnet 37). Each subtle faculty may be activated by coming into contact with the corresponding evolutionary impulse. In several of his counsels, the Guide refers to the subtle faculties as roses of various colours (i.e., "beauty's Rose might never die" in Sonnet 1, "the perfumed tincture of the Roses" in Sonnet 54, "his Rose is true" in Sonnet 67, "like a canker in the fragrant Rose" in Sonnet 95, "the deep vermilion in the Rose" in Sonnet 98. "a third nor red, nor white, had stol'n of both" in Sonnet 99). As indicated in Sonnet 99, the poet has so far been exposed to yellow, red, and white impulses.

Sonnet 127 marks the first appearance of an impulse that is designated for the purification of an inner aspect of the intellect faculty. In accordance with this spiritual methodology, this aspect may be activated once an inner aspect of the heart has been at least partially purified. The heart faculty was initially purified during the first cycle (see Sonnet 46). This "red faculty" was further developed during the second phase (see Sonnets 80, 115). Now, the poet is ready for exposure to a purifying "black" impulse. The Black Lady symbolically represents this evolutionary impulse needed for the activation of the "black faculty".

In accordance with Shakespeare's presentation, the methodology of activation of the black faculty was introduced in Europe in the Middle Ages. (Coincidentally, it was in the Middle Ages that the cult of the Black Madonna appeared in Europe.) In other words, this inner faculty was still latent prior to that time. The first two lines of the Sonnet refer to this fact, i.e., in the olden days "black beauty" was not known or recognized. ("in the old age black was not counted fair, or if it were, it bore not beauty's name"). Once this particular faculty became operational, some corrupted forms of it started to spread around ("but now is black beauty's successive heir, and beauty slandered with a bastard shame"). Some people tried to mimic the black beauty's natural power by inventing the black art, and in this way they give it a bad name ("for since each hand hath put on nature's power, fairing the foul with art's false borrowed face"). The next line of the Sonnet makes a reference to the cult of the Black Madonnas, i.e., the black beauty should not be personalized or worshiped ("sweet beauty hath no name no holy bower"). Therefore, any attempts at portraying it or worshipping it are the marks of profanation ("but is profaned, if not lives in disgrace"). The poet explains that the Lady's eyes became black because they are lamenting those who ignore their developmental potential ("her eyes so suited, and they mourners seem, at such who not born fair no beauty lack"). Being driven by their selfish desires, those people remain in an ignorant state ("slandering creation with a false esteem"). The Black Lady is mourning because those ignorant people, instead of learning, started to worship her ("that every tongue says beauty should look so").

Here is Berowne's description of Rosaline[127], i.e., the Black Lady of "Love's Labour's Lost":

> "Her favour turns the fashion of the days,
> For native blood is counted painting now;
> And therefore red, that would avoid dispraise,
> Paints itself black, to imitate her brow."

---

[127] See "French impulse" (Shakespeare for the Seeker, Volume 2, Chapter 5.3).

"Do I envy those Jacks that nimble leap,
To kiss the tender inward of thy hand" (Sonnet 128)

SONNET CXXVIII

How oft when thou my music music play'st,
Upon that blessed wood whose motion sounds
With thy sweet fingers when thou gently sway'st,
The wiry concord that mine ear confounds,
Do I envy those Jacks that nimble leap,
To kiss the tender inward of thy hand,
Whilst my poor lips which should that harvest reap,
At the wood's boldness by thee blushing stand.
To be so tickled they would change their state,
And situation with those dancing chips,
O'er whom thy fingers walk with gentle gait,
Making dead wood more bless'd than living lips,
    Since saucy Jacks so happy are in this,
    Give them thy fingers, me thy lips to kiss.

In its outward content the Sonnet gives a sensual description of the Black Lady playing on the virginals ("that blessed wood"). The poet compares himself to a post ("blushing stand") that watches with envy his mistress' fingers playing with the wooden keys of the keyboard ("do I envy those jacks that nimble leap, to kiss the tender inward of thy hand"). He expresses the wish that his lips would take the place of the keys ("to be so tickled they would change their state and situation with those dancing chips").

In its inner content, the Sonnet indicates that the poet, despite the Guide's warning ("Yet fear her, O thou minion of her pleasure", in Sonnet 126), has already allowed himself to be overtaken by the sensual impact of the Black Lady. Instead of paying attention to the content ("music"), he is preoccupied with the container, i.e., her lips ("since saucy jacks so happy are in this, give them thy fingers, me thy lips to kiss").

Shakespeare uses "music" as a symbol of divine guidance. For example, when Pericles reached Pentapolis, he became "a music's master". In "The Winter's Tale" music enabled the resurrection of Hermione of Sicily. Othello was assisted by "music that may not be heard" when he raised a tempest that completely destroyed the Turkish fleet. Prospero in "The Tempest" could exercise his powers only in the presence of "heavenly music". Similarly, assisted by the harmony of "immortal souls" in "The Merchant of Venice", Portia of Belmont was able to destroy and then miraculously recover Antonio's ships. Lorenzo's comment (see Sonnet 8) about "such harmony" in "The Merchant of Venice" applies directly to the poet's current state:

> "Such harmony is in immortal souls;
> But whilst this muddy vesture of decay
> Doth grossly close it in, we cannot hear it".

In other words, the poet's fascination with his mistress' "lips to kiss" is a sign that his inner state is still enclosed by "this muddy vesture of decay". The poet's fascination with the Lady's lips does not allow him to perceive the "heavenly music".

In was for the same reason that Duke Vincentio in "Measure for Measure" warned against the arbitrary listening to music[128]:

> "music oft hath such a charm
> To make bad good, and good provoke to harm."

---

[128] See "Corruption" (Shakespeare for the Seeker, Volume 4, Chapter 7.2).

The Guide's thirteenth counsel (Sonnet 129)

SONNET CXXIX

The expense of Spirit in a waste of shame
Is lust in action, and till action, lust
Is perjured, murderous, bloody full of blame,
Savage, extreme, rude, cruel, not to trust,
Enjoyed no sooner but despised straight,
Past reason hunted, and no sooner had
Past reason hated as a swallowed bait,
On purpose laid to make the taker mad.
Made in pursuit and in possession so,
Had, having, and in quest, to have extreme,
A bliss in proof and proved a very woe,
Before a joy proposed behind a dream,
    All this the world well knows yet none knows well,
    To shun the heaven that leads men to this hell.

This counsel is addressed to the readers, so that it will be easier for them to follow and understand the poet's upcoming experiences. In particular, the Guide explains why the poet's reaction to "music" in the previous Sonnet is a sign of his inner impurities. He refers to these impurities as "lust". It is lust that will put the poet in trouble during his encounters with the Black Lady. It is only when he will be able to purify his inner self from such desires that he may hope to fulfill his quest. We may notice that this is the sixth counsel of the second cycle. Therefore, it marks a particularly challenging stage of the poet's journey.

The Guide emphasizes the fact that man's spiritual development ("spirit") is marred by his earthly attractions. He draws a parallel between earthly attachments and sexual urge ("lust"). The desire to turn spiritual experiences into personal advantages is as damaging as being driven by lust ("the expense of spirit in a waste of shame is lust in action, and till action, lust is perjured, murderous, bloody full of blame"). Therefore, it is unwise to follow it ("savage, extreme, rude, cruel, not to trust"). Earthly attractions are misleading and short-lived ("enjoyed no sooner but despised straight"). People go to absurd lengths in their pursuit of worldly pleasures, only to hate them as soon as they have obtained them ("past reason hunted, and no sooner had past reason hated"). Then they discover that these pleasures were like a bait, that was specially prepared to distract them ("as a swallowed bait, on purpose laid to make the taker mad"). In spite of this, such attractions are strongly desired and frantically pursued ("made in pursuit and in possession so, had, having, and in quest, to have extreme"). However, as soon as they are obtained, they turn anticipated joy into sorrow ("a bliss in proof, and proved, a very woe, before a joy proposed behind a dream"). Although these distractive influences have been known, their nature has not been understood yet ("all this the world well knows yet none knows well"). This is why imposing some rigid moralistic or dogmatic limitations is not effective in dealing with them ("To shun the heaven that leads men to this hell"). Expert knowledge and an updated methodology are needed to deal with them effectively.

Viola in "Twelfth Night" alluded to such expert knowledge in her comment about Feste[129]:

> "This fellow is wise enough to play the fool;
> And to do that well craves a kind of wit:
> He must observe their mood on whom he jests,
> The quality of persons, and the time,
> And, like the haggard, cheque at every feather
> That comes before his eye. This is a practise
> As full of labour as a wise man's art
> For folly that he wisely shows is fit;
> But wise men, folly-fall'n, quite taint their wit."

This expert knowledge includes the understanding of to whom, what, how, and when to administer specific procedures.

---

[129] See "Feste". (Shakespeare for the Seeker, Volume 4, Chapter 7.1).

Purification (Sonnets 130 - 142)

SONNET CXXX

My Mistress' eyes are nothing like the Sun,
Coral is far more red, than her lips red,
If snow be white, why then her breasts are dun:
If hairs be wires, black wires grow on her head:
I have seen Roses damasked, red and white,
But no such Roses see I in her cheeks,
And in some perfumes is there more delight,
Than in the breath that from my Mistress reeks.
I love to hear her speak, yet well I know,
That Music hath a far more pleasing sound:
I grant I never saw a goddess go,
My Mistress when she walks treads on the ground.
    And yet by heaven I think my love as rare,
    As any she belied with false compare.

The poet gives details that further specify the nature of his mistress. Shakespeare uses a colour code to emphasize the developmental functionality of the poet's mistress. Namely, the description clearly indicates that the mistress' completion is neither red nor white ("coral is far more red, than her lips red, if snow be white, why then her breasts are dun"). Her hair is black ("if hairs be wires, black wires grow on her head"). The Lady's completion is "one of the four"; she is wholly "black". She is a symbolic representation of an impulse of evolutionary energy that, in accordance with this colour code, is destined for the activation of a purified aspect of the intellect faculty. In other words, she is the black Rose. The poet claims that it is irrelevant, therefore, to try to use such terms as delight or pleasing to describe the effect of her appearance ("and in some perfumes is there more delight than in the breath that from my mistress reeks; I love to hear her speak, yet well I know that music hath a far more pleasing sound"). Neither is it relevant to try to compare her to a goddess-like persona ("I grant I never saw a goddess go, my mistress, when she walks, treads on the ground"). The encounter with the Black Lady corresponds to a specific spiritual experience. This is why the poet stresses that his encounter with the Black Lady is unique and incomparable to any ordinary experience ("and yet by heaven I think my love as rare, as any she belied with false compare).

The Sonnet provides the context in which the following Sonnets are composed. Namely, the outward effect is deliberately interwoven with sexual innuendoes, which act as a veil behind which is hidden the description of the evolutionary process. The veil acts as a trap for those minds that are skewed by sensual overreactions and are conditioned by ordinary thinking patterns.

King Ferdinand demonstrated such an ordinary reaction. He could not understand Berowne's attraction to Rosaline, the Black Lady of "Love's Labour's Lost". For him black was the badge of hell, the colour of darkness, and a symbol of black art[130]:

> "O paradox! Black is the badge of hell,
> The hue of dungeons and the suit of night;
> And beauty's crest becomes the heavens well."

---

[130] See "French impulse" (Shakespeare for the Seeker, Volume 2, Chapter 5.3).

SONNET CXXXI

Thou art as tyrannous, so as thou art,
As those whose beauties proudly make them cruel;
For well thou know'st to my dear doting heart
Thou art the fairest and most precious Jewel.
Yet in good faith some say that thee behold,
Thy face hath not the power to make love groan;
To say they err, I dare not be so bold,
Although I swear it to myself alone.
And to be sure that is not false I swear
A thousand groans but thinking on thy face,
One on another's neck do witness bear
Thy black is fairest in my judgment's place.
    In nothing art thou black save in thy deeds,
    And thence this slander as I think proceeds.

The Black Lady symbolically represents experiences associated with the manifestation of a subtle aspect of the intellect. Such an encounter may be very challenging and confusing at first, because it leads to the realization of the limitation of ordinary knowledge and understanding. This is why such an experience is described as "tyrannous" and "cruel" ("thou art as tyrannous, so as thou art, as those whose beauties proudly make them cruel"). As long as sensual attractions are the prime driving forces, this inner "jewel" will remain beyond the poet's reach ("for well thou know'st to my dear doting heart thou art the fairest and most precious Jewel"). Yet some people say that the Lady is not beautiful enough to make them sigh with love ("yet in good faith some say that thee behold, thy face hath not the power to make love groan"). The poet realizes that there is no point in arguing with them ("to say they err, I dare not be so bold"). But he swears, to himself, that the Lady's blackness is the source of his most beautiful experiences ("I swear a thousand groans but thinking on thy face, one on another's neck do witness bear, thy black is fairest in my judgment's place"). And it is such an effect of her "blackness", or her secret functionality, that has contributed to the Black Lady's bad reputation ("In nothing art thou black save in thy deeds, and thence this slander as I think, proceeds").

Orsino's encounter with Olivia in "Twelfth Night" was also referred to as "cruel". Here is Orsino's comment about Olivia[131]:

> "Once more, Cesario,
> Get thee to yond same sovereign cruelty."

---

[131] See "Cruel maid" (Shakespeare for the Seeker, Volume 4, Chapter 7.1).

SONNET CXXXII

Thine eyes I love, and they as pitying me,
Knowing thy heart torment me with disdain,
Have put on black, and loving mourners be,
Looking with pretty ruth upon my pain.
And truly not the morning Sun of Heaven
Better becomes the grey cheeks of the East,
Nor that full star that ushers in the Even
Doth half that glory to the sober West
As those two morning eyes become thy face:
O let it then as well beseem thy heart
To mourn for me since mourning doth thee grace,
And suit thy pity like in every part.
    Then will I swear beauty herself is black,
    And all they foul that thy complexion lack

The poet describes his present state by comparing it to the expression of his mistress' eyes. Her eyes express pity as she tortures him with her contempt ("thine eyes I love, and they as pitying me, knowing thy heart torment me with disdain"). He admits that he is one of those men whose ignorance contributed to blackness of his mistress' eyes ("have put on black, and loving mourners be, looking with pretty ruth upon my pain"). A similar effect is described in the Sonnet 127. However, there is a substantial difference. Previously, the mistress' eyes were blackened as the result of other people's ignorance. Now the blackening of her eyes is caused by the poet's foolishness.

Like the rising sun in the morning or the appearance of the evening star, the blackening eyes are the sign of a transition, i.e., a certain predictable stage of the process ("and truly not the morning sun of heaven better becomes the grey cheeks of the east, nor that full star that ushers in the even doth half that glory to the sober west"). In other words, the poet's experience is part of the process, which may be compared to the gradual unveiling of the Black Lady's face ("as those two morning eyes become thy face"). Specifically, this experience marks the poet's entry onto the stage of spiritual purification. This is why the mourning of his earthly attachments contributes to his mistress' grace ("O let it then as well beseem thy heart to mourn for me since mourning doth thee grace, and suit thy pity like in every part"). This particular experience is referred to as "to die before dying" (see Sonnet 45). It is the stage where emotional and intellectual attachments are gradually removed. The poet's re-entry in the stage of purification is a sign of his gradual progress along the path. This is why all those who have not yet experienced "blackness" will remain ignorant of their own potentiality ("then will I swear beauty herself is black, and all they foul that thy complexion lack").

Othello led Desdemona through such a very difficult transition[132]. Desdemona had to "die" to her worldly attachments, so she could save others:

> "Yet I'll not shed her blood;
> Nor scar that whiter skin of hers than snow,
> And smooth as monumental alabaster.
> Yet she must die, else she'll betray more men."

---

[132] See "Transition" (Shakespeare for the Seeker, Volume 3, Chapter 6.2).

SONNET CXXXIII

Beshrew that heart that makes my heart to groan
For that deep wound it gives my friend and me;
Is't not enough to torture me alone,
But slave to slavery my sweet'st friend must be.
Me from myself thy cruel eye hath taken,
And my next self thou harder hast engrossed,
Of him, myself, and thee I am forsaken,
A torment thrice three-fold thus to be crossed:
Prison my heart in thy steel bosom's ward,
But then my friend's heart let my poor heart bail,
Whoe'er keeps me, let my heart be his guard,
Thou canst not then use rigour in my Jail.
    And yet thou wilt, for I, being pent in thee,
    Perforce am thine and all that is in me.

Now we witness reappearance of the three elements of an advanced evolutionary triad, i.e., the poet, the Black Lady, and the Guide. More precisely, it is the poet's partially purified aspect of the intellect that constitutes the third part of the triad. Previously, the poet experienced the manifestation of the triad during his initiation (Sonnet 40). Afterwards, he alluded to it in his meditation about the unity of trinity in Sonnet 105. It helps to understand the poet's present situation to realize that the appearance of the Black Lady was induced by the Guide (as the Guide is in control of "all hues" - see Sonnet 29). In other words, the Black Lady is part of the Guide's essence.

Presently, the poet curses the Black Lady for wounding him and, supposedly, the Guide ("beshrew that heart that makes my heart to groan for that deep wound it gives my friend and me"). The poet assumes that the Black Lady has also seduced the Guide ("is't not enough to torture me alone, but slave to slavery my sweet'st friend must be"). He accuses the Lady of destroying him and his friend, whom he considers to be his second self ("me from myself thy cruel eye hath taken, and my next self thou harder hast engrossed"). He refers to his state as being tree-fold injury, because the Guide, the poet, and the Black Lady have been affected ("of him, myself, and thee I am forsaken, a torment thrice three-fold thus to be crossed"). He does not realize yet, that his present experience is driven by the operation of an evolutionary triad. Previously, he referred to the triad in Sonnet 105 as "Fair, kind, and true". But he does not understand that the overall process requires the unity of these three elements. Unity may be realized through the poet's complete submersion within the Guide's essence. Only in this way may he be united with the Guide and the Black Lady. The poet, however, is still not able to grasp the concept of the unity of trinity, the state when all three become one. Therefore, he pleads with the Lady that she should free his friend, while he himself will remain her prisoner ("prison my heart in thy steel bosom's ward, but then my friend's heart let my poor heart bail"). And he asks that his heart be put in charge of guarding his friend. So, in this prison, the Lady will not be able to exercise her cruelty ("whoe'er keeps me, let my heart be his guard, thou canst not then use rigour in my jail"). Yet, the poet realizes that the Lady is in control of his entire being ("and yet thou wilt, for I, being pent in thee, perforce am thine and all that is in me"). Therefore, he has no hope for any signs of mercy.

The poet's sufferings are the results of disappointment and jealousy, which are the manifestations of spiritual impurities. The Guide induces these feelings, so the poet may discover how easily he can be disturbed by his ordinary emotions. Let's recall, that Othello also used jealousy to unmask Iago's villainy. It is only at the end of the play that Iago understood that Othello outsmarted him. Here is Iago's final remark to Othello[133]:

> "Demand me nothing: what you know, you know:
> From this time forth I never will speak word."

---

[133] See "Transition" (Shakespeare for the Seeker, Volume 3, Chapter 6.2).

SONNET CXXXIV

So now I have confessed that he is thine,
And I my self am mortgaged to thy will,
Myself I'll forfeit, so that other mine,
Thou wilt restore to be my comfort still:
But thou wilt not, nor he will not be free,
For thou art covetous, and he is kind,
He learned but surety-like to write for me,
Under that bond that him as fast doth bind.
The statute of thy beauty thou wilt take,
Thou usurer that put'st forth all to use,
And sue a friend, came debtor for my sake,
So him I lose through my unkind abuse.
    Him have I lost; thou hast both him and me,
    He pays the whole, and yet am I not free.

The poet still does not understand the Guide's actions. He thinks that the Guide, while wooing the Black Lady on the poet's behalf, fell in love with her. Therefore, the poet pleads with the Lady that she should accept his love instead but let his friend go free ("myself I'll forfeit, so that other mine, thou wilt restore to be my comfort still"). So his friend's freedom will bring him some comfort ("thou wilt restore to be my comfort still"). But the poet is convinced that the Lady will not let his friend go ("but thou wilt not, nor he will not be free"). He tells the Lady that she is greedy, and he refers to his friend as kind ("for thou art covetous, and he is kind"). According to the poet, his friend became the Lady's slave, because he mortgaged himself to bail out the poet ("he learned but surety-like to write for me, under that bond that him as fast doth bind"). The poet accuses the Lady of acting as a usurer by using her beauty ("the statute of thy beauty thou wilt take, thou usurer, that put'st forth all to use"). His friend became the Lady's debtor for the sake of the poet; and now the Lady pursues him. As a result, the poet lost his friend ("and sue a friend, came debtor for my sake, so him

I lose through my unkind abuse"). Now the Lady has both, the poet and his friend. Although the poet's friend paid off the entire debt, yet the poet is not free ("him have I lost; thou hast both him and me, he pays the whole, and yet am I not free").

The Sonnet indicates that the poet's inner state is still fragmented and disunited. The poet uses the terms "thine", "my self", and "other mine" to describe three elements of the triad, i.e., the Lady, himself, and the Guide. It is only when he will experience the unity of all three elements of the triad that he will be able to move forward along the path.

Shakespeare described a similar situation in "Much Ado About Nothing". In the play Don Pedro performed the same role as the Guide, i.e., he wooed Hero on Claudio's behalf[134]:

> "I will assume thy part in some disguise
> And tell fair Hero I am Claudio,
> And in her bosom I'll unclasp my heart
> And take her hearing prisoner with the force
> And strong encounter of my amorous tale."

---

[134] See "The Guide" (Shakespeare for the Seeker, Volume 3, Chapter 6.3).

SONNET CXXXV

Whoever hath her wish, thou hast thy *Will*,
And *Will* to boot, and *Will* in over-plus,
More than enough am I that vexed thee still,
To thy sweet will making addition thus.
Wilt thou whose will is large and spacious,
Not once vouchsafe to hide my will in thine,
Shall will in others seem right gracious,
And in my will no fair acceptance shine:
The sea all water, yet receives rain still,
And in abundance addeth to his store,
So thou being rich in *Will* add to thy *Will*,
One will of mine to make thy large *Will* more.
    Let no unkind, no fair beseechers kill,
    Think all but one, and me in that one *Will*.

The important thing is to recognize that this Sonnet is addressed by the poet to the Guide. The poet refers to the Guide as "no unkind" and to himself as "no fair". Let's recall that "fair, kind, and true" are the three parts of the evolutionary triad. In this way Shakespeare indicates that the poet remains an incongruent part of the triad. In his interaction with the Black Lady, the poet has breached proper conduct. Now, he pleads with the Guide for his forgiveness.

The poet starts to understand the difference between "her wish" and "thy Will". There is a subtle but a significant difference. In the context of the Sonnet, the "wish" is expressed by her, i.e., the Black Lady. It applies to the poet's sensual desires. The "Will", on the other hand, applies to the supreme priority that is represented by the intention and the actions of the Guide ("whoever hath her wish, thou hast thy Will"). This meaning is further emphasized by the italicisation of the word "Will". The Guide's "will" is to make extra ordinary efforts that are compliant with the supreme priority ("and Will to boot, and Will in over-plus"). The poet admits that his behaviour was much below the Guide's expectations ("am I that vexed thee still"). Now he asks the Guide for one more chance ("to thy sweet will making addition thus"). Namely, the poet asks whether it is possible to invoke the Guide's evolutionary functionality and erase the poet's previous mistakes ("wilt thou whose will is large and spacious, not once vouchsafe to hide my will in thine"). How is it, asks the poet, that others' actions seem to be acceptable, while his efforts are disapproved ("shall will in others seem right gracious, and in my will no fair acceptance shine"). The poet argues that even Nature, in her abundance, grants benefits to all ("the sea all water, yet receives rain still, and in abundance addeth to his store"). Therefore, the poet expects that the Guide should follow the example and override the poet's free but misleading will, and in this way benefit himself ("so thou, being rich in Will add to thy Will, one will of mine, to make thy large Will more"). The poet implies that it is not right for the Guide to punish him ("let no unkind, no fair beseechers kill"). The poet hopes that the Guide's mercy will allow him to continue the journey ("Think all but one, and me in that one Will").

The poet's pleading for mercy was echoed by Portia's appeal[135] to Shylock in "The Merchant of Venice":

> "The quality of mercy is not strain'd,
> It droppeth as the gentle rain from heaven
> Upon the place beneath: it is twice blest;
> It blesseth him that gives and him that takes."

---

[135] See "Final touches" (Shakespeare for the Seeker, Volume 3, Chapter 6.4).

SONNET CXXXVI

If thy soul check thee that I come so near,
Swear to thy blind soul that I was thy *Will*,
And will thy soul knows is admitted there,
Thus far for love, my love-suit sweet fulfil.
Will, will fulfil the treasure of thy love,
I fill it full with wills, and my will one,
In things of great receipt with ease we prove,
Among a number one is reckoned none.
Then in the number let me pass untold,
Though in thy store's account I one must be,
For nothing hold me, so it please thee hold,
That nothing me, a something sweet to thee.
    Make but my name thy love, and love that still,
    And then thou lovest me for my name is *Will*.

The poet continues his appeal to the Guide. He tries to convince the Guide that he is worthy of his love. If the Guide's soul announces that the poet is near, the Guide should admit that it was his will that brought the poet there ("if thy soul check thee that I come so near, swear to thy blind soul that I was thy will"). The Guide's soul knows that the poet is to be admitted for the sake of love, so his loving suit may be accepted ("and will thy soul knows is admitted there, thus far for love, my love-suit sweet fulfil"). The Guide's will, therefore, will be fulfilled ("*Will*, will fulfil the treasure of thy love"). The poet admits that he is full of many desires, but only one of them may prove to be important ("I fill it full with wills, and my will one, in things of great receipt with ease we prove"). Within unity, one counts for nothing ("among a number one is reckoned none"). So, within unity the poet disappears, although he is an essential part of it ("then in the number let me pass untold, though in thy store's account I one must be"). He claims that he is not attached to anything ("for nothing hold me"). He asks to be considered as nothing, so he may be of some value within the unity ("that nothing me, a something sweet to thee"). The poet claims that he is nothing but a mark of love, and he is constant in loving his Guide ("make but my name thy love, and love that still"). So the Guide should love him because he is the manifestation of the Guide's will ("and then thou lovest me for my name is *Will*"). The notion of "nothing me" or "thou single wilt prove none" was introduced by the Guide in his first counsel (see Sonnet 8).

Richard II[136] arrived at a similar conclusion, i.e., he was of some value only once he realized that he was nothing:

> "And straight am nothing: but whate'er I be,
> Nor I nor any man that but man is
> With nothing shall be pleased, till he be eased
> With being nothing."

---

[136] See "Preliminary realization" (Shakespeare for the Seeker, Volume 1, Chapter 1).

SONNET CXXXVII

Thou blind fool love, what dost thou to mine eyes,
That they behold and see not what they see:
They know what beauty is, see where it lies,
Yet what the best is, take the worst to be.
If eyes corrupt by over-partial looks,
Be anchored in the bay where all men ride,
Why of eyes falsehood hast thou forged hooks,
Whereto the judgment of my heart is tied?
Why should my heart think that a several plot,
Which my heart knows the wide world's common place?
Or mine eyes seeing this, say this is not
To put fair truth upon so foul a face,
>   In things right true my heart and eyes have erred,
>   And to this false plague are they now transferred.

After experiencing a first taste of union with the Guide ("I one must be"), the poet discovers the folly of ordinary and sensual love. Shakespeare uses Cupid, who is usually depicted as a blind boy, as a symbol of sensual and emotional attractions. This is why the poet refers to ordinary love as a blind fool ("thou blind fool love, what dost thou to mine eyes"). Ordinary love is governed by the ordinary physical senses ("mine eyes"), which are immune to objective truth ("that they behold and see not what they see"). Therefore, the poet realizes that he cannot rely on them to judge what "the best" and what "the worst" is ("they know what beauty is, see where it lies, yet what the best is, take the worst to be"). The eyes can only see the distorted and fragmented world of ordinary men ("if eyes corrupt by over-partial looks, be anchored in the bay where all men ride"). The poet complains that his emotions have been induced by this distorted image ("why of eyes falsehood hast thou forged hooks, whereto the judgment of my heart is tied?)" Why should he think that there is anything special in the world, when his heart knows it is a common and ordinary thing ("why should my heart think that a several plot, which my heart knows the wide world's common place"). Or why should he think that there is no truth in something, because his eyes see it as unattractive ("or mine eyes seeing this, say this is not to put fair truth upon so foul a face"). In the final couplet, the poet accuses his senses and emotions of misleading him ("in things right true my heart and eyes have erred, and to this false plague are they now transferred"). Previously, he has entirely relied on his physical senses (see Sonnets 46 and 47). Now he starts to realize the limitations of ordinary senses and emotions.

In the final scene of "Twelfth Night", Duke Orsino also discovered the limitations of ordinary senses[137]:

> "One face, one voice, one habit, and two persons,
> A natural perspective, that is and is not!"

---

[137] See "Evolutionary impulse" (Shakespeare for the Seeker, Volume 4, Chapter 7.1).

SONNET CXXXVIII

When my love swears that she is made of truth,
I do believe her though I know she lies,
That she might think me some untutored youth,
Unlearned in the world's false subtleties.
Thus vainly thinking that she thinks me young,
Although she knows my days are past the best,
Simply I credit her false-speaking tongue,
On both sides thus is simple truth suppressed:
But wherefore says she not she is unjust?
And wherefore say not I that I am old?
O love's best habit is in seeming trust,
And age in love, loves not to have years told.
    Therefore I lie with her, and she with me,
    And in our faults by lies we flattered be.

In the previous Sonnet, the poet alluded to the limitations of physical senses, which drive ordinary emotions. In this Sonnet he uses the terms "love" and "her" to describe the working of ordinary emotions ("her false-speaking tongue"). The poet presents himself as being driven by a deceiving self ("vainly thinking"). Prior to his recent experiences, the poet's modus operandi was driven by the interactions between his emotions and his deceiving self. He would, therefore, accept whatever pleased him, even though he knew that it was not true ("when my love swears that she is made of truth, I do believe her though I know she lies"). The poet starts to recognize that such a way of living corresponds to that of an untutored boy, who is ignorant of the deceitfulness of the ordinary world ("that she might think me some untutored youth, unlearned in the world's false subtleties"). Now the poet realizes that by relying on his emotions he would be deceiving himself ("thus vainly thinking that she thinks me young, although she knows my days are past the best"). This is exactly what the Guide warned him against in Sonnet 3: instead of developing his inner being the poet would be wasting his precious time by indulging in trivial pursuits. As long as the poet remains in such a state of sleep, he is cut-off from the possibility to experience truth ("simply I credit her false-speaking tongue, on both sides thus is simple truth suppressed"). He asks himself why he does remain in such a deceiving state of sleep ("but wherefore says she not she is unjust; and wherefore say not I that I am old"). And he answers himself that the reason is self-flattery and the illusions of emotions ("love's best habit is in seeming trust, and age in love, loves not to have years told"). The poet concludes with the observation that, by accepting the flattery of his deceiving self, he is led further into the abyss ("therefore I lie with her, and she with me, and in our faults by lies we flattered be").

In his famous soliloquy, Hamlet also referred to such a deceiving state of sleep[138]:

> "To sleep; no more; and by a sleep to say we end
> The heart-ache and the thousand natural shocks
> That flesh is heir to, 'tis a consummation
> Devoutly to be wish'd."

---

[138] See "To be or not to be" (Shakespeare for the Seeker, Volume 4, Chapter 7.3).

SONNET CXXXIX

O call not me to justify the wrong,
That thy unkindness lays upon my heart,
Wound me not with thine eye but with thy tongue,
Use power with power, and slay me not by Art,
Tell me thou lov'st elsewhere; but in my sight,
Dear heart forbear to glance thine eye aside,
What need'st thou wound with cunning when thy might
Is more than my over-pressed defence can bide?
Let me excuse thee, ah my love well knows,
Her pretty looks have been mine enemies,
And therefore from my face she turns my foes,
That they else-where might dart their injuries:
  Yet do not so, but since I am near slain,
  Kill me outright with looks, and rid my pain.

It is not an easy task to overcome emotional attachments. It is going to take several attempts before the poet is able to accomplish it. The poet can achieve his goal only with the help of the Black Lady. Let's remember that the Black Lady's unkindness is a reflection of the poet's behaviour, and her eyes are a mirror reflection of the poet's inner state (see Sonnet 132). This is why the poet protests against being called to justify the Lady's unkindness ("call not me to justify the wrong that thy unkindness lays upon my heart"). It is easier for him to face her words than her look ("wound me not with thine eye but with thy tongue"). Yet, he realizes, that there is no point in allowing his deceiving self to influence his behaviour anymore. To make progress, he has to eliminate the influence of his corrupted self ("use power with power, and slay me not by art"). So, he asks the Lady to use all her might to kill his emotional and sensual attachments ("what need'st thou wound with cunning when thy might is more than my over-pressed defence can bide"). He says that he will excuse her for doing it ("let me excuse thee"). He knows that the Lady's eyes have been his enemies and this is why she turns her eyes away from him ("her pretty looks have been mine enemies, and therefore from my face she turns my foes"). The Lady's eyes blast the poet's self-conceit. It is a painful experience. The poet realizes, however, that although the Black Lady's looks are painful, they are needed. Therefore he asks the Black Lady to finish her job and kill his attachments, so he may be freed from emotional pain ("yet do not so, but since I am near slain, kill me outright with looks, and rid my pain").

The poet's present experience is paralleled by that of Berowne in "Love's Labour's Lost". Berowne discovered that women's eyes were the most effective way leading towards inner development. Here is Berowne's assessment of the effect of women's eyes[139]:

> "From women's eyes this doctrine I derive:
> They sparkle still the right Promethean fire;
> They are the books, the arts, the academes,
> That show, contain and nourish all the world:
> Else none at all in ought proves excellent."

---

[139] See "The being of Navarre" (Shakespeare for the Seeker, Volume 2, Chapter 5.3).

SONNET CXL

Be wise as thou art cruel, do not press
My tongue-tied patience with too much disdain:
Lest sorrow lend me words and words express,
The manner of my pity wanting pain.
If I might teach thee wit, better it were,
Though not to love, yet love to tell me so,
As testy sick-men when their deaths be near,
No news but health from their Physicians know.
For if I should despair I should grow mad,
And in my madness might speak ill of thee,
Now this ill wresting world is grown so bad,
Mad slanderers by mad ears believed be.
    That I may not be so, nor thou be lied,
    Bear thine eyes straight, though thy proud heart go wide.

The poet appeals to the Black Lady to be gentle with him while he is going through this very difficult experience ("be wise as thou art cruel, do not press my tongue-tied patience with too much disdain"). He is afraid that he might start to complain about his sufferings ("lest sorrow lend me words and words express, the manner of my pity wanting pain"). The poet suggests to the Lady that she might help by telling him, even if it is not true, that she does love him ("If I might teach thee wit, better it were, though not to love, yet love to tell me so"). This would make things much easier for him. He compares his situation to that of impatient dying men, who cannot listen to anything but good prognosis from their physicians ("as testy sick-men when their deaths be near, no news but health from their Physicians know"). Otherwise, the poet is afraid of going mad and in his madness he may speak ill of her ("for if I should despair I should grow mad, and in my madness might speak ill of thee"). Ignorant people may overhear him and start to spread rumours and lies about her ("now this ill wresting world is grown so bad, mad slanderers by mad ears believed be").

So, to prevent him from going mad and to protect her against lies, the poet asks the Lady to look straight into his eyes, even though her heart wanders in some other direction ("that I may not be so, nor thou be lied, bear thine eyes straight, though thy proud heart go wide").

Feste in his song in "Twelfth Night" also referred to such a fair but cruel maid[140]:

> "Come away, come away, death,
> And in sad cypress let me be laid;
> Fly away, fly away breath;
> I am slain by a fair cruel maid."

---

[140] See "Cruel maid" (Shakespeare for the Seeker, Volume 4, Chapter 7.1).

SONNET CXLI

In faith I do not love thee with mine eyes,
For they in thee a thousand errors note,
But 'tis my heart that loves what they despise,
Who in despite of view is pleased to dote.
Nor are mine ears with thy tongue's tune delighted,
Nor tender feeling to base touches prone,
Nor taste, nor smell, desire to be invited
To any sensual feast with thee alone:
But my five wits, nor my five senses can
Dissuade one foolish heart from serving thee,
Who leaves unswayed the likeness of a man,
Thy proud heart's slave and vassal wretch to be:
    Only my plague thus far I count my gain,
    That she that makes me sin, awards me pain.

In the previous four Sonnets, the poet has discovered the limitations imposed by ordinary senses. This is why he says that he does not love the Lady because of her external appearance ("in faith I do not love thee with mine eyes, for they in thee a thousand errors note"). The poet admits that in his present state he is not driven by his ordinary emotions ("but 'tis my heart that loves what they despise, who in despite of view is pleased to dote"). He knows that true love is not dependent on the physical senses of sight, hearing, touch, taste, or smell ("nor are mine ears with thy tongue's tune delighted, nor tender feeling to base touches prone, nor taste, nor smell, desire to be invited to any sensual feast with thee alone"). Neither his ordinary faculties can deter him from loving her ("my five wits, nor my five senses can dissuade one foolish heart from serving thee"). He knows that his love is going to destroy his ordinary self and his present slavery ("who leaves unswayed the likeness of a man, thy proud heart's slave and vassal wretch to be"). His only hope is that the pain caused by his present state may force him to make further efforts towards freeing himself from slavery ("only my plague thus far I count my gain, that she that makes me sin, awards me pain").

Rosalind in "As You Like It" tried to explain to Silvius that his love was driven by his ordinary emotions[141]:

> "You foolish shepherd, wherefore do you follow her,
> Like foggy south puffing with wind and rain?
> You are a thousand times a properer man
> Than she a woman: 'tis such fools as you
> That makes the world full of ill-favour'd children."

---

[141] See "The Forest of Arden" (Shakespeare for the Seeker, Volume 2, Chapter 5.2).

SONNET CXLII

Love is my sin, and thy dear virtue hate,
Hate of my sin, grounded on sinful loving,
O but with mine, compare thou thine own state,
And thou shalt find it merits not reproving,
Or if it do, not from those lips of thine,
That have profaned their scarlet ornaments,
And sealed false bonds of love as oft as mine,
Robbed others' beds' revenues of their rents.
Be it lawful I love thee, as thou lov'st those,
Whom thine eyes woo as mine importune thee,
Root pity in thy heart that when it grows,
Thy pity may deserve to pitied be.
> If thou dost seek to have what thou dost hide,
> By self-example mayst thou be denied.

It helps to interpret the Sonnet to keep in mind that the term "love" and the poet's attraction to the Lady are not driven by ordinary emotions. But ordinary emotions interfere with it and make his experience very difficult. This is why he says that his current love is painful, but the Lady's disapproval of his present state is constructive ("love is my sin, and thy dear virtue hate, hate of my sin, grounded on sinful loving"). Although the poet has understood a few things about himself and about the path, he still reacts as an immature boy. Instead of focusing his attention on his own shortcomings, he quarrels with the Lady about her behaviour ("but with mine, compare thou thine own state, and thou shalt find it merits not reproving"). The presence of the Lady is intentionally induced as part of the developmental sequence. The poet keeps forgetting that the Lady's behaviour is a mirror reflection of his own inner self ("and sealed false bonds of love as oft as mine, robbed others' beds' revenues of their rents"). In his folly, the poet demands to be allowed to harass the Lady with his desires in the same way as she seduces others ("be it lawful I love thee, as thou lov'st those, whom thine eyes woo as mine importune thee"). So, by having pity for the poet, she may earn pity for herself ("root pity in thy heart that when it grows, thy pity may deserve to pitied be"). He arrogantly warns the Lady that if she does not give away what she is hiding, then by the same example, she herself will be deprived of it ("if thou dost seek to have what thou dost hide, by self-example mayst thou be denied").

The same degree of ignorance and arrogance was demonstrated by Hamlet, when he assumed that he could control the afterlife of another man[142]:

> "A villain kills my father; and for that,
> I, his sole son, do this same villain send to heaven.
> O, this is hire and salary, not revenge."

Whenever the poet derails from the right path, the Guide intervenes with a corrective counsel. So it is in this case. The last couplet of the Sonnet clearly marks the poet's departure from the right track. It is time for the Guide's next and last counsel.

---

[142] See "The players' performance" (Shakespeare for the Seeker, Volume 4, Chapter 7.3).

The Guide's fourteenth counsel (Sonnet 143)

SONNET CXLIII

Lo as a careful housewife runs to catch,
One of her feathered creatures broke away,
Sets down her babe and makes all swift dispatch
In pursuit of the thing she would have stay:
Whilst her neglected child holds her in chase,
Cries to catch her whose busy care is bent,
To follow that which flies before her face:
Not prizing her poor infant's discontent;
So runn'st thou after that which flies from thee,
Whilst I thy babe chase thee afar behind,
But if thou catch thy hope, turn back to me:
And play the mother's part, kiss me, be kind.
    So will I pray that thou mayst have thy Will,
    If thou turn back and my loud crying still.

Each time the poet starts to divert from the straight path, the Guide has to intervene into the process. It looks that the poet's latest "offence" towards the Black Lady was the sign of another departure from the prescribed path.

The Guide draws a parallel between the poet and a housewife who, distracted by a runaway hen, left her own child unattended ("as a careful housewife runs to catch, one of her feathered creatures broke away, sets down her babe and makes all swift dispatch"). Similarly, preoccupied with his emotions the poet ignores the Guide and his counsels ("in pursuit of the thing she would have stay: whilst her neglected child holds her in chase"). The Guide tells the poet that he has not valued enough his developmental opportunity. The Guide compares himself to a "child", whom the poet has abandoned while chasing after fleeting emotions ("not prizing her poor infant's discontent; so runn'st thou after that which flies from thee"). The Guide appeals to the poet to return to him ("but if thou catch thy hope, turn back to me: and play the mother's part, kiss me, be kind"). Only then the Guide will be able to invoke his evolutionary functionality and grant the poet his will, i.e., the request that the poet made in Sonnet 135 ("so will I pray that thou mayst have thy will"). By returning, the poet will fulfil the Guide's demand ("if thou turn back and my loud crying still").

This is the Guide's last counsel. All that which the poet has needed was given to him. Now it is up to him to use it correctly.

Bertram in "All's Well That Ends Well" went through a similar experience when he run away from Helena. At that time he declared that he would never return[143]:

> "When thou canst get the ring upon my finger which
> never shall come off, and show me a child begotten
> of thy body that I am father to, then call me
> husband: but in such a 'then' I write a 'never'."

Yet, as we have seen in the quote that is inserted in the discussion of Sonnet 110, Helena was able to bring him back onto the right track. So, there is still hope for the poet of the Sonnets.

---

[143] See "Pilgrimage" (Shakespeare for the Seeker, Volume 2, Chapter 5.1).

Dying (Sonnets 144 - 152)

SONNET CXLIV

Two loves I have of comfort and despair,
Which like two spirits do suggest me still,
The better angel is a man right fair:
The worser spirit a woman coloured ill.
To win me soon to hell my female evil,
Tempteth my better angel from my sight,
And would corrupt my saint to be a devil:
Wooing his purity with her foul pride.
And whether that my angel be turn'd fiend,
Suspect I may, yet not directly tell,
But being both from me both to each friend,
I guess one angel in another's hell.
    Yet this shall I ne'er know but live in doubt,
    Till my bad angel fire my good one out.

The Guide is using the Lady to help the poet get rid of his weaknesses. Therefore, both the Guide and the Lady are working together. The poet constitutes the third part of this evolutionary triad, which consists of the kind (the Guide), the true (the Lady), and the fair (the poet). The Guide's and the Lady's aim is to bring the poet onto a higher level of being by uniting all three parts into one. In this way a new inner being may be formed. But the poet does not understand the situation he is in. Instead, he is looking at the Guide and the Lady as two opposite forces pulling him in two different directions ("two loves I have of comfort and despair, which like two spirits do suggest me still"). In accordance with moralistic convention, he assumes that one force is good, while the other is bad ("the better angel is a man right fair: the worser spirit a woman coloured ill"). He does not see that these two opposites are working together. The poet thinks that the Lady is trying to seduce the Guide, so it will be easier for her to gain further control over him ("to win me soon to hell my female evil, tempteth my better angel from my sight"). According to the poet, the Lady is using her charm to corrupt the Guide ("and would corrupt my saint to be a devil: wooing his purity with her foul pride"). And he suspects that the Guide will be trapped by the Lady ("and whether that my angel be turn'd fiend, suspect I may, yet not directly tell"). Driven by his jealousy, he imagines that the Guide has already been seduced by the Lady ("but being both from me both to each friend, I guess one angel in another's hell"). Yet, the poet is not quite sure what is going on. His suspicions may be confirmed only when the Lady frees the Guide from her prison; till that time the poet will live in doubt ("yet this shall I ne'er know but live in doubt, till my bad angel fire my good one out").

A situation of constructive use of jealousy was also implemented by Othello. Here is Othello setting up Iago[144]:

> "No, Iago;
> I'll see before I doubt; when I doubt, prove;
> And on the proof, there is no more but this,
> Away at once with love or jealousy!"

The target of Iago's deception was not Othello, but the readers and the audiences watching the play.

---

[144] See "Transition" (Shakespeare for the Seeker, Volume 3, Chapter 6.2).

SONNET CXLV

Those lips that Love's own hand did make,
Breathed forth the sound that said I hate,
To me that languished for her sake:
But when she saw my woeful state,
Straight in her heart did mercy come,
Chiding that tongue that ever sweet,
Was used in giving gentle doom:
And taught it thus anew to greet:
I hate she altered with an end,
That followed it as gentle day,
Doth follow night who like a fiend
From heaven to hell is flown away.
    I hate, from hate away she threw,
    And saved my life, saying not you.

It is the first time that the poet is able to experience a moment of true sincerity. During this brief moment he raised himself above his ordinary emotions. This is further indicated by the structure of the Sonnet, which breaks off with the form of the iambic pentameter. Instead, Sonnet 145 is written in the iambic tetrameter, i.e., a less sophisticated form. So is the poet's reflection. Somehow, his previous over-sophisticated and over-intellectualized meditations have been put aside. In its place the poet delivers a simpler but sincere reflection. It is this moment of sincerity that allows him to recognize another side of the Black Lady. This time he is able to feel her warmth and compassion ("but when she saw my woeful state, straight in her heart did mercy come"). The poet was expecting the usual reproach and scolding ("chiding that tongue that ever sweet, was used in giving gentle doom"). And he anticipated an expression of hatred ("and taught it thus anew to greet: I hate she altered with an end"). Instead, the Lady told him that she does not hate him; she hates his inner corrupted self. And this gave the poet much hope ("I hate, from hate away she threw, and saved my life, saying not you"). For the poet it was like the arrival of day after night, or an evil spirit departing to hell ("that followed it as gentle day, doth follow night, who like a fiend from heaven to hell is flown away").

Proteus in "Two Gentlemen of Verona" went through a similar experience[145] when he discovered the inner beauty of Julia:

> "What is in Silvia's face, but I may spy
> More fresh in Julia's with a constant eye?"

---

[145] See "Implementation" (Shakespeare for the Seeker, Volume 3, Chapter 6.7).

SONNET CXLVI

Poor soul the centre of my sinful earth,
My sinful earth these rebel powers that thee array,
Why dost thou pine within and suffer dearth
Painting thy outward walls so costly gay?
Why so large cost having so short a lease,
Dost thou upon thy fading mansion spend?
Shall worms inheritors of this excess,
Eat up thy charge? is this thy body's end?
Then soul live thou upon thy servant's loss,
And let that pine to aggravate thy store;
Buy terms divine in selling hours of dross:
Within be fed, without be rich no more,
    So shall thou feed on death, that feeds on men,
    And death once dead, there's no more dying then.

The moment of sincerity allows the poet not only to perceive the other side of the Black Lady. Through this experience he also gained insights into his inner self. Now he compares his inner being to the vital centre of his body ("poor soul the centre of my sinful earth"). And he saw that his earthly attachments were preventing his inner being to grow ("my sinful earth these rebel powers that thee array"). The poet is asking how it is possible that his inner being is starving while his exterior is so richly decorated? ("Why dost thou pine within and suffer dearth painting thy outward walls so costly gay?") And why is he spending so much on that deteriorating and short-lived body? ("Why so large cost having so short a lease, dost thou upon thy fading mansion spend?") He realizes that all of this investment on his body is simply preparation of food for worms. He asks himself, is this the overall purpose of life? ("Shall worms inheritors of this excess, eat up thy charge? is this thy body's end?") If this is the case, then let the inner being be fed at the body's expense, and let the body fade away while his inner being accumulates the riches ("then soul live thou upon thy servant's loss, and let that pine to aggravate thy store"). Let the inner being grow at the expense of worldly pursuits ("buy terms divine in selling hours of dross: within be fed, without be rich no more"). In this way, the inner being may be fed on death, while death is fed on ordinary men ("so shall thou feed on death, that feeds on men"). And this meditation leads the poet to grasping the meaning of the formula "to die before dying". The poet concludes that once he manages to die to the worldly riches, he will be beyond death's reach ("and death once dead, there's no more dying then"). At this point the poet enters the stage of "dying".

Hamlet also managed to arrive at the stage of "dying". The moment of his "dying" was clearly defined[146]:

"I am dead, Horatio."

It was then that he was able to experience the state "to be". It lasted till Hamlet's physical death. During that time Hamlet understood everything that had happened to him.

---

[146] See "The fencing match" (Shakespeare for the Seeker, Volume 4, Chapter 7.3).

SONNET CXLVII

My love is as a fever longing still,
For that which longer nurseth the disease,
Feeding on that which doth preserve the ill,
The uncertain sickly appetite to please:
My reason the Physician to my love,
Angry that his prescriptions are not kept
Hath left me, and I desperate now approve,
Desire is death, which Physic did except.
Past cure I am, now Reason is past care,
And frantic made with ever-more unrest,
My thoughts and my discourse as madmen's are,
At random from the truth vainly expressed.
    For I have sworn thee fair, and thought thee bright,
    Who art as black as hell, as dark as night.

The poet describes his experience of "dying before dying". He says that his love is like longing for fever, which sustains his illness ("my love is as a fever longing still, for that which longer nurseth the disease"). In other words, his love is fed on that which leads to death ("feeding on that which doth preserve the ill"). His love lives on whatever feeds his illness by promising to satisfy his insatiable desires ("feeding on that which doth preserve the ill, the uncertain sickly appetite to please"). His reasoning, i.e., the doctor who was treating his love, has abandoned him because the poet was ignoring his prescription ("my reason the physician to my love, angry that his prescriptions are not kept hath left me"). Now, the poet agrees with the doctor's diagnosis, which said that his desires were killing him ("and I desperate now approve desire is death, which physic did except"). The poet is now incurable and it is too late for any reasonable solutions ("past cure I am, now reason is past care"). He has become anxious and restless ("frantic made with ever-more unrest"). He thinks and speaks like a madman, uttering erratic statements ("my thoughts and my discourse as madmen's are, at random from the truth vainly expressed"). As an example of his madness he quotes his inconstant view of the Lady, whom sometimes he sees as beautiful and radiant, and then perceives as vile and gloomy ("for I have sworn thee fair, and thought thee bright, who art as black as hell, as dark as night").

Duke Orsino in "Twelfth Night" was in a similar state when for the first time he saw Olivia[147]:

> "That instant was I turn'd into a hart;
> And my desires, like fell and cruel hounds,
> E'er since pursue me."

---

[147] See "Cruel maid" (Shakespeare for the Seeker, Volume 4, Chapter 7.1).

SONNET CXLVIII

O me! what eyes hath love put in my head,
Which have no correspondence with true sight,
Or if they have, where is my judgment fled,
That censures falsely what they see aright?
If that be fair whereon my false eyes dote,
What means the world to say it is not so?
If it be not, then love doth well denote,
Love's eye is not so true as all men's: no,
How can it? O how can love's eye be true,
That is so vexed with watching and with tears?
No marvel then though I mistake my view,
The sun itself sees not, till heaven clears.
    O cunning love, with tears thou keep'st me blind,
    Lest eyes well seeing thy foul faults should find.

The poet wonders what kind of eyes, which cannot see correctly, has love put into his head ("what eyes hath love put in my head, which have no correspondence with true sight"). Or if his eyes see correctly, then what has happened to his judgement that makes him criticize what they see ("or if they have, where is my judgment fled, that censures falsely what they see aright"). If his eyes really see true beauty, why does the rest of the world not agree with him? ("If that be fair whereon my false eyes dote, what means the world to say it is not so?") But if this is not true beauty, then this means that love blurs lover's eye so that he does not see in the same way as other men do ("if it be not, then love doth well denote, love's eye is not so true as all men's"). This is possible because lover's eyes are distressed from crying and keeping constant watch ("O how can love's eye be true, that is so vexed with watching and with tears?") No wonder then that the poet's vision is blurred ("no marvel then though I mistake my view"). The same happens to the sun when it is veiled by clouds ("the sun itself sees not, till heaven clears"). The poet exclaims: how clever true love is! It blinds the poet's eyes with his own tears ("O cunning love, with tears thou keep'st me blind"). Otherwise, eyes unaffected by love would see many faults in true beauty ("Lest eyes well seeing thy foul faults should find").

This is a reoccurrence of the poet's previous experiences described in Sonnets 113 and 114. Like in those previous Sonnets, he refers to the subtle faculty as "eye in my mind". But this faculty is not fully functional yet, because it is still partially veiled. This time the poet is able to identify the cause of his blindness. Namely, his imperfections prevent him from seeing true beauty.

Romeo discovered the blurring effect of ordinary, i.e., sensual love. When Romeo met Juliet, his sensual attraction to Rosaline melted right away[148]:

> "It is the east, and Juliet is the sun.
> Arise, fair sun, and kill the envious moon,
> Who is already sick and pale with grief,
> That thou her maid art far more fair than she."

---

[148] See "Romeo" (Shakespeare for the Seeker, Volume 3, Chapter 6.6).

SONNET CXLIX

Canst thou o cruel, say I love thee not,
When I against myself with thee partake:
Do I not think on thee when I forgot
Am of my self, all tyrant, for thy sake?
Who hateth thee that I do call my friend,
On whom frown'st thou that I do fawn upon,
Nay if thou lour'st on me do I not spend
Revenge upon myself with present moan?
What merit do I in my self respect,
That is so proud thy service to despise,
When all my best doth worship thy defect,
Commanded by the motion of thine eyes.
    But love hate on for now I know thy mind,
    Those that can see thou lov'st, and I am blind.

The poet has a great difficulty to keep the constancy of his inner states. He keeps switching between the two states of "to be" and "not to be". Only when he manages to die to his worldly attachments, may he have a chance to experience true love. One might expect that, at the conclusion of the previous Sonnet, the poet has finally arrived at an unwavering state. Yet, this Sonnet indicates that he is still like a ball bouncing up and down. Now he accuses the Lady of cruelty for telling him that she does not love him ("canst thou o cruel, say I love thee not, when I against myself with thee partake"). What the Lady does and says is a reflection of the poet's inner state. It is obvious that he has not yet arrived at the state of true love. So, there should be no surprise that the Lady tells him just that.

The poet lists a number of facts to prove that he does deserve the Lady's love. For example, he thinks about her, even when he has forgotten about himself ("do I not think on thee when I forgot am of my self, all tyrant, for thy sake"); he does not befriend those who hate her ("who hateth thee that I do call my friend"); he does not respect anyone whom the Lady frowns at ("on whom frown'st thou that I do fawn upon"); and he moans each time the Lady scolds him ("nay if thou lour'st on me do I not spend revenge upon myself with present moan"). Then he asks her which of his qualities are so flawed that she despises him? ("What merit do I in my self respect, that is so proud thy service to despise"). The poet assumes that he does his best by worshiping the Lady's faults and by following the commands of her eyes ("when all my best doth worship thy defect, commanded by the motion of thine eyes"). In the concluding lines the poet declares that he knows why the Lady hates him ("but love hate on for now I know thy mind"). Namely, she loves those who can see and she hates him because he is blind ("those that can see thou lov'st, and I am blind"). In this context "to see" means to be able to use the purified faculty of the intellect, i.e., the black faculty. It is in this sense that the poet is still partially blind.

Shakespeare uses Cupid as a god of sensual love. This is how Berowne in "Love's Labour's Lost" described Dan Cupid, i.e., the blind god of love[149]:

> "This whimpled, whining, purblind, wayward boy;
> This senior-junior, giant-dwarf, Dan Cupid;
> Regent of love-rhymes, lord of folded arms,
> The anointed sovereign of sighs and groans,
> Liege of all loiterers and malcontents,
> Dread prince of plackets, king of codpieces,
> Sole imperator and great general
> Of trotting 'paritors."

---

[149] See "The Fair Youth, the Dark Lady, and Cupid" (Shakespeare for the Seeker, Volume 2, Chapter 5.3).

SONNET CL

Oh from what power hast thou this powerful might,
With insufficiency my heart to sway,
To make me give the lie to my true sight,
And swear that brightness doth not grace the day?
Whence hast thou this becoming of things ill,
That in the very refuse of thy deeds,
There is such strength and warrantise of skill,
That in my mind thy worst all best exceeds?
Who taught thee how to make me love thee more,
The more I hear and see just cause of hate,
Oh though I love what others do abhor,
With others thou shouldst not abhor my state.
 If thy unworthiness raised love in me,
 More worthy I to be beloved of thee.

As in the previous Sonnet, the poet struggles with overpowering feelings. Something is happening to him, which he neither can control nor understand. There is only one thing that he can recognize. Namely, that the Lady is the source of this overwhelming power ("Oh from what power hast thou this powerful might, with insufficiency my heart to sway"). The Lady has such power that she is able to alter the poet's ordinary sight and her radiance overshadows his wits ("to make me give the lie to my true sight, and swear that brightness doth not grace the day"). The poet wonders from where did the Lady derive this capacity to turn her most reprehensible deeds into thing which he considers to be the best of all ("there is such strength and warrantise of skill, that in my mind thy worst all best exceeds"). And who did teach her how to make him love her, despite the fact that all his physical senses hate her ("who taught thee how to make me love thee more, the more I hear and see just cause of hate"). Even though the poet loves what other people scorn, the Lady should not despise his present state ("though I love what others do abhor, with others thou shouldst not abhor my state"). The poet claims that he deserves her love, because his love was induced by her unworthiness ("if thy unworthiness raised love in me, more worthy I to be beloved of thee"). In reality - it is just the very opposite: the Lady's supposed "unworthiness" is a mark of the poet's inconstancy.

Benedick in "Much Ado About Nothing" alluded to similar contradictions[150]:

> "And, I pray thee now, tell me for
> which of my bad parts didst thou first fall in love
> with me?"

---

[150] See "Assimilation of creative energy" (Shakespeare for the Seeker, Volume 3, Chapter 6.3).

SONNET CLI

Love is too young to know what conscience is,
Yet who knows not conscience is born of love,
Then gentle cheater urge not my amiss,
Lest guilty of my faults thy sweet self prove.
For thou betraying me, I do betray
My nobler part to my gross body's treason,
My soul doth tell my body that he may,
Triumph in love, flesh stays no farther reason,
But rising at thy name doth point out thee,
As his triumphant prize, proud of this pride,
He is contented thy poor drudge to be
To stand in thy affairs, fall by thy side.
    No want of conscience hold it that I call,
    Her love, for whose dear love I rise and fall.

The poet is gradually getting closer and closer to discovering the source of all his difficulties. He starts to recognize the limitations of ordinary and sensual love. He states that Dan Cupid is too immature to know what is constructive and what is destructive ("love is too young to know what conscience is"). But everyone knows that such knowledge is the result of true love ("yet who knows not conscience is born of love"). Therefore, he should not be blamed by the Lady for his faults, because by doing so, she would be making the same error ("then gentle cheater urge not my amiss, lest guilty of my faults thy sweet self prove"). By betraying the poet, the Lady causes him to deceive his inner being for the sake of his worldly desires ("for thou betraying me, I do betray my nobler part to my gross body's treason"). The poet's ordinary soul tells his body that it may have its way in love, and the body is happy with such reward ("my soul doth tell my body that he may, triumph in love, flesh stays no farther reason"). It puffs-up itself proudly when hearing the Lady's name and points towards her as its prize ("but rising at thy name doth point out thee, as his triumphant prize, proud of this pride"). The body is fully satisfied to serve as a drone and be destroyed afterwards ("he is contented thy poor drudge to be, to stand in thy affairs, fall by thy side"). The poet insists, however, that it is not ordinary conscience that makes him rise and fall while chasing after his love ("no want of conscience hold it that I call, her love, for whose dear love I rise and fall").

King Richard III in the History Plays also claimed that he was not driven entirely by ordinary conscience. He was just ignoring it[151]:

> "Conscience is but a word that cowards use,
> Devised at first to keep the strong in awe:
> Our strong arms be our conscience, swords our law."

---

[151] See "Completion of purification" (Shakespeare for the Seeker, Volume 1, Chapter 1).

SONNET CLII

In loving thee thou know'st I am forsworn,
But thou art twice forsworn to me love swearing,
In act thy bed-vow broke, and new faith torn,
In vowing new hate after new love bearing:
But why of two oaths' breach do I accuse thee,
When I break twenty: I am perjured most,
For all my vows are oaths but to misuse thee:
And all my honest faith in thee is lost.
For I have sworn deep oaths of thy deep kindness:
Oaths of thy love, thy truth, thy constancy,
And to enlighten thee gave eyes to blindness,
Or made them swear against the thing they see.
    For I have sworn thee fair: more perjured eye,
    To swear against the truth so foul a lie.

It helps to interpret this Sonnet to remember that the Black Lady's acts and sayings are a reflection of the poet's inner state. Therefore, by describing the Lady's behaviour the poet gives away his own self-description. In this way the Lady helps him to recognize his shortcomings. It is only by recognizing his weaknesses that the poet may be able to get rid of them.

The poet accuses the Lady of double forswearing ("in loving thee thou know'st I am forsworn, but thou art twice forsworn to me love swearing"). According to the poet, the Lady broke two promises, i.e., her oath of love and her oath of hate ("in act thy bed-vow broke, and new faith torn, in vowing new hate after new love bearing"). Then the poet reflects and admits that he himself is guilty of breaking plenty of his promises ("but why of two oaths' breach do I accuse thee, when I break twenty"). He confesses that all his promises were just manipulations to exploit her ("I am perjured most, for all my vows are oaths but to misuse thee"). And he realizes that he is not able to be true to her ("and all my honest faith in thee is lost"). The poet recalls that he has sworn that he loved her, that she was faithful and true ("for I have sworn deep oaths of thy deep kindness: oaths of thy love, thy truth, thy constancy"). And to give her even more glory, he has blinded himself and pretended to see something that he was unable to see ("and to enlighten thee, gave eyes to blindness, or made them swear against the thing they see"). He sincerely admits that it was a big lie to swear against the truth, as he was incapable to recognize her true beauty ("For I have sworn thee fair: more perjured eye, to swear against the truth so foul a lie"). It is this moment of sincerity and recognition of his mistakes and faults that will allow the poet to advance onto the next stage of the path. The next stage is symbolically presented in the two concluding Sonnets.

Katharina in "The Taming of the Shrew" also arrived at a similar recognition of her inner state[152]:

> "And when she is froward, peevish, sullen, sour,
> And not obedient to his honest will,
> What is she but a foul contending rebel
> And graceless traitor to her loving lord?"

---

[152] See "Taming school" (Shakespeare for the Seeker, Volume 3, Chapter 6.5).

Epilogue (Sonnets 153 - 154)

"And so the General of hot desire,
Was sleeping by a Virgin hand disarm'd" (Sonnet 154)

SONNET CLIII

Cupid laid by his brand and fell asleep,
A maid of *Dian's* this advantage found,
And his love-kindling fire did quickly steep
In a cold valley-fountain of that ground:
Which borrowed from this holy fire of love,
A dateless lively heat still to endure,
And grew a seething bath which yet men prove,
Against strange maladies a sovereign cure:
But at my mistress' eye love's brand new-fired,
The boy for trial needs would touch my breast,
I sick withal the help of bath desired,
And thither hied a sad distempered guest.
    But found no cure, the bath for my help lies,
    Where *Cupid* got new fire; my mistress' eyes.

Sonnets 153 and 154 are an allegorical conclusion of the poet's quest. This conclusion consists of two sequential encounters with Dan Cupid, the little love-god. In Shakespeare's presentation Cupid's role is limited to triggering only ordinary, i.e., sensual and emotional love. Cupid's interference is greatly diminished at the moment when the poet's inner faculties are purified. It is only then that he may become immune to Cupid's influence. In other words, the poet's confusion and despair that were caused by his encounter with the Black Lady may be overcome by the symbolic disarming of Cupid. The scenes with Cupid presented in Sonnets 153 and 154 are based on the same episode. Namely, Cupid put down his torch and fell asleep. One of Diana's maidens took advantage of this situation, took Cupid's love-inducing torch and plunged it in a cold spring ("and his love-kindling fire did quickly steep in a cold valley-fountain of that ground"). The spring acquired heat from the fire of the torch ("which borrowed from this holy fire of love, a dateless lively heat still to endure"). And the babbling water of the spring became an all powerful cure for love-affected men ("and grew a seething bath which yet men prove against strange maladies a sovereign cure"). Through the Black Lady's eyes, Cupid was able to rekindle his torch ("but at my mistress' eye love's brand new-fired"). Then, he decided to test it on the poet ("the boy for trial needs would touch my breast"). The poet became infected with sensual love and sought remedy in the soothing bath ("I sick withal the help of bath desired, and thither hied a sad distempered guest"). But he found no cure. He thinks that the cure for his love-sickness is where Cupid got his fire from, i.e., in the Lady's eyes ("the bath for my help lies, where Cupid got new fire; my mistress' eyes"). This conclusion is in agreement with the poet's previous observation, i.e., the Lady's eyes are a mirror reflection of his inner state (see Sonnet 132). As long as his inner state is impure, he remains vulnerable to Cupid's torch. The poet assumes that by improving his inner state he may be cured from his love-sickness.

Prospero in "The Tempest" was able to protect Miranda and Ferdinand from Cupid's interference into their relationship[153]. Here is a comment by goddess Iris to goddess Ceres about Cupid, i.e., Mars' and Venus' "waspish-headed son":

> "Mars's hot minion is returned again;
> Her waspish-headed son has broke his arrows,
> Swears he will shoot no more but play with sparrows
> And be a boy right out."

Iris assured Ceres that Cupid got frustrated and gave-up further attempts at corrupting the young couple.

---

[153] See "Prospero's challenges" (Shakespeare for the Seeker, Volume 4, Chapter 8.1).

SONNET CLIV

The little Love-God lying once asleep,
Laid by his side his heart-inflaming brand,
Whilst many Nymphs that vow'd chaste life to keep,
Came tripping by, but in her maiden hand,
The fairest votary took up that fire,
Which many Legions of true hearts had warm'd,
And so the General of hot desire,
Was sleeping by a Virgin hand disarm'd.
This brand she quenched in a cool Well by,
Which from love's fire took heat perpetual,
Growing a bath and healthful remedy,
For men diseased, but I my Mistress' thrall,
    Came there for cure and this by that I prove,
    Love's fire heats water, water cools not love.

The poet again refers to Cupid, the General of hot desire, who fell asleep with his heart-inflaming torch by his side ("the little love-god lying once asleep, laid by his side his heart-inflaming brand"). Then one of Diana's maidens took his torch away from him ("whilst many nymphs that vow'd chaste life to keep, came tripping by, but in her maiden hand, the fairest votary took up that fire"). In this way the virgin was able to disarm the little love-god ("and so the general of hot desire, was sleeping by a virgin hand disarm'd"). The maiden quenched the torch in a nearby well, which turned into a hot spring ("this brand she quenched in a cool well by, which from love's fire took heat perpetual"). The hot spring acquired curing quality ("growing a bath and healthful remedy, for men diseased"). The poet went there to be cured from his love-sickness ("but I my Mistress' thrall, came there for cure"). This time he discovered that the hot well was a cure for sensual love, but that it was incapable of providing cure for true love ("and this by that I prove, love's fire heats water, water cools not love").

At first look there is no difference between this Sonnet and the previous one. Yet, Sonnet 154 provides a subtle but a significant piece of information that allows to distinguish between the nature of sensual love and the nature of true love. In the previous Sonnet the poet's conclusion applied to the cause of his love-sickness, i.e., he assumed that he might be cured from his illness by improving his inner state. In this Sonnet the poet indicates that men affected by ordinary love may be cured. But true love is not curable.

The explanation of the two last Sonnets is given in "A Midsummer Night's Dream" in the episode involving Oberon and the juice from Cupid's flower. The juice had the same effect as Cupid's arrows or his torch. The magical love-inducing juice, i.e., Cupid's flower, was at Oberon's disposal. But Oberon had also access to antidote to the juice, i.e., an equivalent to the bath mentioned in the Sonnets. The antidote was described as an herb called Diana's bud[154]:

> "Dian's bud o'er Cupid's flower
> Hath such force and blessed power."

The episode with Diana's bud indicates that only corrupted men may be affected by Cupid's arrow, his torch, or his flower. By the same token, the remedy of Diana's bud or the hot bath works only on sensual and emotional attractions. Spiritually purified men, or women, are beyond Cupid's reach. True love is affected neither by Cupid's flower nor can be cured by Diana's bud. In other words, the Sonnet indicates that the poet was able to discover the nature of true love.

---

[154] See "Oberon" (Shakespeare for the Seeker, Volume 4, Chapter 8.3).

CONCLUSION

Cupid's role is diminished at the moment when the subtle faculties are reformed, purified, and united to form a new inner being. It is only then that a person becomes immune to Cupid's arrows.

We may now realize that it was Cupid who was disturbing the relationship between the poet and the Black Lady. Sonnet 154 indicates that the poet overcame Cupid's influence by taking a hot "bath". But this did not cure him from true love. "Water cools not love" means that the poet has finally understood what true love means. By overcoming Cupid's influence, the poet was able to remove the veil preventing him from seeing the true beauty of the Black Lady. Only then was he able to become a true lover, hear "heavenly music", and reach the state of "secret knowledge".

At this point it is worthwhile to recall Berowne's sonnet that Shakespeare inserted into "Love's Labour's Lost". The sonnet was addressed to Rosaline, i.e., the Black Lady of the play:

> "If love make me forsworn, how shall I swear to love?
> Ah, never faith could hold, if not to beauty vow'd!
> Though to myself forsworn, to thee I'll faithful prove:
> Those thoughts to me were oaks, to thee like osiers bow'd.
> Study his bias leaves and makes his book thine eyes,
> Where all those pleasures live that art would comprehend:
> If knowledge be the mark, to know thee shall suffice;
> Well learned is that tongue that well can thee commend,
> All ignorant that soul that sees thee without wonder;
> Which is to me some praise that I thy parts admire:
> Thy eye Jove's lightning bears, thy voice his dreadful thunder,
> Which not to anger bent, is music and sweet fire.
> Celestial as thou art, O, pardon, love, this wrong,
> That sings heaven's praise with such an earthly tongue."

Let's notice that Berowne's sonnet is the only one, among all Shakespearean Sonnets, in which the poet is able to hear "music" in his mistress' thundering voice. It is the first time that the author of the Sonnets is able to perceive the true beauty of his mistress. Such a state is the result of the experiences described in the Sonnets. Now, therefore, the poet is ready to enter onto the final stage of his "heavy journey on the way".

This means that Berowne's poem, which was inserted into "Love's Labour's Lost", contains the conclusion of Shakespeare's Sonnets. This Sonnet marks the poet's entry onto the final stage of the process. Yet, the final stage has not been described. Does it mean that neither the poet, nor Mr. W.H. to whom the Sonnets were dedicated, were able to fulfill their evolutionary potentiality?

The two concluding Sonnets, similarly to the concluding words of Timon of Athens and Othello, carry a two-fold message. The first message (Sonnet 153) applies to Mr. W.H., i.e., an ordinary man and an aspirant to higher learning. Ordinary man is under the influence of Cupid. He sees things piecemeal and cannot distinguish the hidden trend in events because his mind is fixed on conditioned patterns; he follows a linear thinking that relies on intellectual speculations, socially imposed terms of reference, and emotional stimuli. The message says that such a man, like Berowne in "Love's Labour's Lost", would have to wait for another occasion to advance further his evolutionary state. This delay was symbolically indicated by Shakespeare in "Love's Labour's Lost" as "a twelvemonth and a day". The analysis of Shakespeare plays points out that such a time period corresponded historically to 400 years[155]. This means that Mr. W.H. symbolically encompasses many generations of Western European society.

The second message (Sonnet 154) applies to the poet, i.e., Shakespeare himself. Shakespeare wrote the plays in which he precisely described the entire process of man's inner growth and the evolutionary history of Western European civilization. This clearly indicates that Shakespeare reached a higher stage of human

---

[155] See "Conclusion" (Shakespeare for the Seeker, Volume 4).

development. He was able to overcome Cupid's influence and hear the "heavenly music" which guided his writings. In accordance with the Guide's prediction, the poet, "the inspired adventurer who undertook the task of writing the Sonnets", was the first among ordinary men who earned access to "secret knowledge". In this way he found out that the door to the "secret" was opened for him and for all the future generations.

....

Another digression may be helpful in understanding Shakespeare's writings. Namely, Shakespeare delegated Holofernes, a know-it-all schoolmaster, to deliver an interpretation of Berowne's sonnet. Here is Holofernes' review of the Sonnet:

> "Here are
> only numbers ratified; but, for the elegancy,
> facility, and golden cadence of poesy, caret.
> Ovidius Naso was the man: and why, indeed, Naso,
> but for smelling out the odouriferous flowers of
> fancy, the jerks of invention? Imitari is nothing:
> so doth the hound his master, the ape his keeper,
> the tired horse his rider."

It seems that Shakespeare knew very well how his Sonnets would be analyzed by his critics and the future generations of scholars, poets, and writers. Holofernes' "erudite" comment is a caricature of those artificial comparative analyses that are limited to such factors as originality, composition, elegance, sublimity, delicacy, sensuality, etc. By providing such a hint, Shakespeare points out that there is another dimension in his writings that is invisible to such ordinary rational and scholarly approaches.

References

- W. Jamroz, "Shakespeare for the Seeker", Volume 1, Troubadour Publications (2012)

- W. Jamroz, "Shakespeare for the Seeker", Volume 2, Troubadour Publications (2013)

- W. Jamroz, "Shakespeare for the Seeker", Volume 3, Troubadour Publications (2013)

- W. Jamroz, "Shakespeare for the Seeker", Volume 4, Troubadour Publications (2013)

www.ingramcontent.com/pod-product-compliance
Lightning Source LLC
Chambersburg PA
CBHW071646160426
43195CB00012B/1369